Oxford

D0924077

Idioms and Phrasal Verbs

Intermediate

Ruth Gairns and Stuart Redman

CALGARY PUBLIC LIBRARY

MAR 2015

OXFORD
UNIVERSITY PRESS

OXFORD
UNIVERSITY PRESS

Great Clarendon Street, Oxford OX2 6DP

Oxford University Press is a department of the University of Oxford.
It furthers the University's objective of excellence in research, scholarship,
and education by publishing worldwide in

Oxford New York

Auckland Cape Town Dar es Salaam Hong Kong Karachi
Kuala Lumpur Madrid Melbourne Mexico City Nairobi
New Delhi Shanghai Taipei Toronto

With offices in

Argentina Austria Brazil Chile Czech Republic France Greece
Guatemala Hungary Italy Japan Poland Portugal Singapore
South Korea Switzerland Thailand Turkey Ukraine Vietnam

OXFORD and OXFORD ENGLISH are registered trade marks of
Oxford University Press in the UK and in certain other countries

© Oxford University Press 2011

The moral rights of the author have been asserted

Database right Oxford University Press (maker)

First published 2011
2015 2014
10 9 8 7 6 5 4 3

No unauthorized photocopying

All rights reserved. No part of this publication may be reproduced,
stored in a retrieval system, or transmitted, in any form or by any
means, without the prior permission in writing of Oxford University
Press, or as expressly permitted by law, or under terms agreed with the
appropriate reprographics rights organization. Enquiries concerning
reproduction outside the scope of the above should be sent to the ELT
Rights Department, Oxford University Press, at the address above

You must not circulate this book in any other binding or cover
and you must impose this same condition on any acquirer

Any websites referred to in this publication are in the public domain
and their addresses are provided by Oxford University Press for
information only. Oxford University Press disclaims any responsibility
for the content

ISBN: 978 0 19 462012 3

Printed in China

This book is printed on paper from certified and well-managed sources.

ACKNOWLEDGEMENTS

The authors and publisher are grateful to those who have given permission to
reproduce the following extracts and adaptations of copyright material: p.12
Extracts from Oxford Advanced Learner's Dictionary; p.101 Adapted extract
from 'A new goal for football stars: to spread love of languages' by
Richard Garner, 8 October 2008 from The Independent. Reproduced by
permission.

Sources: p.124 adapted from www.dearmrsweb.com.

Illustrations by: Chris Davidson pp.57, 76; Colin Elgie p.144; Clive Goddard
17, 45, 47, 52, 110, 118; Sarah Kelly 14, 19, 24, 42, 43, 74, 79, 126, 132;
Harry Venning 20, 58, 130.

Cover illustration by: Carol Verbyst.

The authors and publisher would also like to thank the following for permission
to reproduce the following photographs: Alamy pp.9 (Mark Andersen/
RubberBall), 29 (Lisa F. Young), 31 (Photosindia Batch5/PhotosIndia.com
LLC), 39 (Ben/David J. Green - Lifestyle), 39 (Emily/DMAc), 41 (Picturenet/
Picturenet), 61 (Steve Nagy/Design Pics Inc.), 64 (couple/Gino's Premium
Images), 64 (terraced street/Greg Balfour Evans), 65 (Erik Isakson/Tetra
Images), 68 (couple/moodboard), 69 (Radius Images), 70 (Yuri Arcurs/
INSADCO Photography), 73 (Leosceptic/AKP Photos), 80 (Chloe/81a),
80 (Luke/Chris Rout), 82 (Jo Ann/MatthiolaC), 82 (blond 23/foodfolio),
87 (IE006/Image Source), 89 (Ralph Henning), 95 (Frank and Helena/
Cultura RM), 96 (Peter Titmuss), 97 (duck/D. Hurst), 99 (Charles Stirling
(Travel)), 102 (Plattform/Johner Images), 125 (Mark Boulton), 134 (Black
Forest/Matthias Dietrich), 134 (skiing/Cultura/Philip Lee Harvey),
134 (broken marriage/artpartner-images.com), 134 (dog/lantapix);
Construction Photography p.113 (Damian Gillie); Getty Images
pp.18 (Kraig Scarbinsky/Digital Vision), 32 (Chris Ryan/OJO Images),
33 (Barry Austin Photography/Riser), 51 (Hill Street Studios/Blend Images),
60 (Digital Vision), 62 (Susan Wides/UpperCut Images), 63 (rubberball),
71 (Stockbyte), 83 (Photodisc/Marshall Gordon/Cole Group), 84 (Thinkstock
Images/Comstock Images), 94 (Justin Lightley/Photographer's Choice
RF), 97 (woman photo/Digital Vision), 98 (Adam Burto/Robert Harding
World Imagery), 100 (Melissa Majchrzak/MLS via Getty Images), 101 (Phil
Cole), 112 (Takuya Matsunaga/Aflo), 115 (John Lund/Marc Romanelli/
Blend Images); image100 p.30 (woman); iStockphoto.com pp.78 (Mike
Cherim), 82 (Kima/Niko Guido), 97 (woman illustration/Janne Ahvo),
105 (Crazy cat/Regina Makhonko), 105 (Erin/Jim Snyder), 105 (Leroy/
shino-b), 106 (David Mingay); Photolibrary.com p.66 (Peter Gridley);
Royalty-free pp.26 (Chris King), 68 (woman/Gareth Boden),
73 (Moonlover/Photodisc), 73 (Stargirl/Digital Vision), 73 (Discoman/
Photodisc), 73 (Amal/Digital Vision), 73 (Indy/Image Source), 97 (man/
Photodisc)

Artwork sourced by: Pictureresearch.co.uk

The authors and publishers would like to thank the teachers and students from
Argentina, Brazil, Czech Republic, France, Greece, Indonesia, Italy, Norway, Serbia,
and Poland who helped with the development of this book.

They would also like to thank Maggie Baigent, Rachel Godfrey, Carol Tabor, Michael
Terry, and Scott Thornbury for their valuable comments on early drafts of the text;
and Suzanne Williams for the picture research.

For About You answers, they would like to thank Leticia Ansaldi, Eleni Babaliouta,
Abd ul-Qadir Dar'ouzy, Karla Dědková, Raquel Montaleão, Carla Montebello, Silvia
Santinelli, Melanie Steyn, Eva Trubacova, Mayra Aixa Villar, and Maria Wenger.

Contents

Introduction   5
Abbreviations   7

Introduction to idioms and phrasal verbs

1   What are idioms?   8
2   Types of idiom   10
3   Finding idioms in a dictionary   12
4   The grammar of phrasal verbs   14
5   Core meanings 1   16
6   Core meanings 2   18
7   Different meanings of phrasal verbs   20
Review   22

Thinking, learning, and knowledge

8   I can follow classroom language   26
9   I can talk about learning   28
10   I can talk about exams   30
11   I can talk about ability and progress   32
12   I can talk about thought processes   34
13   I can talk about knowledge and skills   35
Review   36

Communicating with people

14   I can talk about getting in touch   39
15   I can describe ways of saying things   40
16   I can talk about phoning   41
17   I can use short spoken phrases   42
18   I can use phrases with *say*, *tell*, and *see*   44
19   I can use common spoken responses   46
20   I can understand and leave messages   48
21   I can say what I think   50
22   I can talk about jokes that go wrong   52
Review   54

People and relationships

23   I can describe actions   58
24   I can talk about my family   60
25   I can talk about different generations   62
26   I can talk about neighbours   64
27   I can describe my feelings   66
28   I can describe romantic relationships   68
29   I can describe annoying habits   70
30   I can talk about astrology   72
Review   74

Everyday topics

31 I can describe the weather   78
32 I can talk about sleep   79
33 I can talk about spending and saving   80
34 I can talk about diets and cooking   82
35 I can understand crime reporting   84
36 I can talk about work experience   86
37 I can describe a small business   88
38 I can talk about shopping   90
    Review   91

Out and about

39 I can describe social activities   94
40 I can describe outdoor activities   96
41 I can talk about holidays   98
42 I can talk about team sports   100
43 I can talk about situations on the road   102
    Review   104

Concepts

44 I can say what I want or need   107
45 I can discuss plans and arrangements   108
46 I can talk about likes and interests   109
47 I can describe damage and repair   110
48 I can say how things begin and end   112
49 I can talk about time   114
50 I can talk about numbers   116
51 I can talk about problems and solutions   118
52 I can give advice   120
    Review   121

Language

53 I can use link phrases   125
54 I can use fixed phrases with two key words   126
55 I can use prepositional phrases   128
56 I can use phrasal verbs as commands   130
57 I can use verb-based idioms   132
58 I can use key verbs: *get*   134
59 I can use key verbs: *take* and *look*   136
60 I can use key verbs: *come* and *go*   138
    Review   140

Idioms – some interesting histories   144
Answer key   145
Answer key to review units   166
List of spotlight boxes   175
Word list/Index   176
Key words   187

Introduction

Idioms and Phrasal Verbs

Idioms and Phrasal Verbs forms part of the *Oxford Word Skills* vocabulary series. It is a series of two books for students to learn, practise, and revise everyday English idioms and phrasal verbs.

Intermediate:	intermediate and upper-intermediate (CEF levels B1 and B2)
Advanced:	advanced (CEF levels C1 and C2)

There are over 1,000 new idioms and phrasal verbs in each level, and all of the material can be used in the classroom or for self-study.

How are the books organized?

Each book contains 60 units of vocabulary presentation and practice. Units are one or two pages long, depending on the topic. New vocabulary is presented in manageable quantities for learners, with practice exercises following immediately, usually on the same page. The units are grouped together thematically in modules of five to nine units. At the end of each module there are further practice exercises in the review units, so that learners can revise and test themselves on the vocabulary learned.

At the back of each book you will find:

- an answer key for all the exercises
- an answer key for the review units
- a list of all the idioms and phrasal verbs taught, with a unit reference to where each item appears
- a separate list of key words with unit references
- a page featuring the histories behind some of the idioms in the book (👁 look on the website www.oup.com/elt/wordskills for more).

What are idioms and phrasal verbs? Why teach them together?

Idioms are usually defined as groups of words whose overall meaning is different from the meanings of the individual words. So, *over the moon* has nothing to do with the literal meaning of 'the moon'; it means 'extremely happy or excited'. An organization that *changes hands* passes from one owner to another; and if you are *in someone's way*, you are stopping them from moving or doing something. As these examples illustrate, in some idioms the meaning can be almost impossible to guess out of context, while others are more transparent.

Phrasal verbs consist of two and occasionally three words: a base verb and at least one particle (preposition or adverb). Many phrasal verbs are idiomatic: in other words, the meaning of the verb and particle is different from the base verb on its own. For example, the meanings of *give up* and *give in* are quite different from the meaning of *give*. As with idioms, some phrasal verbs are more transparent than others, e.g. *stand up* and

the most common sense of *stand* are very similar in meaning, as are *sit down* and *sit*. In other words, phrasal verbs can be seen as a type of idiom, although they are often singled out for specific attention in language-teaching materials.

Putting idioms and phrasal verbs together has a linguistic rationale, but perhaps an even greater pedagogic one. A relatively short passage of text – a practical necessity in most language-teaching materials – does not normally produce nine or ten naturally occurring phrasal verbs, but it can easily yield that number if the target language includes both phrasal verbs <u>and</u> idioms. This makes it easier to present the target language in continuous text rather than disconnected sentences, and gives learners more opportunity to see the expressions being used naturally.

Which idioms and phrasal verbs are included?

When people think of idioms, they tend to come up with imaginative and colourful examples: *kick the bucket, have a bone to pick with someone, full of beans, be barking up the wrong tree,* etc. These vivid expressions can be extremely difficult to understand, so they are often the ones that teachers are called on to explain in the classroom. It is also undeniably true that idioms – and especially the more vivid ones – hold a particular fascination for some learners. However, there are thousands of idioms, less exotic and often more transparent than the ones above, which are of a higher frequency and probably greater value in everyday English to the vast majority of learners.

These are typical examples:
it depends, in the end, have had enough of sth/sb, at the last minute, give my love to sb, first of all, it's no good (doing sth), by the way, get hold of sb, keep in touch, do your best, to a certain extent, get on sb's nerves, here you are, as usual, see how it goes, yes and no, I beg your pardon, make fun of sb, have second thoughts about doing sth, can't wait (to do sth), all over the place, make the most of sth, cover the cost (of sth), all of a sudden, cost a fortune.

In fact, some of these will appear so mundane that they often pass unnoticed as idioms. In some cases the meaning may be quite easy to guess, especially in context, but the same concept is often expressed in a different way in the learner's mother tongue, so these expressions need to be learnt, and are equally deserving of our attention.

At the intermediate / upper-intermediate level, we have concentrated on idioms and phrasal verbs which are likely to be of greatest value to learners in everyday English. To this end, you will find some vivid and colourful examples, but the majority are closer to the list above.

One final note on selection. Dictionaries do not always agree on what constitutes an idiom: *hold the line* is listed as an idiom in one dictionary, but a collocation in another. The same is true for *cross your legs, be careful with money, have an early / a late night,* etc. Our criterion for inclusion in this series is that an item has to be listed as an idiom in at least one of the following ELT dictionaries (and they are almost always in more than one):

Oxford Advanced Learner's Dictionary

Oxford Wordpower Dictionary

Oxford Idioms Dictionary for learners of English

Longman Dictionary of Contemporary English

Macmillan English Dictionary for Advanced Learners

Cambridge Advanced Learner's Dictionary

Collins COBUILD Advanced Learner's English Dictionary

How can teachers use the material in the classroom?

New idioms and phrasal verbs are presented through different types of text, including dialogues, tables, and visuals. The meaning of the new vocabulary is explained in an accompanying glossary unless it is illustrated in visuals or diagrams. Important or additional information is included in the 'spotlight' boxes.

Here is a procedure you could follow:

- Students study the presentation for five to ten minutes (longer if necessary).

- You answer any queries the students may have about the items, and provide a pronunciation model of the items for your students to repeat.

- Students do the first exercise, which they can check for themselves using the answer key, or you can go over the answers with the whole class.

- When you are satisfied, you can ask students to go on to further exercises, while you monitor them as they work individually or in pairs, and assist where necessary.

- When they have completed the written exercises, students can often test themselves on the new vocabulary. The material has been designed so that students can cover the new vocabulary and look at the meaning, or vice versa. This is a simple, quick, and easy way for learners to test themselves over and over again, so there is no pressure on you to keep searching for different exercises.

- After a period of time has elapsed, perhaps a couple of days or a week, you can use the review exercises for further consolidation and testing.

- You will often notice the heading ABOUT YOU or ABOUT YOUR COUNTRY. This indicates a personalized exercise which gives learners an opportunity to use the new vocabulary within the context of their own lives. Students can write answers to these in their notebooks, but they make ideal pair-work activities for learners to practise their spoken English while using the new vocabulary. If you use these as speaking activities, students could then write their answers (or their partner's answers) as follow-up. In the answer key, possible answers for these activities are provided by native and proficient non-native speakers from different parts of the world.

- 👁 To extend page 144, which gives the histories behind a number of idioms in this book, go to the website **www.oup.com/elt/wordskills** to find a regular feature. You and your students should find this interesting.

How can students study alone?

- Choose the topics that interest you. You don't need to do the units in any particular order.

- Each page will probably take you about 20–25 minutes. Firstly, spend at least ten minutes studying the presentation, which may be a text, a dialogue, a table, etc. Use the glossaries to help you understand the meaning of new items. Practise saying the idioms and phrasal verbs a few times to help you remember them.

- Keep a notebook where you can write down the new idioms and phrasal verbs with the meaning and an example sentence to help you remember them. If you are using a bilingual dictionary, you could also add a translation.

- Do the exercises in pencil; then you can rub them out, and do them again in a few days' time. Check your answers in the answer key on pages 145–65. At the end of many units you will find a section called ABOUT YOU or ABOUT YOUR COUNTRY. This gives you an opportunity to use the vocabulary more freely to write in your notebook about yourself, your country, etc. You will find some possible answers in the answer key, written by native and proficient non-native speakers of English. You may find it interesting to compare your answers with theirs.

- You can usually **test yourself** on the new vocabulary. Look at the idioms and phrasal verbs in the glossaries, and cover the meanings. See if you can remember the meanings. You can do this when you have finished the exercises, or several days later as a way of revising the idioms and phrasal verbs.

- You can use the further practice exercises in the review sections which follow each module. Either do them immediately after a unit, or do them a few days later to help you revise the idioms and phrasal verbs.

- If you haven't got a good dictionary in English, we recommend *The Oxford Advanced Learner's Dictionary*. You may also be interested in two specialist dictionaries: *Oxford Idioms Dictionary for learners of English* and *Oxford Phrasal Verbs Dictionary for learners of English*.

- 👁 Go to the website **www.oup.com/elt/ wordskills** to find a regular feature on the histories behind a number of idioms in this book.

Abbreviations

The following abbreviations are used:

N	noun	sth	something
V	verb	sb	somebody
ADJ	adjective	etc.	You use 'etc.' at the end of a list to show there are other things, but you aren't going to say them all.
ADV	adverb		
PL	plural		
OPP	opposite		
SYN	synonym	i.e.	that is
INF	informal	e.g.	for example
FML	formal		

1 What are idioms?

1 An idiom is a phrase with a meaning that is often difficult to understand by looking at the individual words. For example, it isn't easy to guess the meaning of the idiom **lose face**, but seeing it in context will help you to understand it:

He could **lose face** if other people see that he got everything wrong.	**lose face** be less respected or look stupid because of sth you have done.

Here are more examples:

The teacher **turned a blind eye to** some of the children's bad behaviour.	**turn a blind eye (to sth)** pretend not to see or notice sth, usually sth bad.
My uncle just arrived **out of the blue**.	**out of the blue** INF suddenly and unexpectedly.

2 Not all idioms are so difficult to guess. Many phrases that are easier to understand are still listed as idioms in dictionaries because they have a fixed form which you need to know and learn:

We could see lights **in the distance**.	**in the distance** far away, but able to be seen or heard.
I ring my mother every day **without fail**.	**without fail** always.
If all else fails, I'll have to sell the car.	**if all else fails** used to say what sb can do if nothing else they have done is successful.

3 Most idioms have a fixed form. For example, if a name **rings a bell**, it means it is a name that sounds familiar to you. The idiom is *ring a bell*, but not *ring ~~the~~ bell*. However, with some idioms alternative words *are* possible:

Do you want to go out? ~ **That/It depends**.	**that/it depends** used to say that you are not certain about something because other things have to be considered.
I would **steer/stay clear of** that place; it's not very safe.	**steer/stay clear of sth/sb** take care to avoid sth or sb, because it or they may cause problems.
Why on earth are you shouting? Be quiet! **How on earth** did he pass the exam? He did no work at all.	**why/how/where/who**, etc. **on earth** INF used to emphasize a question when you are angry or surprised, or cannot think of an obvious answer.

Sometimes additional words can be used within an idiom, especially to change the emphasis:

She **was in a** <u>terrible</u> **state**, so I decided to stay and look after her.	**be in / get into a state** INF be/become anxious or upset. (*Terrible* here means 'extreme', so 'she was extremely anxious'.)
It **makes** <u>a lot of</u> **sense** to buy now while houses are cheap.	**make sense** be a practical and logical thing to do. (*A lot of* here adds emphasis.)

4 Idioms are very common in spoken English, and dictionaries show when they are particularly informal. In this book, informal idioms are labelled 'INF', like this: **be in / get into a state** INF. Here are more examples:

How come you're here so early?	**how come** INF used to ask the reason for something which is surprising. (Notice the word order after **how come** is in statement form, although it is a question.)
I had to run **like mad** to catch the bus.	**like mad** INF very fast, hard, much, etc. SYN **flat out** INF.

5 To sum up, idioms:
   * are phrases which are often difficult to understand out of context;
   * usually have a fixed form;
   * are very common in spoken English, and many are informal.

1 **Circle the correct answer(s). Sometimes both answers are correct.**

1 We should *steer* | *stay* clear of those people; they're dangerous.
2 Who *in* | *on* earth is that?
3 We will *lose face* | *lose our face* if we just accept their lowest offer.
4 Does it matter if we're late? ~ *It* | *That* depends.
5 I could hear the drums *in distance* | *in the distance*.
6 Have you heard of a place called Dinster? ~ Er, it rings a *bell* | *noise*.

2 **The words or phrases in the box are missing from the sentences below. Where do they go? Write them at the end.**

> on earth   out of the blue ✓   if all else fails   a lot of   like mad   terrible   without fail

▶ Our cousin arrived ⁄ just after we got home last night. *out of the blue*
1 He was in a state last night when he heard about the accident. ....
2 How is your sister going to buy a car if she hasn't got any money? ....
3 It makes sense to give up sweet things if you are overweight. ....
4 My brother loves that car, and he cleans it every day. ....
5 The police came after us, so we ran. ....
6 He's in a bad situation, but he can always work for his father. ....

3 **Replace the underlined word(s) with a word or phrase that has a similar meaning.**

▶ Her name <u>sounds familiar</u>. *rings a bell*
1 I'm going to <u>stay</u> clear of that part of town in future. ....
2 We had to work <u>like mad</u> to finish the project. ....
3 Do you think he'll stay? ~ <u>It</u> depends. ....
4 They arrived <u>suddenly and unexpectedly</u>. ....
5 I could see the church <u>far away</u>. ....
6 He felt he would <u>look stupid</u> if he refused to go in the icy water. ....

4 **Complete the last word in each sentence or dialogue. Then underline the full idiom.**

▶ I got this cheque for $300 <u>out of the blue</u>.
1 Promise me you'll post this letter without ....
2 Do you know Alan Davies? ~ The name rings a ....
3 He always buys the cheapest trainers. ~ Really? I don't think that makes a lot of ....
4 The boys shouldn't be in there, but I'm just going to turn a blind ....
5 After her dog died, she was in a terrible ....
6 I can't get out; the door is locked. ~ How .... ?

5 **In this short text Leona is talking about last night. The idioms are shown in bold. Try to guess what they mean, then check in a dictionary.**

> I **was in two minds about** going to Paul's last night — it's a long way to his place. But **in the end** I decided to go, and it**'s a good thing that** I did because Mike and Jean couldn't go, so there were only three of us. A friend of Paul's called Malcolm was there — he was **a good laugh**, and apparently, he**'s rolling in money**.

1 be in two minds (about doing sth) = ...
2 in the end = ...
3 be a good thing (that) = ...
4 a good laugh INF = ...
5 be rolling in money INF = ...

2 Types of idiom

There are many different types of idiom. The following extract from a story includes some typical patterns. Read it, then look at the table below.

We left camp **bright and early** to **take advantage of** the good weather, but by the afternoon we were getting tired, so I asked Simon which was the quickest way back.

'**Don't ask me**,' he said.

'It's all right,' said Magnus. 'I know the way back from here. It's **a piece of cake**.'

Famous last words! We followed him in one direction for half an hour, before he **changed his mind** and set off in another direction. But by five o'clock, Simon and I were fed up with walking round in circles. Even Magnus agreed we **were getting nowhere** and announced that we were lost.

'Well, **in that case**, we should give Tim a ring,' I said. Tim Collier was **in charge of** our group and I knew he'd be furious that we'd got lost. But we were deep in a valley and there was no signal on my mobile, so we couldn't **get through**. Just then, Simon realized where we were. **Thank heavens** for that, I thought. We followed him up a steep path, and at the top we could see we were only **a stone's throw** from the main road, which **more or less** took us back to camp. We finally got there just before seven.

As we passed Tim, I tried to **laugh it off**. 'Ah, well, **better late than never**, eh?'

'You **were supposed to** be back by five,' he said. And with that, he marched off.

Type of idiom	Example	Meaning
1 verb-based idioms	**take advantage of sth** **change your mind** **get nowhere** **be supposed to do sth**	make good use of sth. change your decision or opinion about sth. make no progress, or have no success. If you **are supposed to do sth**, you should do it because sb told you to do it, or because it is your responsibility to do it. SYN **be meant to do sth**.
2 prepositional phrases	**in that case** **in charge (of sb/sth)**	used to say what will happen, or what you will do, as a result of a particular situation. having control or command (of sb/sth).
3 noun phrases	**a piece of cake** **a stone's throw**	INF a thing that is very easy to do. a short distance. (See page 144.)
4 sayings/proverbs	**famous last words** **better late than never**	used when you think sb is speaking with too much confidence about sth that they think will happen. = it is better to arrive late than not at all.
5 fixed phrases with two key words, usually joined by *and* or *or*	**bright and early** **more or less**	early in the morning. almost or approximately.
6 idiomatic phrasal verbs	**get through (to sb)** **laugh sth off**	make contact with sb by phone. joke about sth to show you think it is not serious or important.
7 exclamations or short spoken phrases	**don't ask me** **thank heavens**	INF used to say that you don't know the answer to sth. SYN **search me** INF. used to say you are pleased and relieved about sth.

1 Circle the correct answer.

1 I'm here. ~ Well, better late than *ever* | *never*, I suppose.
2 We got up *quick* | *bright* and early because we had to catch the seven o'clock train.
3 It looked a bad injury, but Matt just laughed it *off* | *away*, saying it didn't hurt.
4 The teacher who is in *charge* | *responsibility* of the boys must stay with them at all times.
5 Don't worry. Everything's under control. ~ Yeah, famous last *phrase* | *words*.
6 You should take *care* | *advantage* of being in Canada to practise your English.

2 Complete the idioms in this conversation. They are all from page 10.

A OK. I'm going now.
B Fine. By the way, did you get (1) _____ to your mother?
A Yes. She's fine, but she asked me to get some things from the chemist for her.
B Oh well, there's one in the shops near the park.
A Great. In that (2) _____ I can walk.
B Oh yes, it's just a stone's (3) _____ from here.
A Would you like to come into town afterwards?
B No, I'd better not. I'm (4) _____ to be at my sister's at four, and it's more or (5) _____ half
   past two now.
A OK, but if you change your (6) _____ , just text me.

3 Replace the underlined words and phrases with idioms that have a similar meaning.

▶ Who is <u>responsible for</u> the sales department? *in charge of*
1 What's wrong? ~ I'm <u>not making any progress</u> with this essay. _____
2 How was your exam? ~ <u>Easy</u>. _____
3 When's Ben arriving? ~ <u>I've no idea</u>. He never tells me anything. _____
4 The kids got back safely. ~ Oh, <u>I'm so relieved to hear that</u>. _____
5 Did you try phoning? ~ Yes, but I couldn't <u>contact</u> him. _____
6 Is the bank far? ~ No, it's only a <u>short distance</u> from here. _____

4 Identify the types of idioms in bold in these sentences and write the correct number in the spaces provided. Then look up the meanings in the answer key on page 145.

▶ There were lots of keys, but we found the right one by **trial and error**. *Type 5*
1 You can't **live on** £50 a week. _____
2 She's just lost $1000. ~ **Good grief!** _____
3 The food here is quite good **in the main**. _____
4 It was a completely new job, so it took me a while to **find my feet**. _____
5 They say **absence makes the heart grow fonder**. I'm not sure I believe it, though. _____
6 I'm afraid that wars happen – it's **a fact of life**. _____

5 It can be difficult to identify an idiom, and know where it begins and ends. Underline the idioms in the dialogue below. (You will check the meanings in the next exercise.)

pam I ▶ <u>can't stand</u> sitting next to Nigel – he's always making fun of me. Would you swap places with me?
livy No way! He gets on my nerves too – all those stupid jokes. Oh, no, he's here!
nigel Hi, girls. Do you want to hear a joke?
pam No. Get lost, Nigel! You're a pain in the neck! Just go away!

6 Complete the table with the idioms you underlined. Then look up the meanings on page 145.

Spoken phrase	Verb-based idiom	Noun phrase	Phrasal verb
1 _____	▶ *can't stand*	1 _____	1 _____
2 _____	1 _____		
	2 _____		
	3 _____		

3 Finding idioms in a dictionary

Where are idioms explained?

Dictionaries don't always enter idioms in the same place, or in the same way. Read the introduction to your dictionary to discover where to find idioms. In the *Oxford Advanced Learner's Dictionary*, idioms are explained after the symbol **IDM**▶. For example, the idiom **in vain** is in the IDM section after the main meanings of the word **vain**.

If there is more than one idiom, they are listed in alphabetical order (not including grammatical words such as *a*, *the*, *sb/sth*, *his*, *her*, etc.). So, with idioms listed at the word *way*, you will find **all the way** before **by the way** (*a* before *b*).

> **vain** /veɪn/ *adj.* **1** that does not produce the result you want **SYN** **useless**: *She closed her eyes tightly in a vain attempt to hold back the tears.* ◇ *I knocked loudly in the vain hope that someone might answer.* **2** (*disapproving*) too proud of your own appearance, abilities or achievements **SYN** **conceited**: *She's too vain to wear glasses.* ⊃ see also VANITY
> **IDM**▶ **in 'vain** without success: *They tried in vain to persuade her to go.* ◇ *All our efforts were in vain.* ⊃ more at NAME *n.*

Which word in an idiom do I look up?

There isn't one simple rule, but in the *Oxford Advanced Learner's Dictionary* most idioms are explained at the first *meaningful* word in the idiom (noun, verb, adjective, or adverb). For example, with these idioms, you need to look up the underlined word:

on <u>purpose</u> N   **<u>pull</u> sb's leg** V   **it's a <u>long</u> story** ADJ   **<u>once</u> in a blue moon** ADV

With most idioms, there is also cross-referencing. For example, if you look up **blue** to find the meaning of **once in a blue moon**, there will be a reference telling you to look up **once**. (👁 See also page 144.)

> BLUE ▶ blue-ness *noun* [U, sing.]: *the blueness of the water.*
> **IDM**▶ **do sth till you are blue in the 'face** (*informal*) to try to do sth as hard and as long as you possibly can but without success: *You can argue till you're blue in the face, but you won't change my mind.* ⊃ more at BLACK *adj.*, DEVIL, ONCE *adv.*, SCREAM *v.*

However, some common verbs, e.g. *have* and *go*, and some common adjectives, e.g. *good*, have so many idioms that they cannot be listed in one place. In this case, the dictionary tells you to look up the next noun, verb, adjective, etc. in the idiom. For example, if you look up *have* to find the meaning of the idiom **have sth in common (with sb)**, you will see this:

> **IDM**▶ Most idioms containing **have** are at the entries for the nouns and adjectives in the idioms, for example **have your eye on sb** is at **eye** *n.*   **have 'done with sth** (*especially*

To find the meaning of **have sth in common**, you need to look up *common*:

> **IDM**▶ **have sth in common (with sb)** 0→ (of people) to have the same interests, ideas, etc. as sb else: *Tim and I have nothing in common./I have nothing in common with Tim.*

[Extracts from *Oxford Advanced Learner's Dictionary*, 8th edition.]

What information can I find?

- Dictionaries explain the meaning of an idiom and sometimes give an example.
- Most idioms can be used in spoken English and informal written English, but a dictionary will tell you if an idiom is especially *informal*, *formal*, *humorous*, *old-fashioned*, and so on. It will tell you if an idiom is more common in British English (BrE) or North American English (NAmE).
- Dictionaries will show you if one word in an idiom can be replaced by another with the same meaning, e.g. **it/that depends.**

These exercises are based on the way idioms are listed in the *Oxford Advanced Learner's Dictionary*. Other dictionaries may not enter idioms in the same way, or at the same place.

1 **Which word should you look up to find the meaning of these idioms? (Think carefully before you answer 6 and 7.)**

▶ **if you ask me** (Look up *ask*.)
1 **(at) any moment** ....
2 **catch sb's eye** ....
3 **out of breath** ....
4 **it's early days** ....
5 **not just yet** ....
6 **go public** ....
7 **be a good thing (that)** ....

2 **Are these sentences true (T) or false (F)? They contain idioms from page 12 and Exercise 1, so you may have to use a dictionary.**

1 If you do something **on purpose**, it is your intention to do it. ....
2 If you **catch somebody's eye**, you do something stupid and somebody else notices. ....
3 If something is going to happen **at any moment**, it is going to happen very soon. ....
4 If you **pull somebody's leg**, you play a joke on them, usually by telling them something that isn't true. ....
5 If somebody is **out of breath**, they are dead. ....
6 If you do something **once in a blue moon**, you do it once a month. ....
7 If you **go public**, you tell people about something that is a secret. ....
8 If you do something **in vain**, you do it successfully. ....
9 If you say '**by the way**', you are going to say something that is not directly connected to what you have just been talking about. ....
10 If you say '**it's a long story**' to someone, you want them to sit down so that you can explain the story with all the details. ....

3 **The idioms in bold have one word that can be replaced by another without changing the meaning. Look them up in your dictionary and write the idiom again using the alternative word.**

▶ Are you going? ~ **It depends**. *That depends.*
1 We've got a fantastic Italian restaurant **on the doorstep**. ....
2 He arrived **at the last minute**, as usual. ....
3 She **was a bag of nerves** before her exam. (Look up *nerve*.) ....
4 Please **send my love to** Grace. (Look up *love*.) ....
5 He's very angry, so just **keep out of his way**. (Look up *way*.) ....
6 The company is always looking for **new blood**. (Look up *blood*.) ....

4 **Does your dictionary label the style of the idioms in these sentences? What label does it use?**

▶ Could I borrow the car? ~ **No chance**. *informal*
1 **As regards** a solution to the problem, we're a long way off. ....
2 She's a very attractive woman. ~ **I'll say**. ....
3 We'll see you soon. **Lots of love**, Terry. ....
4 I think these DVDs might have **fallen off the back of a lorry**. ....
5 Put your coat on or you'll **catch your death of cold**! ....
6 I've never had an accident on my motorbike – **touch wood**! ....
7 I'm sorry, we**'re fresh out of** coffee. ....
8 I'm ringing **with reference to** your advertisement in today's newspaper. ....

4 The grammar of phrasal verbs

Phrasal verbs consist of a verb, e.g. *put*, *take*, *show*, and one or two particles, e.g. *off*, *out*, *by*, *up*, etc. These are the three main types of phrasal verbs.

1 Phrasal verbs with no object ('intransitive')

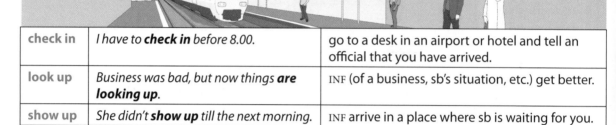

The train's just **coming in** now.
(Come in = arrive.)

check in	I have to **check in** before 8.00.	go to a desk in an airport or hotel and tell an official that you have arrived.
look up	Business was bad, but now things **are looking up**.	INF (of a business, sb's situation, etc.) get better.
show up	She didn't **show up** till the next morning.	INF arrive in a place where sb is waiting for you.

2 Phrasal verbs which can be separated by an object ('transitive, separable')

She **wrote** his name **down** in her notebook. (Write sth down = write sth on paper.)

look sth up	I had to **look** the word **up**.	look for information in a book or online.
make sth up	I didn't want to see him, so I **made up** an excuse and left.	invent a story or an explanation for sth.
try sth on	I **tried** the jacket **on** but it was too small.	put on a piece of clothing to see if it fits or looks good on you.

With these transitive verbs, you can usually put the object before or after the particle.
*She **wrote** his name **down**.* OR *She **wrote down** his name*.

If the object is a long phrase, it will usually come after the phrasal verb.
*She **wrote down** everything she could remember about him*.

If the object is a pronoun, e.g. *him*, *her*, it **must** go between the verb and the particle.
*She **wrote** it **down**.* NOT ~~She wrote down it~~.

3 Phrasal verbs which cannot be separated by an object ('transitive, inseparable')
These may have one or two particles.

He **looked after** the baby. NOT ~~He looked the baby after.~~
(Look after sb/sth = take care of or be responsible for sb/sth.)

look into sth	I complained to the airline, and they**'re looking into** it.	investigate and try to discover the facts about sth, e.g. a crime, a problem.
come across sth/sb	I **came across** the word in an article.	meet sb or find sth by chance.
stand for sth	What does WWW **stand for**?	represent or mean (WWW **stands for** World Wide Web).
go out with sb	Marisa**'s going out with** Tom's brother.	spend time with sb and have a romantic relationship with them.
cut back on sth	I must **cut back on** sweets to try and lose weight.	reduce the amount of sth that you eat, spend, use, etc.

spotlight Intransitive and transitive verbs

Some verbs can be both intransitive and transitive, but a difference in structure indicates a difference in meaning: e.g. **look up** = get better, but **look sth up** = look for information in a book or online; **take off** = (of a plane) leave the ground, but **take sth off** = remove a piece of clothing.

spotlight Phrasal verbs in dictionaries

Dictionaries usually list phrasal verbs after the entry for the main verb and any idioms.
They show you if a verb takes an object (*sb/sth*). If the phrasal verb is separable, you will find *sb/sth* between the verb and the particle, e.g. **make sth up**. If the verb and particle are inseparable, you will see *sb/sth* after the particle, e.g. **look after sb/sth**.

1 **Tick ✓ the sentences which are correct.**

1 He wrote a few words down. ......
2 He wrote down. ......
3 Did he write down her address? ......
4 Don't write it down yet. ......

5 I've cut back on smoking. ......
6 I'm trying to cut back on. ......
7 She's cut chocolate back on. ......
8 There are easy ways to cut back on it. ......

2 *It* **is missing in __some__ of these sentences. Where does it go?**

▶ If you don't know the meaning, look ∧ up in the dictionary.
1 Someone has stolen our car, and the police are looking into at the moment.
2 It wasn't a true story; I'm sure he just made up.
3 They said they'd be here early, but they didn't show up till 9.00.
4 Can I ask you about your cat? Who looks after when you go on holiday?
5 I don't know what MP3 stands for. Do you?
6 I hadn't seen the website before; I came across yesterday on the Internet.
7 If you try on and it's too big, you could always give it to me.
8 The train was delayed but it finally came in at midday.

3 **Organize the words into sentences and add one word.**

▶ cut | to | should | sugar | you | try | back You should try to cut back **on** sugar.
1 5.00 | can | you | check | at | ....
2 look | you | could | the | number ? ....
3 today | daughter | after | friend's | I'm | my ....
4 David's | out | he's | going | sister ....
5 Cable | CNN | Network | stands | News ....
6 this | like | try | would | to | you | skirt ? ....

4 **Rewrite the sentences using a phrasal verb from page 14. The meaning must stay the same.**

▶ I found the information by chance on the Internet. I came across the information on the Internet.
1 She wasn't happy, but now things are getting better. ....
2 The committee investigated the cause of the problem. ....
3 I didn't know the answer, so I invented something. ....
4 The train's arriving on platform five. ....
5 We can reduce the electricity we use. ....
6 What do the letters FAQ represent? ....
7 I had to check the meaning in a dictionary. ....
8 Our meeting was at 5.00, but Sue never arrived. ....

5 **ABOUT YOUR DICTIONARY Use your dictionary to find out if these verbs are transitive or intransitive, and separable or inseparable. In your notebook, write a sentence example for one meaning of the verb.**

▶ put back put sth back (transitive, separable) e.g. I put the book back on the shelf.
rub out, go in for, settle down, take after, take back, fall out with

5 Core meanings 1

A On

Some particles can express a particular meaning when they are used with certain verbs.
For example, **on** can indicate continuation.

Example	Meaning
The meeting **dragged on** for hours.	**drag on** continue for too long.
I **carried on** painting while the light was still good.	**carry on** (**doing sth**) continue with an activity for a period of time.
Michael's very annoying – he **keeps on** taking my pens.	**keep on doing sth** repeat sth many times, often in an annoying way.
Be quiet and **get on with** your work.	**get on with sth** continue doing sth, often after an interruption.
The weather was great, so we **stayed on** for a couple more days.	**stay on** continue enjoying yourself, studying, or working in a place, often after others have left.
We **drove on** for several kilometres.	**drive on** continue driving.

spotlight *go on* (see also page 65)

The traffic noise goes on all night. = continues without changing.
He went on (and on) about his car. = talked about his car for a long time in a boring way.
Let's go on to Exercise 2. = pass from doing the first exercise to doing the next exercise. SYN **move on to sth**.

1 Match 1–8 with a–h.

1 Pat went home but I stayed on ....
2 I was angry because I kept on ....
3 We had a coffee, then got on with ....
4 The company can't go on ....
5 The lecture dragged on ....
6 The teacher told us to move on ....
7 He's always going on about ....
8 We weren't tired, so we carried on ....

a his collection of DVDs. No one's interested.
b some more work.
c like this; we're losing too much money.
d to the next section of the text.
e until the party finished.
f making the same mistake.
g for a few more miles.
h for ages; everyone was bored.

2 Replace the underlined word(s) with a phrasal verb from the box in the correct form.

drag on   go on   go on to   carry on ✓   keep on   drive on   stay on   go on and on   get on with

▶ We played cards in the garden and just <u>continued</u> until it got dark. *carried on*
1 He <u>is always</u> interrupting me; it's very annoying. ....
2 We've talked enough about this. Let's <u>move on to</u> the next item on the list. ....
3 Some students leave at sixteen, while others <u>continue</u> for two more years. ....
4 I thought it would be a short speech, but it <u>continued</u> for almost an hour. ....
5 The train service is getting worse and worse; we can't <u>continue</u> like this. ....
6 She <u>talked for hours</u> about her boyfriend – I nearly fell asleep. ....
7 When the children have gone to school, I can <u>do</u> the housework. ....
8 The petrol station was closed, so we <u>continued</u> to the next one. ....

B Off and *around*

Off sometimes adds a meaning of departure or separation. **Around** can add the meaning, 'with no particular purpose or aim'. **About** and **around** are interchangeable in the examples below.

'My sister was going skiing and I went to the airport to **see** her **off**. But when we got there it was snowing heavily, and the plane couldn't **take off**, so we had to come home. By the morning the snow was very deep, and we **were cut off** from the rest of the village.'

'I **went off** to do some shopping, and left my husband **messing about with** his motorbike while the boys **lazed around** in the garden. When I got back, there were tools **lying around** everywhere, and Mike and the boys had disappeared.'

'There were some boys **hanging around** the school entrance, and one or two were **messing about with** other pupils' bikes, so I told them to **clear off**.'

Glossary

see sb off	go to an airport, station, etc. with sb in order to say goodbye to them.
take off	(of a plane) leave the ground.
cut sth off	(often passive) separate sth from sth else, so it is difficult to leave or enter. (**Cut sth off sth** remove sth from sth larger by cutting it.)
go off	leave a place, especially in order to do sth.
mess about/around (with sth)	INF 1 spend time doing sth or repairing sth in a relaxed way (Text 2). 2 do sth or use sth in a careless or annoying way (Text 3).
laze around/about	relax, enjoy yourself, and do nothing.
lie around/about	(of a number of things) be left in a place, usually untidily or where they shouldn't be.
hang around/about	INF spend time in a place doing nothing.
clear off	INF go away (often used angrily as a command).

3 Write six more sentences using words from the table.

He leaves his shoes lying ✓		at the airport.
I saw my dad		the street corner.
We lazed	**off**	until 7.00.
The town was cut	**around**	and leave her alone.
We didn't take		by the flood water.
She told me to clear		by the pool.
The boys often hang		on the floor. ✓

▶ He leaves his shoes lying around on the floor.

4 Complete the sentences with a suitable verb in the correct form.

1 After the concert, there were lots of people .... around, waiting for taxis.
2 My husband spends most of the weekend .... about on the river with his boat.
3 We .... a branch off the tree because it was getting too big.
4 My son always leaves his CDs .... around in the living room.
5 He .... off to buy a paper, but he'll be back in a minute.
6 My brother's leaving for Singapore tomorrow, so we're all going to .... him off.
7 A lot of teenagers just .... around the centre of town: they have nothing better to do.
8 I don't like that boy following me. I wish he'd .... off.

6 Core meanings 2

A *Up* and *through*

When **up** is used with certain verbs, it doesn't change the meaning of the verb, but emphasizes the idea of completing or finishing something. The verbs in the text are separable.

Karen made her son **eat up** his breakfast and **drink up** his milk before he went to school. Then, as soon as he'd left, she **cleared** the breakfast things **up** and put the dirty stuff in the dishwasher. Today, she was also going to wash the floor, but then she remembered she**'d used up** the floor cleaner the previous day, so she **tidied up** the living room instead.

Through sometimes suggests going from the beginning to the end of something. The verbs below are inseparable.

Example	Meaning
I'd like to go through *the homework.*	look at, check, or discuss sth carefully.
His father has lived through *two wars.*	experience and survive sth very difficult.
I flicked through *his new book.*	look through sth quickly, without reading it.
I looked through *your report yesterday.*	look at the pages of sth, reading it only in part.
I managed to sleep through *the storm.*	continue sleeping while there is a lot of noise around you.

1 Match 1–8 with a–h.

1 I picked up the book and flicked through ....
2 My grandfather lived through ....
3 We sat down and went through ....
4 I managed to sleep through ....
5 I had to clear up ....
6 Please don't use up ....
7 I couldn't eat up ....
8 I offered to tidy up ....

a all the milk from the fridge.
b the first few pages.
c the noise of my neighbour's party.
d the sugar that was on the floor.
e years of depression.
f all the rice; she gave me too much.
g her desk.
h the report together.

2 Complete the sentences with suitable verbs.

1 After the party we had to .... up all the mess that people had left.
2 I .... through the brochure while I was waiting, but I only read part of it.
3 I'd .... up all my travel tickets, so I had to buy some more.
4 The teacher usually .... through the exercises when we've finished them.
5 My mother makes me .... my room up every week.
6 Many of these people have had to .... through years of civil war.
7 OK. .... up your coffee and we can go.
8 The music was really loud, but Jake .... through it without waking up.

3 ABOUT YOU Write your answers in your notebook, or talk to another student.

1 Do you normally go through homework in class?
2 When did you last tidy up your bedroom?
3 Do you ever sleep through the alarm clock?
4 Do you always clear up as soon as you've finished a meal?
5 Do you often flick through magazines without buying them?

B Back

In phrasal verbs, the particle **back** usually has the meaning of returning somewhere, or returning something to a place.

The radio was faulty so I took it back to the shop.

She took his car key by mistake, but gave it back this morning.

She read a few pages then put the book back on the shelf.

Example	Meaning
If you borrow that brush, please bring it back.	return to this place with sth that you have taken or borrowed.
I'll go there by bus, and Jim can bring me back.	return sb to a place, usually by car.
The books were damaged so I sent them back.	return sth by post, messenger, waiter, etc.
He rang at 2.00. I said I'd phone him back later.	return sb's phone call. SYN **ring sb back**.
Dad lent me the money, but I've paid him back.	return to sb the money that you borrowed from them.

> **spotlight** *get back*
>
> *When do you get back?* = return, especially to your home or workplace.
> *Can we get the money back?* = have something returned to you.
> *I woke up and couldn't get back to sleep.* = return to an earlier state, situation, etc.

4 Tick ✓ the most likely answers. One, two, or three may be possible.

1 The jumper wasn't right, so I .... it back to the shop.
took ☐ rang ☐ sent ☐ got ☐
2 I was out when he called me this morning, so I'll have to .... him back.
ring ☐ get ☐ bring ☐ phone ☐
3 When you've finished with the books, please .... them back.
take ☐ pay ☐ bring ☐ put ☐
4 If your train arrives more than an hour late, you .... half your money back.
take ☐ ring ☐ get ☐ pay ☐
5 I borrowed the books yesterday and .... them back to Pat this morning.
gave ☐ put ☐ took ☐ rang ☐
6 The shirts weren't the ones I ordered, so I .... them back.
gave ☐ sent ☐ took ☐ put ☐

5 Complete the dialogues with the correct verb.

1 Did you complain about the steak? ~ Yes, the waiter .... it back to the kitchen.
2 Did Angela phone? ~ Yes, but I was out, so I'll .... her back later.
3 Did you have to borrow the money? ~ Yes, but I can .... it back easily.
4 Do you pay a deposit when you move in? ~ Yes, but you .... it back when you leave.
5 Did you go there by train? ~ Yes, but my uncle .... me back in his car.
6 The injury affected him a lot. ~ Yes, he never .... back to the same level of fitness.
7 I'm leaving soon. ~ OK, fine. What time do you .... back?
8 Do you want to borrow this book? ~ Yes, please. I'll .... it back to you tomorrow.

7 Different meanings of phrasal verbs

Many phrasal verbs can have more than one meaning.

Go off

The alarm goes off *at 5.00.* = rings.

The lights suddenly went off.
= stopped working.

The bomb went off. = exploded.

Put sth on

I put my best suit *on.* =
dressed myself. OPP take sth off.

He put *the light* on.
SYNS turn sth on, switch sth on.

I put on *a lot of weight last year.*
= became fatter.

Break down

The car broke down. = stopped working.

She broke down *at the news.* = started crying.

Go down

The sun's going down.
= disappearing below the
horizon. OPP come up.

Prices went down *by
10 per cent.* = became lower.
OPP go up.

Do sth up

I can't **do** *this zip* up. = fasten.

They're doing the flat up.
= redecorating.

Turn up

When did they turn up?
= arrive.

Look! My ring's turned up!
= be found by chance.

Tie sb up

They tied *him* up. = tied
his arms so that he
couldn't move.

She's tied up *at the
moment.* = very busy
(used in the passive).

1 Tick (✓) the answers which are possible. One, two, or all three may be correct.

1 He's put on *about five kilos* ☐ *a lot of weight* ☐ *fat* ☐.
2 Did you hear the *fire alarm* ☐ *television* ☐ *car alarm* ☐ go off?
3 I'm hoping that the *temperature* ☐ *price of meat* ☐ *age limit* ☐ will go down.
4 She's very young and she can't do her *shoes* ☐ *jacket* ☐ *socks* ☐ up yet.
5 The *taxi* ☐ *car* ☐ *train* ☐ broke down on the way back from the mountains.

2 Correct the mistake in each sentence.

▶ We sat and watched the sun ~~come~~ down over the horizon. *go* ....
1 I see Beverley's got on a few kilos again; her diet's not working, is it? ....
2 Could you put the lights down? I can't see a thing in here. ....
3 I don't know what's happened to my keys; I hope they turn out. ....
4 We've decided to make the living room up; Pat's going to do the painting. ....
5 She was tidied up this week, so I made an appointment to see her next Monday. ....
6 When I heard what had happened to the animals, I broke away and cried. ....
7 They tied me out and ran off with the money. ....
8 The zip on my coat has broken and I can't do it on. ....

3 Complete the email.

Hi Laura, What a morning! My alarm clock (1) .... off unexpectedly at 4.00
a.m., and I couldn't get back to sleep. I just lay there worrying till the sun (2) ....
up, and then I got up, feeling terrible. I had an important business meeting in town, so I
(3) .... my best suit on, then I spilt coffee all over the trousers and had to change.
I decided to drive, but that was a big mistake – the car (4) .... down on the
way to the meeting. I rang the man I was meeting and tried to explain, but he said that if I
didn't (5) .... up in the next five minutes, he would have to leave, and he added
that he would be (6) .... up for the rest of the week. I sat in the car and just
(7) .... down in tears. And it was still only 9.30!

4 Replace the underlined words with a suitable phrasal verb in the correct form.

1 What time did they <u>arrive</u> in the end? ....
2 My hands were so cold I couldn't <u>fasten</u> the buttons on my coat. ....
3 I'm worried about my gas bill; I've heard the prices are <u>increasing</u> again. ....
4 Excuse me, Mr Salter, but are you <u>busy</u> at the moment? ....
5 We're planning to <u>redecorate</u> the flat before we move in. ....
6 There was a terrible bang, and we realized that a bomb had <u>exploded</u>. ....
7 Has the missing dog <u>been found</u> yet? ....
8 He just <u>started crying</u> for no reason I could understand. ....

5 Complete the questions. (You will answer them in Exercise 6.)

1 Do car alarms .... off very often where you live?
2 Do you tend to .... weight on at certain times of the year? If so, when?
3 Have you ever been in a car that .... down late at night? If so, what happened?
4 Is your home newly decorated, or would you like to .... it up?
5 What happens if you .... up late for class?
6 Are prices generally .... down, up, or staying the same at the moment?

6 ABOUT YOU Write your answers to the questions in Exercise 5 in your notebook,
or talk to another student.

Review: Introduction to idioms and phrasal verbs

Unit 1

1 Complete the definitions.

1 If someone arrives *out of the blue*, it means they arrive _____ and unexpectedly.
2 If you're driving *like mad*, it means you're driving _____ .
3 If you ring your mother every morning *without fail*, it means you _____ ring your mother in the morning.
4 If someone thinks they have *lost face*, it means they feel that they look _____ because of something they have done.
5 If someone is *in a terrible state*, it means they are feeling very _____ .
6 If you *turn a blind eye* to something, it means you pretend not to _____ it.

2 One word is missing in each line. Where does it go? Write it at the end.

1 A How you're still doing that grammar exercise? _____
   B Because when I checked my answers I realized they didn't sense. _____
2 A Ooh, that awful David Leventon – just steer of him! _____
   B David Leventon? That name rings a – didn't he go to prison for burglary? _____
3 A What's happening over there in distance? _____
   B It looks like a man chasing some boys and they're running flat. _____
4 A How earth did the accident happen? _____
   B She was running mad for the bus and didn't see the cyclist. _____

Unit 2

1 Find answers to the clues by moving horizontally or vertically, backwards or forwards.

GET	HEAVENS	DON'T	FAMOUS	LAST
NOWHERE	THANK	ASK	ME	WORDS
OF	CAKE	EARLY	BETTER	NEVER
PIECE	BRIGHT	AND	LATE	THAN
A	LESS	A	CHANGE	YOUR
MORE	OR	STONE'S	THROW	MIND

▶ Very early in the morning. *bright and early*
1 You say this when you don't know the answer to something. _____
2 Almost or approximately. _____
3 You might say this when someone has arrived late. _____
4 Only a short distance away. _____
5 Used to say you are pleased and relieved about something. _____
6 An informal phrase meaning 'very easy'. _____
7 You say this when you think someone is too confident that something is going to happen. _____
8 Change your decision or opinion about something. _____
9 Make no progress, or have no success. _____

2 Complete the words in the sentences. Then underline the full idiom in each one.

1 If something is generally true, you can also say it's true in the m_____ .
2 Do you agree with the saying that absence makes the heart grow f_____ ?
3 'Good g_____ !' is quite a common exclamation to express surprise.
4 If somebody gets on your n_____ , you find them very irritating.
5 Many people think that trial and e_____ is a good way of learning.
6 We all have to face disappointments; that's a fact of l_____ .

Unit 3

1 Replace the underlined words with an idiom that includes the word in capital letters. The meaning must stay the same.

▶ It was <u>lucky</u> that he left early. THING *a good thing* _____
1 Mo and I see each other <u>very rarely</u>. MOON _____
2 She was just <u>playing a joke on me</u>. LEG _____
3 I've got a market <u>very close to my flat</u>. DOORSTEP _____
4 We need some <u>new members</u> in the club. FRESH _____
5 She's planning to <u>tell everyone the secret</u>. PUBLIC _____
6 I am writing <u>about</u> the advertisement. REFERENCE _____

2 Cross out one unnecessary word in each line.

1 He said the watch had fallen off the back part of a lorry. I was right not to trust him.
2 She's made good progress at work, but it's still too early days. We'll see what happens.
3 A beautiful blue silk shirt caught up my eye in the shop window.
4 I think she just said it on her purpose to annoy me. And she succeeded.
5 I'd better go or I'll be late. Oh, and by in the way, what time's the meeting tomorrow?
6 Why were you in your pyjamas in the street at 1.00? ~ Well, it's a long time story.

Unit 4

1 Read the sentences on the left. Circle the phrase on the right which expresses the meaning most accurately.

1 We need to cut back on coffee.	*drink less coffee | stop drinking coffee*
2 I'm looking after the children.	*looking for them | taking care of them*
3 She tried it on.	*put on a piece of clothing | made an effort*
4 He takes after his father.	*looks after him | behaves like him*
5 The girls have fallen out.	*they've had a row | they've had an accident*
6 What does it stand for?	*represent | show*

2 Complete the dialogues with a suitable phrasal verb.

1 There's a mistake here. ~ That's OK, it's in pencil. I'll _____ it _____ .
2 Did you find the book by chance? ~ Yes, I _____ it in a second-hand bookshop.
3 Is business getting better? ~ Yes. Things have started to _____ recently.
4 Were the two girls late? ~ Yes. They didn't _____ until 9.30.
5 What time should we be at the airport? ~ We're meant to _____ an hour and a half before take-off.
6 He didn't invent the story, did he? ~ Yes, he just _____ it _____ .
7 Is that her boyfriend? ~ Yes. They've been _____ each other for months.
8 I don't know what this word means. ~ Well, _____ it _____ , then.

Unit 5

1 Put the words in the correct order and add one more word.

▶ the | at | uncle | I | my | off | station   *I saw my uncle off at the station.*
1 on | illness | about | and | she | went | her   ....
2 in | was | Brenda | garden | messing | the   ....
3 the | was | deep | by | cut | village | snow   ....
4 lunchtime | working | children | the | carried | until   ....
5 club | outside | boys | the | hanging | the | were   ....
6 a | of | lying | there | lot | was | money   ....

2 Complete the dialogues using a phrasal verb.

1 A Did you have a relaxing time?
  B Yes, I just .... in the garden. It was lovely.
2 A Did she interrupt your work?
  B Yes, and I really needed to .... with my project.
3 A Why are you going to the airport?
  B I'm going to .... my brother ....
4 A He's very boring, isn't he?
  B Yes, he's always .... about his job.
5 A Is Ella very untidy?
  B Definitely! She leaves all her clothes ....
6 A Jenny's very annoying.
  B Yes, she .... losing things – it drives me mad.
7 A Was it a good play?
  B Well, the acting was OK, but it just .... for hours.
8 A Did you leave the party late?
  B Yes, I .... after it finished to help clear up.

Unit 6

1 Circle the correct answer(s). Both answers may be correct.

1 When you go to John's, would you *bring* | *put* my coat back home, please? I left it there.
2 Come on, eat *up* | *out* that salad; it's good for you.
3 The room was a terrible mess and it took me ages to *clear* | *tidy* it up.
4 I paid him too much, but I'm sure I'll *pay* | *get* it back if I ask for it.
5 Did you *live* | *go* through the list and discuss everything?
6 She took a book from the shelf and *looked* | *flicked* through it.

2 Rewrite the sentences using a phrasal verb. Use the words in capital letters.

▶ If you borrow the key, please return it. BACK *If you borrow the key, please put it back.*
1 Please put everything in order in the office. UP
2 I'll have to return these trousers to the shop. BACK
3 When do you think he'll return from lunch? BACK
4 I looked quickly at the magazine. THROUGH
5 Maggie rang – she wants you to return her call. BACK
6 Did you check the figures? THROUGH

Unit 7

1 Complete the phrasal verbs.

1 When the sun .... down, it's getting near the end of the day.
2 If someone .... up at 7.00, it means they arrive at 7.00.
3 If you .... on weight, it means you get heavier.
4 If you're .... up at work, it means you're busy.
5 If someone's .... their living room up, it means they're decorating it.
6 If your car .... down on the way home, it means you can't get home.
7 If an alarm .... off, it makes a loud noise.
8 If you .... your coat up, it means you fasten the buttons of your coat.
9 If someone .... down, it means they start crying.
10 If the lights suddenly .... off, it means the room goes dark.
11 If your salary .... down, it means you'll earn less money.
12 If something .... up, it means you find it by chance.

2 Complete the crossword. Replace the words in italics in the clues with a phrasal verb.

		▶ T	A	K	E	O	F	F	
					1	O			
					2	O			
					3	O			
4						O			
					5	O			
		6				O			
7						O			
					8	O			
					9	O			

▶ I was told to *remove* my shoes as soon as I went in the building.
1 The bomb landed, but luckily it didn't *explode*.
2 Do you think the prices will *fall* before the end of the year?
3 They always tell you to *fasten* your seat belt when you get on the plane.
4 Could you *turn on* the lights, please? It's a bit dark in here.
5 Did you watch the sun *rise* this morning? It was beautiful.
6 I *got dressed in* an old pair of boots and a raincoat and went for a walk.
7 The photocopier in our office *stopped working*, so I couldn't send him the documents.
8 My flat has been *redecorated* in bright colours.
9 Why did the lights suddenly *stop working* in the middle of the evening?

8 I can follow classroom language

A Teachers' instructions

Teachers often use certain idioms and phrasal verbs when they give instructions in class.

First of all, let's **go over** the homework.
You can **leave out** Exercise 2.
If you make a mistake, **rub** it **out**.
Take it in turns to read the dialogue.
Pascal, **swap places with** Marcel, please.
Finish it **off** at home and **hand it in** tomorrow.
Put all the books **away** before you leave.
OK, let's **call it a day**.

Glossary

first of all	before doing anything else.
go over/through sth	look at, check, or discuss sth carefully.
leave sth out	not do sth, e.g. an exercise (**leave sb out** = not include sb).
rub sth out	remove marks made by a pencil, chalk, etc. using a rubber.
take it in turns	do sth one after another so that everyone has an opportunity to do it (also **take turns at sth**).
swap places (with sb)	take sb's seat or position so they can take yours.
finish sth off	do the last part of sth.
put sth away	put sth where you usually keep it, especially after using it.
call it a day	INF decide to stop what you are doing (often work).

spotlight *hand sth in/out/round*

If you **hand sth in**, you give something to a person in authority, e.g. a teacher or the police.
If you **hand sth out**, you give something to each person in a group, e.g. *Hand out the books.* SYN **give sth out**.
If you **hand sth round**, you pass something, especially food or drink, to people in a group: *Lars, could you hand the cakes round, please?*

1 Complete the phrases below using words in the box.

> it   of   it   a day   places   over something   all   in turns   something out

call	swap	take ....
go	hand	first ....

2 Complete the teacher's instructions.

Silvia, first of (1) ...., could you (2) .... out these worksheets, please? Thanks. Now everyone, I want you to do the first exercise and we'll go (3) .... the answers when you've finished. If you use pencil, you can rub (4) .... the answers afterwards, and do it again later. Marco, I know you have to leave in a minute, so why don't you finish it (5) .... at home and hand it (6) .... to me tomorrow?

3 Complete the last word in each sentence.

1 If you want to talk to Joe, we'll have to swap ....
2 After you've used the CD player, remember to put it ....
3 Paul, you can't use the computer all the time; you'll have to take it in ....
4 I think we've done enough; let's call it a ....
5 If you can't do one of the questions, just leave it ....
6 As it was our last lesson, the teacher made cakes for the class and handed them ....

B Teachers' advice

At different times, teachers have given me the following advice.

> If you're doing an English course, **take** it **seriously**.

> Do written work **in rough** first, then it doesn't matter if you **cross** something **out**.

> Practising with classmates will help you to **build up** your confidence.

> If you're not sure of the meaning of a word, **look** it **up** rather than guess.

> **It's no good** writing things in a notebook if you don't **go back** and study them again.

> What you learn in class is just **the tip of the iceberg**. You need to study **at home** as well.

Glossary

take sth seriously	think that sth is important and should be given careful attention.
look sth up	look for information about sth in a reference book or online.
in rough	If you write sth **in rough**, you do it for a first time without worrying about mistakes because you will write it correctly later.
cross sth out	In this sentence, *it* is **crossed out**: *Look* ~~it~~ *something up.*
it's no good (doing sth)	= it will have no positive result (doing sth). SYN **it's no use (doing sth)**.
go back (to…)	return to a person, place, subject, or activity.
build sth up	increase or develop sth over a period of time (**build up confidence / strength / a reputation**, etc.).
the tip of the iceberg	only a small part of a much larger problem or matter.
at home	in your own house or flat.

4 Correct the mistake in each sentence. Write the correct word at the end.

1 If you see a mistake, you can just cross it off. ....
2 I think it's a real problem, and what you can see is just the top of the iceberg. ....
3 It's no use to study grammar if you don't practise it. ....
4 My brother's in home at the moment. ....
5 It's not good trying to learn English without a dictionary. ....
6 When you've finished the text, get back to the beginning and read it again. ....

5 Complete the sentences.

1 I always write essays in .... first, then I copy them out later.
2 They think they've solved the problem, but this is just the tip of the ....
3 My name was on the list, but somebody .... it out – I don't know why.
4 When I studied English at school, I didn't really .... it seriously.
5 I wrote the answers quickly, then I went .... and checked them carefully later.
6 It's no .... telling him to work harder. He just won't listen to you.
7 He missed last term with a serious illness, and he'll need time to .... up his strength.
8 Give me the dictionary and I'll .... it up.

6 ABOUT YOU Do you do any of the things suggested at the top of the page? Is it all good advice or is there any bad advice, in your opinion? Write your answers, or talk to another student.

....
....
....
....
....

9 I can talk about learning

A How to make progress

Dos and don'ts

- Don't be embarrassed about speaking: the main thing is to **make yourself understood**.

- Don't be afraid to make mistakes: you learn from **trial and error**.

- The classroom is an opportunity to practise speaking, so **make the most of** it.

- There are certain things, such as irregular verbs, that you can **learn by heart**.

- **Saying** something **out loud** can help you to practise the pronunciation and remember it.

- Don't miss lessons, or you**'ll get behind with** your work and find it difficult to **catch up**.

- Don't **give up**. **Stick at** it and you'll **get there** in the end.

Glossary

dos and don'ts	things you should and shouldn't do.
make yourself understood	speak in a way that others can understand.
trial and error	a way of solving a problem by trying several possibilities and learning from your mistakes.
make the most of sth	enjoy sth or use sth as much as you can.
learn sth (off) by heart	learn sth by reading or hearing it repeatedly until you remember it exactly.
(say/read sth) out loud	(say/read sth) so that others can hear it.
get behind (with sth)	not do sth on time, and then have more to do later.
catch up (with sb)	reach the level of others who are more advanced.
give up	stop trying to do sth, or accept that you cannot do sth.
stick at sth	continue with sth even though it is difficult.
get there	achieve sth after a period of work or effort.

1 One word is missing in each sentence. Where does it go? Write it at the end.

▶ At school, we had to learn certain poems ⟨ heart. by
1 My pronunciation isn't very good, but I manage to make understood. ....
2 It'll take me a long time to become a doctor, but I'll there eventually. ....
3 He was ill for ages, and unfortunately he got behind his studies. ....
4 It's your only chance, so make the most it. ....
5 I missed several lessons, so now I have to up with the others in the class. ....
6 The teacher started the lesson with a long list of and don'ts. ....

2 Complete the questions. (You will answer them in Exercise 3.)

1 Can you usually .... yourself understood in English?
2 Have you tried to learn certain things by .... ? If so, what?
3 Do you say words out .... to help you to remember them?
4 Do you always .... the most of your time in class?
5 Do you ever .... behind with any of your studies?
6 Do you think trial and .... is a good learning method?
7 If you start something, do you generally .... at it?
8 Have you ever started a course and then .... up?

3 ABOUT YOU Write your answers to the questions in Exercise 2 in your notebook, or talk to another student. Which is the best piece of advice in the *Dos and don'ts* above?

B A learning process

As I had planned a holiday in Spain, I decided to **brush up on** my Spanish before I went, and I enrolled on a local evening course. At first I had to **rack my brains** to remember anything, and I couldn't **make sense of** the grammar, so it was very hard to **keep up with** the other students. Then, after a while, things started **coming back to** me, and I realized there were lots of words **on the tip of my tongue**. But some of the new vocabulary wouldn't **sink in** – words just **went in one ear and out the other**. When you work hard all day, it's not easy to **keep your mind on** a difficult subject in the evening. But I stuck at it, and I began to **pick** things **up** more quickly. All I have to do now is **keep it up**.

Glossary

brush up on sth / brush sth up	improve your knowledge or skill in sth, especially when you have not used it for a period of time. (👁 See page 144.)
make sense of sth	manage to understand sth.
keep up (with sb)	make progress at the same speed as others.
sink in	(of information or experiences) be remembered or understood.
keep your mind on sth	continue to concentrate on sth.
pick sth up	learn sth without making a big effort.
keep it up	continue to do sth as well as you are doing it now.

spotlight Remembering and forgetting

If you **rack your brains** (or **brain**), you try hard to remember something.
If information **comes back to** you, you remember it.
If a word or name is **on the tip of your tongue**, you are sure you know it, but you can't remember it at that moment.
If information **goes in one ear and out the other**, you forget it quickly.

---

4 Complete the six phrases using words in the box.

> the tip   in one ear   your brains   sense of something   of my tongue
> it up   and out the other   your mind on something

rack	on ....
keep	make ....
go	keep ....

5 Complete the sentences.

1 I often find that I have words .... the tip of my ....
2 I often have to .... my brains to remember things I've learnt recently.
3 I think I'm doing really well in English, but I need to .... it up.
4 I'm bad at languages. New words go in one .... and out the ....
5 I'm good at languages. I can usually .... things up quite quickly.
6 I find it quite hard to .... sense of the Present Perfect in English.
7 If I don't write down new words as I learn them, they don't sink ....
8 I need to brush .... on irregular English verbs.
9 When I practise speaking, I find that lots of words .... back to me.

6 ABOUT YOU Read the sentences in Exercise 5 again. Which ones are true for you? Write your answers in your notebook, or talk to another student.

10 I can talk about exams

A Revising for an exam

 Thursday: my last chance to revise for my economics exam. I've worked hard to try and **get on top of** this subject. Not only have I **got into the habit of** reading the business pages in the newspapers, but I also spent the holidays **going through** all my lecture notes. I know it's important not to **get** too **bogged down**, so I decided not to study everything but just try and **work out** which questions might **come up** – and concentrate on those. I also went through some past papers with a friend, which was really useful. Now, I'm just **keeping my fingers crossed** for tomorrow – but the truth is, I can only **do my best**, and **it's not the end of the world** if I fail. Anyway, I'd better **get down** to some work.

Glossary

get on top of sth	manage to control or deal with sth. SYN **get to grips with sth**.
get into the habit of doing sth	develop a particular habit.
go through sth	look at or study notes, papers, etc. SYN **go over sth**.
get bogged down (in sth)	INF become so involved with the details of sth that you can't make any progress.
work sth out	solve a problem by considering the facts.
come up	If a question, number, name, etc. **comes up**, it is selected and appears somewhere (in this case, in an exam paper).
keep your fingers crossed	hope for good luck or success.
it's not the end of the world	INF = it's not the worst thing that could happen.
get down to sth	begin to do sth and give serious attention to it.

> **spotlight** Idioms with *best*
>
> If you **do your best** or **try your best** or **do something to the best of your ability**, you try as hard as possible to achieve something.
> To wish someone luck for an exam, you can say **(The) best of luck!**

1 Cross out one wrong word in each sentence.

▶ It's not the ~~last~~ end of the world.

1 I must get to the grips with this.
2 You can only do to your best.
3 Keep both your fingers crossed!
4 I did it up to the best of my ability.
5 Best of the luck!
6 He works it out answers to problems.

2 Complete the questions. (You will answer them in Exercise 3.)

1 Do you find it easy to .... down to studying in the evening?
2 Do you always do things to the best of your .... ?
3 Do you ever get .... down in details when you're working?
4 Do you go .... your notes when revising for an exam?
5 Do you ever try to guess which topics will .... up in an exam?
6 Is it a good idea to get into the .... of studying regularly?
7 What's the best way to get on .... of a subject?
8 Do you ever feel it'll be the end of the .... if you fail an exam?

3 ABOUT YOU Answer the questions in Exercise 2 in your notebook, or talk to another student.

B What happens on exam day?

- The night before an exam, I **stay up** late and revise. ....
- Outside the exam room, I **steer clear of** other students who are in a panic. ....
- I **keep one eye on** the clock during the exam so that I don't **run out of** time. ....
- I try to **stick to** the question. ....
- If I **get stuck** on a question, I **miss** it **out** and go on to an easier one. ....
- If my mind **goes blank**, I **breathe in** and **out** slowly to calm myself. ....
- I **read through** my answers at the end to check that they **make sense**. ....

Glossary

stay up	go to bed later than usual.
steer/stay clear of sb/sth	take care to avoid sb/sth.
keep/have one eye on sth	look at or watch sth while doing sth else.
run out of sth	use all of sth and have no more left.
stick to sth	talk or write about one particular thing only. SYN **keep to sth**.
get stuck (on sth)	not be able to continue with sth because it is too hard.
miss sth out	not include sth, or fail to include sth. SYN **leave sth out**.
go blank	If your mind **goes blank** you are unable to remember the answer to a question.
breathe in	take air into your lungs. OPP **breathe out**.
read through sth	read sth to check details and look for mistakes.
make sense	have a clear meaning; be logical and easy to understand.

4 Circle the correct answer(s). Both words may be correct.

1 I *stayed | continued* up late last night to finish an essay.
2 Most candidates fail because they don't *keep | stick* to the questions.
3 I was in such a panic my mind just went completely *black | blank*.
4 Try to keep an *ear | eye* on the time during a test so that you finish every question.
5 I finished the letter and then I *went | read* it through carefully to check the spelling.
6 I got *stuck | delayed* on one question, so I *missed | left* it out.

5 One word is missing in each line. Where does it go? Write it at the end.

I know it was very silly, but I ⟨ up very late last night, and
through my notes, so this morning I was really tired. I got to the
exam feeling very stressed, and I tried to in and out slowly to
help myself relax, but I could feel my going blank. Eventually,
I looked at the questions, but none of them sense; I was in
such a state. Of course, I didn't keep one on the clock and
unfortunately, I ran of time. And as a result of that, I had to
out the last question completely, so I knew there was not much
chance that I would pass. I steered of my friends as I left the room.

▶ stayed
1 ....
2 ....
3 ....
4 ....
5 ....
6 ....
7 ....
8 ....

6 ABOUT YOU Are the sentences in the text at the top true about you? Write your answers in your notebook, or talk to another student.

11 I can talk about ability and progress

A Assessing students

University lecturer Peter Rose gives his honest opinion of some of his students.

Patrick's a nice guy, but his work **isn't up to much**, and frankly things have **gone from bad to worse** as the term has progressed. I think he**'d be better off** doing a different type of course, and it wouldn't surprise me if he **dropped out** at the end of the year.

By comparison, Charlotte is **in her element** here. She's bright, she can **think on her feet**, and she's confident in her own ability. She'll **go far**.

With Erin, **it's early days**. At the beginning of term I felt she **sat back** too much and let others do all the talking. But now she's starting to **come up with** more of her own ideas.

Glossary

not be up to much	INF not be very good.
go from bad to worse	(of a bad condition or situation) become even worse.
be better off (doing sth)	used to suggest that sb should do sth differently.
drop out (of sth)	leave school or college without finishing your studies.
by comparison	used for talking about ways in which two people or things are different.
in your element	doing what you are good at and enjoy.
think on your feet	be able to think and react to things very quickly.
go far	be successful in the future.
it's early days	= it's too soon to know how sb/sth will develop.
sit back	relax, especially by not doing anything or not getting involved.
come up with sth	produce ideas or a solution to sth.

1 Cross out the wrong word.

1 think on your *foot* | *feet*
2 by *compare* | *comparison*
3 go from bad to *worse* | *worst*
4 be *better* | *best* off doing something
5 it's *early* | *earlier* days
6 *on* | *in* your element

2 Organize the words into sentences and add <u>one</u> word.

▶ his | on feet | can | he *He can think on his feet.*
1 she | her | far | career | in | will
2 was | element | I | at | my | university
3 came | good | she | ideas | with | some
4 sat | did | and | he | nothing
5 college | drop | did | why | she | of | ?
6 to | went | from | worse | it

3 Complete the sentences. Then underline the full idioms and phrasal verbs.

1 Most of the group are making good progress. By ...., Sam is quite slow.
2 The new waiter is doing quite well at the moment, but it's .... days.
3 It used to be quite a good school, but it's not .... to much now.
4 I hated university, so I .... out at the end of the first year, and got a job.
5 Oscar's not very good at .... on his feet; he needs time to organize his ideas.
6 I think she'd be .... off living at home at her age.

B Assessing the lecturer

Here, the same students give their opinion of Peter Rose.

> PATRICK: He's OK, and he **knows his stuff**, but he's not very encouraging. I always **do my best**, but he **doesn't think much of** me.

> ERIN: At first I thought he **was a bit out of touch**, and he wasn't very friendly, but maybe we just **got off on the wrong foot**. He thought I **wasn't pulling my weight**, when in fact I was just too shy to say anything. But now I like him a lot more.

> CHARLOTTE: I'm **getting on** well, and that's largely **thanks to** Peter Rose. He really motivates me and **brings out the best in** me.

Glossary

know your stuff	INF know a lot about a particular subject.
do your best	try as hard as possible to achieve sth.
get on	make progress.
thanks to sb/sth	used to say that sb/sth is responsible for sth.
bring out the best/worst in sb	make sb behave in the best or worst way that they can.
be out of touch (with sth)	not know or understand recent ideas in a particular subject or area.
get/start off on the wrong foot	INF make a bad start at a relationship.
pull your weight	work as hard as everyone else in a job or activity.

spotlight *think the world of sb/sth, not think much of sb/sth, etc.*

These idioms express a high or low opinion of somebody or something:
We don't think much of the boys. = We have a low opinion of them.
He thinks the world of his niece. = He feels great love or affection for her.
She thinks a lot of Patricia. = She has a high opinion of her.

4 Complete the idioms with a suitable verb.

▶ _be_ out of touch
1 .... on the wrong foot
2 .... your stuff
3 .... your best
4 .... the world of someone
5 .... the best in someone
6 not .... much of something
7 .... your weight

5 Complete the dialogues.

1 How are you .... on? ~ Quite well, actually. I got good marks last term.
2 Is she good at her subject? ~ Not really. She's a bit .... of touch.
3 Did she like the course? ~ No, she didn't think .... of it.
4 What's the problem with Eric? ~ He's just not .... his weight.
5 Is Mr Hall a good teacher? ~ Oh yes, he knows his ....
6 Did Nadia pass the exam? ~ Yes, ... to her uncle; he helped her a lot.
7 What went wrong between you and the teacher? ~ We started off on the wrong ....
8 Good luck. ~ Thanks. I'll .... my best.

12 I can talk about thought processes

What do you think? How do you think?

I'm often surprised by events. I need to **think ahead** more.

I accept other people's opinions too easily. I need to **think for myself** more.

If I have a problem, I like to **talk it over** with friends or family.

If I have a problem, I prefer to **think it over** on my own.

I do things **on the spur of the moment**. I don't think before I **make up my mind**!

I'm not very good at **thinking straight** in stressful situations.

I always **think twice** before lending people money.

I sometimes **think back to** my time at primary school.

Glossary

think ahead (to sth)	think about a future event and plan for it.
think for yourself	form your own opinions rather than simply believing what other people say.
talk it/sth over	discuss sth with sb, especially to help you make a decision.
think it/sth over/through	think carefully about the possible results of sth.
on the spur of the moment	suddenly; without planning in advance.
make up your mind	decide.
think straight	(often used in the negative) think in a clear and logical way.
think twice	think very carefully about sth or before doing sth because you know about the possible dangers and problems.
think back (to sth)	think about things that happened in the past.

1 One word is missing after *think* in each sentence. Write it at the end.

1 I couldn't think; I was nervous and everyone was looking at me. ....

2 We must think and decide where we're going for our holidays this year. ....

3 He needs to think himself rather than go along with everyone else. ....

4 When I think to my school days, I realize how unhappy I was. ....

5 If you have a burglar alarm, it makes burglars think about breaking in. ....

6 Could you give me a few days to think over? ....

2 Complete the sentences.

1 I've got a chance to work abroad, but I'd like to think it .... first.

2 Do you ever think .... to the time you spent in Kenya?

3 We offered Maria the job but she wants to talk it .... with her family.

4 I was under so much stress that I just wasn't thinking ....; I was very confused.

5 I can't make up my .... what to wear to the party tomorrow.

6 Don't listen to what other people say – think for ....

7 I just accepted the offer on the .... of the moment. I wish I hadn't now.

8 After his accident, he'll think .... before driving quite so fast.

3 ABOUT YOU Are the sentences at the top of the page true for you?
   Write your own answers in your notebook, or talk to another student.

13 I can talk about knowledge and skills

A Did you understand the lecture?
B No, I couldn't **take it in**. I was too tired.

A Are you **any good at** maths?
B No, I **haven't got a head for** figures.

A What was her name again?
B I'm afraid it**'s slipped my mind**.

A He's a taxi driver, isn't he?
B Yes, he **knows** London **like the back of his hand**.

A Did Dave really make that chair himself?
B Yeah, well, he's **good with his hands**.

A I've never used this computer before.
B It's OK once you **get the hang of** it.

A Is it OK for Sam to use that machine?
B Yes, sure. He **knows what he's doing**.

A Do you fancy a game of chess?
B Well, I'm a bit **out of practice** but I'll **give** it **a try**.

Glossary

take it/sth in	fully understand and remember what you hear, see, or read.
have got a (good) head for sth	be naturally good at doing calculations, remembering facts, etc.
slip your mind	If sth **slips your mind**, you forget it, or forget to do it.
know sth like the back of your hand	INF know a place very well.
get the hang of sth	INF learn or begin to understand how to do sth.
know what you are doing	INF have experience in doing sth and understand it fully.
out of practice	less good at doing sth than you used to be, because you haven't done it for some time.
give sth a try	make an attempt to do sth.

> **spotlight** Idioms with *good*
>
> *Are you any good at art?* = able to draw/paint well.
> *I'm no good at skiing.* = unable to ski well.
> *He's good with his hands.* = able to use his hands well.
> *He's no good with people.* = unable to deal with people well.

1 Cross out one wrong word in each sentence.

1 I'm a bit out of the practice these days.
2 She knows what that she's doing.
3 Would you like to give to it a try?
4 Are you no any good at making things?
5 I'm no much good at maths.
6 I meant to do it but it slipped out my mind.
7 She knew it like the back side of her hand.
8 Are you any good with for electrical things?

2 Complete the questions. (You will answer them in Exercise 3.)

1 Are you good _____ your hands?
2 Have you got a good _____ for figures?
3 Do you find it easy to take _____ a lot of factual information?
4 Which town do you know like the _____ of your hand?
5 Are you any _____ at cooking? If not, are you prepared to _____ it a try?
6 Do other people's birthdays ever slip your _____ ?
7 Do you think it's easy for a beginner to get the _____ of skiing?
8 Do you cycle much these days, or are you _____ of practice?

3 ABOUT YOU Write answers to the questions in Exercise 2 in your notebook, or talk to another student.

Review: Thinking, learning, and knowledge

Unit 8

1 Tick (✓) the correct meaning.

1 If you *put something away*, you:
   a) hide it where others cannot find it. ☐
   b) put it where you usually keep it, after using it. ☐
2 If you *hand something round*, you:
   a) pass something, such as sandwiches, to people in a group. ☐
   b) stand in a circle with a group of people, holding hands. ☐
3 If you *build up something*, you:
   a) make or construct it. ☐
   b) increase or develop it. ☐
4 If you *take something in turns*, you:
   a) do something one after another so everyone has a chance to do it. ☐
   b) do something by moving round in a circle. ☐
5 If you *hand something in*, you:
   a) give it to each person in a group. ☐
   b) give it to a person in authority. ☐
6 If you *cross something out*, you:
   a) remove it with a rubber. ☐
   b) put a line through it, usually because it is wrong. ☐

2 Rewrite the sentences using an idiom or phrasal verb which includes the word in capitals. Keep the meaning the same.

▶ She drew a line through his name. CROSS *She crossed out his name.*
1 It's just a small part of a larger problem. ICEBERG
2 Make sure you check your work carefully. OVER
3 OK, let's stop now. DAY
4 Mark, sit in Eve's seat, then Eve can sit in yours. SWAP
5 It's a waste of time if you don't listen. GOOD
6 He's working hard on the course. SERIOUSLY
7 Before we do anything else, turn to page 45. ALL
8 You can omit Exercise 3. LEAVE

Unit 9

1 Complete the definitions.

1 *Make sense of something* means to manage to _____ something.
2 *Keep your mind on something* means to continue to _____ on something.
3 *Stick at something* means to continue with something even though it is _____ .
4 If something is *on the tip of your tongue*, it means you _____ it, but can't _____ it at that moment.
5 If you *pick up* a language, it means you _____ it without making a lot of _____ .
6 If something *goes in one ear and out the other*, it means you _____ it quickly.

2 Complete the dialogues.

1 A How's the Italian course going?
   B Oh, I've been so busy recently that I'm (1) _____ behind with my studies. I'm going to spend a few evenings this week trying to (2) _____ up with the rest of the class.
   A Well, try and (3) _____ it up – it would be a shame to give (4) _____ now.

2 A I don't feel I'm making much progress on the photography course. There's a lot of information and it just doesn't seem to sink (5) ....

B Well, a lot of it is about trial and (6) .... , isn't it?

A Yes, I suppose I'll (7) .... there in the end.

3 A When you were at school, did you have to learn poetry by (8) .... ?

B Oh, yes. Actually I was (9) .... my brains this morning to try and remember a poem I learnt as a child. I'm sure it will (10) .... back to me later today.

Unit 10

1 Complete the crossword.

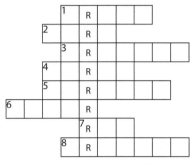

1 get to .... with something = manage to deal with something

2 .... something out = solve a problem by looking carefully at the facts

3 keep your fingers .... = hope that something will be successful

4 it's not the end of the .... = it's not the worst thing that can happen

5 go .... something = look at or discuss something carefully

6 .... clear of someone = avoid someone because meeting them may cause problems

7 .... out of something = have none of something left

8 .... in = take air into your lungs

2 Rearrange the words into sentences, and add one word.

▶ sense | doesn't | this | really | question This question doesn't really **make** sense.

1 the | blank | exam | mind | my | just | in ....

2 question | the | decided | I | miss | to | first ....

3 read | but | the | sense | I | didn't | it | letter ....

4 her | the | to | did | she | it | of | ability ....

5 work | some | down | I | must | to | now ....

6 too | down | I | detail | bogged | in | much ....

Unit 11

1 Match 1–8 with a–h.

1 She's come up ....   a to worse.

2 He doesn't know ....   b doing a different subject.

3 I passed the test, thanks ....   c his stuff.

4 The teacher was really out ....   d of his work.

5 Things went from bad ....   e on your feet.

6 You have to think ....   f with a great idea.

7 I don't think much ....   g to my teacher.

8 She'd be better off ....   h of touch.

2 Read the email from a mother who is worried about her son. One word is missing in each line. Where does it go, and what is it?

… and I'm really worried about Sam; he's talking about dropping ⟨ of   ▸ *out*

university. The thing is, it's days, and he needs time to get to know	1
the teachers. I'm worried that he has got on the wrong foot with one	2
of them; she's accused him of not pulling weight. I know that Sam	3
appears to back and not say anything, but it doesn't mean he's lazy.	4
He's so different from Mary. Her tutor the world of her, and it's clear	5
that she's in element at Oxford and is enjoying it enormously. She	6
always does her, whatever she's involved in, and I know that	7
she'll far and have a brilliant career. And that really makes it	8
harder for Sam. He needs a good teacher to bring the best in him. I	9
hope he gets better with his studies after the Christmas holidays.	10

Unit 12

1 Tick (✓) the correct answer.

1 She'll need some time to think about the situation before .... up her mind.
thinking ☐ doing ☐ making ☐

2 If I were in your position I would think .... about buying that motorbike.
back ☐ twice ☐ straight ☐

3 Before accepting the job, I'd like some time to think ....
for myself ☐ ahead ☐ it over ☐

4 He's very dependent on his parents; he needs to think .... more.
for himself ☐ it over ☐ twice ☐

5 I've decided to talk it .... with my husband and see what we can do.
back ☐ over ☐ up ☐

6 I couldn't think .... because too many people were talking.
twice ☐ ahead ☐ straight ☐

Unit 13

1 Agree with A's questions in the dialogues using a word from the box in each response.

take   good ✓   back   doing   hands   practice   good   slipped

  ▸ A Does he deal with children well?
    B Yes, he's *good with children* ....

1 A She knows this area really well, doesn't she?
  B Yes, she ....

2 A She's not a very skilful cook, is she?
  B No, she's ....

3 A You forgot the appointment, didn't you?
  B Yes, it ....

4 A Was it hard to understand and remember all the information?
  B Yes, I couldn't ....

5 A You're very good at making things, aren't you?
  B Yes, I'm ....

6 A It's ages since you played the piano, isn't it?
  B Yes, I'm ....

7 A Andrew's very good at investing money, isn't he?
  B Yes, he certainly ....

14 I can talk about getting in touch

Ben

BEN	Have you **broken the news** to the family yet?
EMILY	Well, I**'ve been in touch with** most of them, but I can't **get hold of** Uncle Nick.
BEN	No, I **have**n't **heard from** him for a while either. Try **giving** his office **a ring**.
EMILY	I did, but he's not there at the moment, so I've had to **drop him a line**.
BEN	OK. So, shall I **keep quiet about** your move until it**'s common knowledge**?
EMILY	Yes, please. I don't want anyone to feel they**'ve been kept in the dark**.
BEN	Sure. I promise I **won't breathe a word**.

Ben's cousin, Emily

Glossary

break the news	be the first to tell sb about some important news.
get hold of sb	INF find or make contact with sb by email or phone.
hear from sb	be contacted by sb by email, phone, or letter.
give sb a ring	INF phone sb. SYN **give sb a call**.
drop sb a line	INF write a short letter or email to sb.
keep quiet (about sth)	say nothing about sth.
be common knowledge	be sth that everyone knows.
keep sb in the dark	If you **keep sb in the dark**, you don't tell them about sth important.
not breathe a word (about/of sth)	not tell anyone about sth that is secret. SYN **not say a word** (**about sth**).

spotlight *in touch*

If you **are in touch with sb**, you are in contact with them by speaking or writing to them. If you **get in touch with sb**, you make contact with them. If you **keep in touch with sb**, you continue to have contact with them. If you **lose touch with sb**, you no longer have contact with them.

1 Circle the correct answer(s). Both answers may be correct.

1 Have you been *in* | *on* touch with Romi?
2 Who *dropped* | *broke* the news to Mina?
3 Don't *say* | *breathe* a word to the kids.
4 Have you heard *by* | *from* Mari recently?
5 I said we'd give Irina a *call* | *ring*.
6 I'll drop Vincent a *line* | *call*.

2 Complete the dialogues. Then underline the full idiom in each dialogue.

1 You mustn't say anything. ~ Don't worry, I'll keep .... about it.
2 He's upset because we .... him in the dark. ~ Well, that's understandable.
3 Have you got in .... with Michael since last week? ~ No, not yet.
4 Do they know you're getting married? ~ Yes, I .... the news last night.
5 Have you told the class you're having a baby? ~ Yes, it's common .... now.
6 Have you tried to get .... of the manager? ~ Yes, I .... her a ring earlier.

3 ABOUT YOU Write your answers in your notebook, or talk to another student.

1 Which do you use most to get in touch with friends: phone, text, or email?
2 If you thank someone for a present, do you give them a ring or drop them a line?
3 How often do you hear from friends who live in a different town?
4 How often do you get in touch with friends in other countries?
5 Do people find you difficult to get hold of sometimes? If so, why?

15 I can describe ways of saying things

My boss treats me like a child: she's always **talking down to** me.

My sister's very direct and always **speaks her mind**, but at least she never talks about people **behind their backs**.

I shouldn't have mentioned Joey's girlfriend; I think I **put my foot in it**.

My daughter **answers** me **back** when I'm annoyed with her. I'm always **telling** her **off for** being so cheeky!

Ann **gets** things **across** clearly – and she's the only person who **talks sense** around here.

My colleague talks non-stop! You **can't get a word in edgeways**.

My teacher's got a very quiet voice; I wish he'd **speak up**.

Glossary

talk down to sb	talk to sb as if they are less intelligent or important than you.
put your foot in it	INF say or do sth that makes sb embarrassed or upset.
get sth across (to sb)	succeed in making sb understand sth.
talk sense	say things that are sensible and correct. OPP **talk nonsense**.
speak up	speak more loudly.
speak your mind	say exactly what you think in a very direct way.
behind sb's back	without sb knowing about it. OPP **to sb's face**.
answer (sb) back	reply rudely to sb who has more authority than you.
tell sb off (for sth / for doing sth)	INF speak angrily to sb for doing sth wrong.
not get a word in edgeways	not be able to say anything because sb else is talking too much.

1 **Would you be happy or unhappy in these situations? Write H (happy) or U (unhappy).**

1 You ask a child to do something and he answers you back. ......
2 You get advice from a lawyer who talks a lot of sense. ......
3 Someone tells you off for riding your bike through the park. ......
4 You're asked to explain a grammar rule and you manage to get it across. ......
5 Someone talks about you behind your back. ......
6 You go and see a doctor who talks down to you. ......
7 You're in a meeting with your boss and you can't get a word in edgeways. ......
8 You're talking to one of your neighbours and you put your foot in it. ......

2 **Complete the questions. (You will answer them in Exercise 3.)**

1 If you can't hear your teacher, do you ask him/her to .... up?
2 Is there anyone in your family who tends to .... nonsense?
3 Have you ever put your .... in it when talking to a friend?
4 Do you prefer people to criticize you to your ...., or behind your .... ?
5 With a group of strangers, would you always speak your .... ?
6 Have you ever .... someone off for dropping rubbish in the street?
7 Do you ever have problems getting your meaning .... in English?
8 Is it hard to get a word in .... with anyone you know? Who?

3 ABOUT YOU **Write answers to the questions in Exercise 2 in your notebook, or talk to another student.**

16 I can talk about phoning

A Did you **get through to** the complaints department?
B Well, when I rang the first time, I **got cut off**, so I called again. Then someone kept me **hanging on** for ages, and in the end I **hung up**.

A Could I speak to Mr Howey, please?
B **Hold the line**, please, while I **put** you **through** … I'm sorry, he can't take your call at the moment. If you leave your number, he'll **get back to** you later.

A Have you **charged up** your mobile?
B Yes, but I've still got to **top** it **up** before I ring Howard. My phone calls **are costing a fortune**.

Glossary

get through (to sb)	succeed in speaking to sb on the phone.
cut sb off	(usually passive **be/get cut off**) stop or interrupt sb's phone conversation by breaking the connection.
put sb through	make a phone connection that lets sb speak to sb else.
get back to sb	phone or speak to sb later, especially to give a reply.
charge sth (up)	If you **charge (up)** your mobile, you plug it to a supply of electricity until enough is stored in its battery.
top up (your mobile)	pay more money so that you can make more calls.
cost a fortune	INF be very expensive. SYN **cost the earth** INF.

spotlight *hang on, hang up, hang up on sb*

If you **hang on** INF or **hold on**, you wait for a short time (also, in phone calls, **hold the line**). If you **hang up**, you end a phone call and put the phone down. If you **hang up on sb** INF, you end a phone conversation suddenly without saying goodbye.

1 Circle the correct answer(s). Both answers may be correct.

1 There was no answer, so I *hung up | hung up on him*.
2 I was on the phone to the bank when I *cut off | got cut off*.
3 Did you manage to *get | put* through to the accommodation officer?
4 She asked me to *hang | hold* on, then they played some horrible music.
5 It's so expensive to use your mobile abroad; it costs *the earth | a fortune*.
6 Hang on a minute; I've just got to *fill | top* up my mobile before we go out.

2 Complete the dialogues. Then underline the full idioms and phrasal verbs.

1 Could I speak to Mark Lawton, please? ~ Hold the .... – I'll try and put you ....
2 Have you plugged in your mobile? ~ Yeah, but it'll take half an hour to .... it up.
3 Did you .... through to Joe? ~ Yes, but he was in a bad mood and he hung up .... me.
4 Did she ask you to .... on? ~ Yes, but it was costing a .... so I hung ....
5 Did you manage to speak to Mrs Arkle? ~ Yes, briefly, but we got cut ....
6 Are you busy? ~ I'm afraid so, but I promise I'll get .... to you by the end of the day.

3 ABOUT YOU Write your answers in your notebook, or talk to another student.

1 When did you last get cut off during a call?
2 Do you have to top up your mobile, or do you have a monthly plan?
3 Have you ever hung up on someone? Who, and why?
4 Are there certain people you ring who you can never get through to?

17 I can use short spoken phrases

These short idiomatic phrases are commonly used in particular situations in spoken English.

Here's to John and Fiona!

John and Fiona!

Come on! **Hurry up**!
OK, I'm coming!

Did you understand what he said?
Sort of.

Do I pay weekly or monthly?
It's up to you.

OK, everyone. **Time's up**.
Oh no, I haven't finished.

Shall we go there later?
Yeah, **why not**?

Well, see you soon.
Yes, **all the best**.

We can't go on like this.
I know.

What's up?
Steve's late, **as usual**.

Guess what? We won.
Oh, that's brilliant!

I'll pour your coffee. **Say when**.
That's fine. Thanks.

OK, **here goes**. Wish me luck.
Don't worry, you'll be fine.

Here you are.
Thanks a lot.

How come the shop's closed?
I don't know. It should be open.

Glossary

here's to sb/sth	used to wish sb health or success as you lift a glass and drink to them.
hurry up	do sth more quickly because there isn't much time.
time's up	used in exams and competitions to tell people there is no more time left.
I know	used to agree with somebody or to say you feel the same way.
say when	INF used to ask sb to tell you when you should stop pouring their drink or serving their food because they have enough.
here you are	INF used when you are giving sth to sb. SYN **there you are/go**.
sort of	INF to some extent, but in a way that is not easy to explain. SYN **kind of**.
why not?	used to agree to a suggestion. (It can also be used to make a suggestion: *Why not phone her?*)
what's up?	INF = what's the matter?
as usual	as happens most of the time. SYN **as always**.
here goes	INF used when you are telling people you are just going to do sth exciting, dangerous, etc., e.g. go down a ski slope.
how come ...?	INF used to ask the reason for sth. (Notice the word order in the question: *How come you're early?*)
all the best	INF 1 used when you are saying goodbye to sb (as above). SYN **take care**. 2 used to wish sb luck, happiness, etc. SYN **good luck**.
guess what?	INF used before telling sb sth interesting or surprising.

spotlight *be up to sb*

We use this expression to say that something is somebody's decision or responsibility, and usually with the pronoun *it*.
Shall we stay in or go out? ~ *It's up to you.* = it's your decision.
It's up to the government to decide this. = it's their responsibility.

1 Complete the dialogues.

1 What time shall we leave? ~ It's .... to you.
2 How .... we had to pay? ~ I don't know. I thought it was free.
3 Shall we go out tonight? ~ Yeah, why .... ?
4 We must talk to Peter about this. ~ Yes, I .... You're absolutely right.
5 .... up, or we'll miss the bus. ~ Yes, all right. I'm coming.
6 What time did you go to bed last night? ~ Oh, 10.30, as ....
7 Could you follow his map? ~ Yes, sort ....
8 Say .... ~ Yeah, that's plenty, thanks.
9 What's .... ? ~ Oh, I've put my mobile somewhere and I can't find it.
10 .... what? It's snowing! ~ I don't believe it!

2 What do you say in the situations below? Use the phrases in the box.

> Guess what?   Here goes.   Say when.   All the best   Hurry up!   What's up?   Here you are.   Time's up.

1 Your friend is being very slow. ....
2 You're pouring some juice for someone and you don't know how much he wants.
....
3 You're a teacher. It's the end of a test. Tell the class. ....
4 You're going to tell your friend you've passed your exam. .... I passed.
5 Your friend is looking very worried about something. ....
6 You turn and speak quietly to a friend as you stand up to give an important speech.
....
7 Your friend is going to take his driving test. ....
8 Your brother asks you for some cash and you hand it to him. ....

3 Replace the underlined phrase with an idiom that has a similar meaning.

1 Did you understand? ~ <u>Sort of</u>. ....
2 Where's Chris? ~ In bed, <u>as always</u>. ....
3 OK, <u>here you are</u>. ~ Thanks. ....
4 <u>What's the matter</u>? ~ I don't feel well. ....
5 How many people shall we invite? ~ <u>You decide</u>. ....
6 See you next week. ~ Yeah, <u>take care</u>. ....

4 Complete each speech bubble with a suitable idiom.

5 ABOUT YOUR LANGUAGE How would you translate the idioms on page 42 into your own language? Write your answers in your notebook, or talk to another student who speaks your language.

18 I can use phrases with *say*, *tell*, and *see*

A *Say* and *tell*

	Example	Meaning
SAY	*Are you planning to leave your job?* ~ ***I'd rather not say*** *at the moment.*	**I'd rather not say** is a polite way to say you don't want to give sb some information.
	Do you want a coffee? ~ ***I wouldn't say no***.	**I wouldn't say no (to sth)** INF used to say you would like sth, or to accept sth you are offered.
	That was a really awful exam. ~ ***You can say that again!***	**you can say that again** INF = I agree with you completely.
	Did you speak to Mr Ellis? ~ *Yes.* ***I have to say***, *he was very rude.*	**I have to say (that) / I must say (that)** INF used for emphasizing an opinion.
	We need a new carpet in the hall. ~ *OK,* ***whatever you say***.	**whatever you say** used to agree with sb's suggestion, even if you don't like it, because you don't want to argue about it.
TELL	***Tell me***, *how was your trip to Dubai?* ~ *Well, it was hot,* ***to say the least***.	**tell me** INF used before asking a question. **to say the least** used to say that you could have expressed sth in a much stronger way.
	Is Andrea getting married? ~ ***That would be telling***.	**that would be telling** INF used to say that you can't give some information because it is secret.
	Is it going to rain tomorrow? ~ ***I couldn't tell you***.	**I couldn't tell you** INF used to tell sb that you do not know the answer to their question.
	You were right – the train was at 6.00. ~ *You see?* ***I told you so!***	**I told you (so)** INF = I warned you about sth; you didn't listen but now you can see I was right.
	Did you enjoy the play? ~ ***To tell you the truth***, *it was boring.*	**to tell you the truth** INF used to say what you really feel or think.

1 Complete the phrases with *say* or *tell* in the correct form.

1 .... me, why did he leave?
2 I .... you so!
3 You can .... that again!
4 I'd rather not ....
5 That would be ....
6 Whatever you ....
7 I have to .... , it was great.
8 To .... you the truth, I was wrong.
9 I couldn't .... you.
10 It was cold, to .... the least.

2 Complete the dialogues. You may need more than one word.

1 Goodness, it's really hot in here. ~ You can .... ! I can't stand it.
2 I think the best thing would be to take a taxi. ~ OK, ... say. I don't mind.
3 I shouldn't have left the money in the hotel bedroom. ~ Well, I told .... !
4 How was the journey? ~ Well, it was uncomfortable, to ....
5 .... me, how much do you earn? ~ I'd .... That's my business.
6 How much is a litre of olive oil? ~ I couldn't .... ; I don't do the shopping.
7 Shall we have something to eat? ~ Hm, I wouldn't .... I'm really hungry.
8 Are you seeing Henry tonight? ~ To tell .... , I don't really like him, so no.
9 How did you enjoy the show? ~ Well, I have .... , it was very entertaining.
10 Who's going to be in the next Bond movie? ~ Ah, that would .... !

B *See*

I need more help with the horses.	OK, **I'll see what I can do**, but I've got to go now. **See you later**.
Could I have the morning off? **You see**, my brother's arriving from Cairo.	Yeah, **I don't see why not**.
Who's the oldest in your class?	Hmm, **let's see** … It must be Angelo.
Mark thinks I should join a gym.	Well, you could try it and **see how it goes**.
I'm not sure I want to go to the wedding.	Oh, it'll be wonderful – **you'll see**.
Have you finished the painting?	Yes, **see for yourself**.

Glossary

I'll see what I can do	= I'll try to help.
you see	INF used when you are explaining sth.
I don't see why not	INF used to say 'Yes' when sb asks for sth.
let's see / let me see	INF used to say that you are thinking, or trying to remember sth.
see how it goes	INF used to say that you will decide about a situation after letting it develop for a short time. SYN **see how things go**.
you'll see	INF used to tell sb that they will find out you were right about sth.
see for yourself	used to tell sb to look at sth to check that what sb has said about it is true.

spotlight Greetings

Phrases with *see* are commonly used when saying goodbye to someone you know, especially when you expect to see them again soon, e.g. **see you later** / tomorrow or simply **see you! See you around** or **see you soon** are used if you are not sure when you will see the person again.

3 Correct the mistake in each sentence. Write the correct idiom at the end.

1 There isn't much time, but I'll see that I can do. ....
2 Bye, Flora! ~ Bye, Angie – seeing you! ....
3 How long is it since we met? ~ Well, let's me see … Ten years, I think. ....
4 She hasn't cleaned the car, has she? ~ Yes, just go and see yourself! ....
5 Shall I invite Jamie for dinner? ~ I don't see why no. ....
6 I'm hoping the plan will succeed, but we'll see how a thing goes. ....

4 Complete the dialogues. You will need more than one word.

1 Is it OK if I leave my bike here? ~ Yeah, I don't ....
2 Have you put up the new fence yet? ~ You can see .... – it looks great.
3 I'd better go now. ~ OK – .... around!
4 I'm not sure I'll pass this test. ~ Oh, come on, it'll be fine – you ....
5 How far is it to the city centre? ~ Er … .... – it must be about two kilometres.
6 I'm not sure she's the right person for the job. ~ Well, let's see how ....
7 I really need someone to help me with the furniture. ~ OK, well, I'll ....
8 Why were you late? ~ Well, I woke up late .... , and by then the traffic was bad.

19 I can use common spoken responses

A Short responses

Shall we get the bus?
Yeah, **if you like**.

Did you say you'd go?
Not exactly. I said I might.

Can I borrow this?
Sure, **go ahead**.

Thanks a lot.
Not at all.

I've forgotten your book.
Never mind.

It's at Platform Five.
I beg your pardon?

I'm bored with this.
Yeah, **same here**.

Where shall we go?
I'm not bothered.

How are you?
Not bad.

Was the day a success?
Er, **yes and no**.

Glossary

if you like	INF used to agree with sb's suggestion to do sth.
not at all	used as a polite reply when sb thanks you. SYN **you're welcome**.
same here	INF = the same thing is also true for me (or we sometimes say *me too*).
not bad	INF quite good (also **not too bad**).
not exactly	used when you are correcting sth that sb has said.
never mind	used to tell sb not to worry or be upset.
I'm not bothered	= it's not important to me. SYN **it's all the same to me**.
yes and no	used when you cannot give a clear answer to sth.
go ahead	often used to give sb permission to do sth or use sth.

spotlight *I beg your pardon* FML

When you say **I beg your pardon?** with a rising voice, you are politely asking somebody to repeat what they have just said. SYNS **Sorry?** (or **I'm sorry?**).

With a falling voice, you are saying sorry, e.g. for pushing someone (*I beg your pardon – I didn't see you there*.). SYN **I'm very/terribly sorry**.

1 Is the meaning similar or different? Write S or D.

1 Not at all. | Not exactly. ....
2 I'm not bothered. | It's all the same to me. ....
3 Not at all. | You're welcome. ....
4 Me too. | Same here. ....
5 Never mind. | I don't mind. ....
6 I'm very sorry. | I beg your pardon. ....

2 Replace the underlined words and phrases with idioms that have a similar meaning.

1 How are you? ~ <u>Fine</u>. ....
2 I've got two brothers. ~ Yeah, <u>me too</u>. ....
3 Do you want to eat out tonight? ~ Yeah, <u>that's fine by me</u>. ....
4 I'm afraid I can't go tonight. ~ <u>It doesn't matter</u>. ....
5 Thanks a lot. ~ <u>Not at all</u>. ....
6 Ooh! That's my foot! ~ <u>I beg your pardon</u>. ....
7 Was the holiday a success? ~ <u>In some ways it was</u>. ....
8 Shall we have pasta or rice? ~ <u>It's all the same to me</u>. ....
9 Could I borrow this pen? ~ Yes, <u>of course</u>. ....
10 What's the title of the play? ~ <u>Sorry?</u> ....

B Exclamations

An exclamation is a sound, a word, or a short phrase which you say when you are surprised, angry, impressed, etc. When written down it has an exclamation mark (!).

Bless you!

Mind out! SYN **Watch out!**

Well done!

She's got eight children. ~ *You're joking!*	INF used to express surprise. SYN **You're kidding!** INF.
I saw Jamie smoking, and he's only twelve. ~ *Good grief!*	used to express shock or surprise. SYNS **Good heavens! Goodness me!**
I missed the last train home. ~ *Bad luck!*	used to express sympathy. SYN **Hard luck!**
It's my maths exam this afternoon. ~ *Good luck!*	used to wish sb success with sth, e.g. an exam. SYN **(The) best of luck!**
Have you got a new girlfriend? ~ *Mind your own business!*	a rude way to tell sb not to ask questions about sth private. SYN **It's none of your business!**
We need more honesty from politicians! ~ *Hear, hear!*	a way of saying you strongly agree with someone.

> **spotlight** More idioms with *goodness*
>
> The use of *goodness* in these idioms developed so that people could avoid using the word God, which some people found offensive.
> *Where's Tom?* ~ *Goodness knows!* = I don't know (emphatic).
> *I got the job.* ~ *Thank goodness!* used to show you are relieved.
> *I've lost the key again.* ~ *For goodness sake!* used to show you are annoyed or impatient.

3 Circle the correct answer(s). Both answers may be correct.

1 Is your sister married? ~ That's *not | none* of your business!
2 We must improve housing for the poor. ~ *Here! Here! | Hear! Hear!*
3 That boy's cycling really fast. ~ Yes, *watch out! | mind out!*
4 The cinema was full and I couldn't get in. ~ Oh, *best of luck! | hard luck!*
5 There were sixty students in my class. ~ *Good grief! | You're kidding!*
6 The train fares are going up again. ~ *For goodness sake! | Goodness knows!*

4 Complete the responses with a suitable exclamation.

1 We lost the tennis match in the end. ~ Oh, ... !
2 How much money do you earn? ~ .... ! I'm not telling you.
3 It's my job interview tomorrow at the BBC. ~ .... ! I hope you get it.
4 I won first prize in the competition. ~ .... !
5 Ninety per cent of my class failed the exam. ~ .... ! That's shocking.
6 What's the capital of Mali? ~ .... ! Actually, I'm terrible at geography.
7 I'm going to sneeze … ah … ah … atishoo! .... !
8 I finally got a letter to say I don't have to leave my flat. .... ! That's great.

20 I can understand and leave messages

A Informal written messages

Carlos

Really sorry, but could you possibly **put** the rubbish **out**? **By the way**, Joanne rang – she said it was **something to do with** dinner tomorrow.

Must dash, Stuart

Hello Anne

Bad news I'm afraid – I can't meet you for lunch **after all**. Something's **cropped up** at work – an important meeting, and I can't **get out of** it. But **have you got anything on** tomorrow lunchtime? Perhaps we can **get together** then. **Give my love to** Larry.

Claire

Glossary

put sth out	take sth out of your house and leave it outside.
by the way	used when you add a new topic into a conversation.
something to do with	= something connected to or involved with.
(I) must dash	= I must go quickly because I'm in a hurry.
after all	used when sth is different from what you expected.
crop up	happen or appear, especially when it is not expected.
get out of sth	avoid doing sth you should do or said that you would do.
have (got) sth on	have an arrangement to do sth.
get together	meet socially, or in order to discuss sth.

spotlight Sending greetings to other people

When you are talking or writing to someone, you can ask them to give a greeting from you to someone else. Referring to friends or family, you can say: *Give my love to Sam* or *Give Sam my love*; referring to someone you know less well, say: *Give my regards to Sam* or *Remember me to Sam*.

---

1 Cross out one wrong letter, and write the correct word at the end.

▶ Sorry, something's c~~h~~opped up. *cropped*

1 I can't let out of this. ....

2 Sorry, I must bash – I'm late. ....

3 I can't come tonight after ill. ....

4 Did you cut the rubbish out? ....

5 Shall we bet together tonight? ....

6 Have you hot anything on tonight? ....

7 Please give my dove to Lilia. ....

8 Oh, by the day, when's the party? ....

2 Complete the messages.

Hi Jenny

Thanks for your message. I'm afraid something's (1) .... up tonight, and I've got things (2) .... every evening this week, but let's get (3) .... some time soon. (4) .... me to Alec. Love, Judy

---

Hi Gianna

Bad news – I didn't get the job (5) .... all. Well, I'll get over it. Oh, (6) .... the way, did you know Ali's moving next week? Isn't that great? Give my (7) .... to Erno. Love Anne

---

Lauren

Sorry, there's a meeting on Tuesday, and I can't (8) .... out of it. It's (9) .... to do with salaries, so I have to go. Anyway, please give my (10) .... to the rest of the team. Speak soon, Martin.

B Informal voice messages

> Hi, it's me. I'm just **popping out** for half an hour – I've got to **drop** Mum **off** at the station and do a bit of shopping. I'll be back by 6.00 **at the latest**. OK, bye.

> Lucy, hello – it's Dad – I thought I'd just **call by** and see you around lunchtime. I've got a meeting **just round the corner from** you. Let's have a chat then. OK, bye.

> Hi Anton, it's Paddy – thought **it was about time** I gave you a ring. **What have you been up to?** Anyway, can you **ring me back** when you've got a moment? Cheers!

> Hi, it's me. Look, I**'m completely snowed under** with work, and I don't think I'll be able to **get away** before 9.00. And then Mac and I were thinking of having supper together if we **feel up to** it, so don't **wait up for** me, will you? Bye.

Glossary

pop out	INF go somewhere for a short time.
drop sb/sth off	take sb/sth to a place by car and leave them/it there.
at the latest	no later than the time or date mentioned. OPP **at the earliest**.
it's about time	used to say that you think sb should do sth very soon.
What have you been up to?	INF = What have you been doing?
ring sb back	1 phone sb who has called you (as above). 2 ring sb again.
call by	make a short visit to see sb as you pass. SYNS **drop by**, **call in**.
(just) round the corner	nearby (**round the corner from** a place = very near to the place).
be snowed under	have too much work to deal with.
get away (from sb/sth)	succeed in leaving a place or a person.
feel up to (doing) sth	have the strength or energy to do sth.
wait up (for sb)	not go to sleep until sb comes home.

3 Complete the dialogues.

1 Minnie's very boring, isn't she? ~ Yes, I kept trying to get _____ from her at the party.
2 Did you get the message from Nic? ~ Yes. That reminds me, I must ring him _____ .
3 Have you written the report yet? ~ No, I won't finish until Friday at the _____ .
4 I've got to _____ out and buy some food. ~ Yes, it's _____ time you did something!
5 What are you _____ to tonight? ~ Oh, I'm going to a party. Don't _____ up for me.
6 It would be lovely to see you again. ~ OK, well I'll _____ by one evening after work.

4 Rewrite the sentence using the word in capital letters. The meaning must stay the same.

▶ He's just gone out for a few minutes. POP *He's just popped out for a few minutes.*
1 What's she been doing recently? UP
2 Meet me no later than 5.00. LATEST
3 Could you give me a lift to the doctor's? DROP
4 I'll try to leave work by 7.00. GET
5 I'm not sure I have the energy to do it. UP
6 It's very close to where I'm staying. CORNER
7 I've got too much work at the moment. SNOWED
8 I'll come and see you on my way home. CALL

21 I can say what I think

A Giving opinions

What do you make of Mrs Nesbeth?
> She seems nice, and her old boss **thought highly of** her.

How was the film?
> I **didn't think much of** it, **to be honest**.

What do you think of the new doctor?
> Not much. **For one thing**, he's a bit rude.

But that's **beside the point**, isn't it? So long as he's good at his job.

He's the best politician we've got.
> Yeah, **without a doubt**.

Dogs are wonderful companions.
> Yes, **I couldn't agree more**.

The government's made a big mistake, **as far as I'm concerned**.
> Well, **up to a point**, but **in the long run** it won't make any difference.

Glossary

What do you make of sb/sth?	= What's your impression of sb/sth?
think highly / a lot of sb/sth	have a very good opinion of sb/sth. OPP **not think much of sb/sth**.
to be honest	used when telling sb what you really think.
for one thing	used to introduce one or more reasons for sth.
without (a) doubt	used for emphasis to mean 'very definitely'.
I couldn't agree more	= I strongly agree.
as far as I'm concerned	used to introduce your own opinion about sth.
in the long run	not immediately, but at a time in the future. SYN **in the long term**.

spotlight *point*

Point often occurs in idioms used in discussions.
That's beside the point. = not relevant to the thing being discussed.
That's true up to a point. = to some degree but not completely.

---

1 Complete the dialogues. Then underline the full idioms and phrasal verbs.

1 I don't think _____ of this fish. ~ To _____ honest, it was very cheap.
2 What do you _____ of the new boss? ~ As far as I'm _____ , he's the best we've had.
3 If you work hard, you can achieve anything. ~ That's only true _____ to a point.
4 He's a really nice man. ~ But that's beside the _____ – he's no good at his job.
5 I know the manager thinks _____ of him. ~ Yes, I couldn't _____ more.
6 Why didn't you like the hotel? ~ Well, for one _____ , our room wasn't very clean.

2 Correct one word which is wrong in each sentence. Write the correct idiom at the end.

▶ Travel broadens the mind. ~ Well, that's true up to ~~the~~ point. *up to a point*
1 As far that I'm concerned, we don't learn from the past. _____
2 For be honest, I'd be happier if the police didn't carry guns. _____
3 I don't think more of our public transport. _____
4 Most people think lot of our Prime Minister. _____
5 In the large run, we'll need different fuel for cars. _____
6 With a doubt, we're too dependent on computers. _____

3 ABOUT YOU Do you agree or disagree with the statements in Exercise 2? Write your answers in your notebook, or talk to another student.

B Pros and cons

A I've got to write an essay on the **pros and cons** of social networking sites.

B Well, I suppose it's a good way to keep in touch with friends.

A Yes, but you can meet new people too. That's the best thing about them **if you ask me**.

B Yeah, **to some extent**, but **for the most part**, I think face-to-face relationships are most likely to last. And **the thing is**, you don't know if strangers are telling you the truth online.

A Yes, **you've got a point**. But that's also true if you're speaking to someone face to face.

B **Fair enough**, I accept that. But **even so**, I still prefer talking to people face to face. Anyway, these sites are **here to stay** whether we like them or not.

Glossary

pros and cons	the advantages and disadvantages of sth.
if you ask me	INF in my personal opinion.
to some extent	used to say that sth is only partly true. SYNS **to a certain extent, in some ways**.
for the most part	in general. SYNS **by and large, on the whole**.
the thing is	used for emphasizing what you think is the most important point.
you've got a point	used to say that you think sb has made a reasonable statement.
fair enough	INF used to show you understand and accept what sb says.
even so	despite that.
here to stay	If sth is **here to stay**, it is generally accepted and has become part of life.

4 Is the meaning the same or different? Write S (same) or (D) different.

1	That's true, by and large.	That's true to some extent.	
2	On the whole, we agree with him.	For the most part, we agree with him.	
3	If you ask me, it's a big mistake.	In my opinion, it's a big mistake.	
4	The reason is, he's talking nonsense.	The thing is, he's talking nonsense.	
5	What he says is fair enough.	What he says is here to stay.	
6	It's true, but even so, it's not fair.	It's true, but despite that, it's not fair.	

5 One word is missing from each line. Where does it go? Write it at the end.

A What are the and cons of buying a flat? (1) ....

B Well, some ways it's easier to rent than to buy. (2) ....

A I know, but so, your own home eventually increases in value. (3) ....

B You've got a, that's true. But once you buy a flat, it's harder to move. (4) ....
And for the part, it's cheaper to rent than to buy. (5) ....

A Fair, that's an important point. (6) ....

B And the thing, you don't have to decorate it or worry about repairs. (7) ....

A To a certain that's true, but people like to choose their own decor. (8) ....
So, you ask me, owning is far better in the long run. (9) ....

'I said something to Tina in class and she **burst out laughing**. Then the teacher **told** her **off**.'

'I was **pulling his leg** when I said he'd lose the game, but he **took it the wrong way**.'

'The other contestants **made fun of** Max's singing, but I just **felt sorry for** him. Anyway, Max **had the last laugh** because he won the competition for the most original act!'

'I played a trick on my dad, but it **went wrong**. I put salt in the sugar bowl; I only **did it for a laugh**, but he **hit the roof**.'

'I don't know why they're always **laughing at** Mary – she's very nice.'

'Matthew tried to **make a joke of** the fact that I was upset, which was very silly of him.'

'For a laugh, I told my sister that I'd seen her boyfriend with another girl. The trouble is she **can't take a joke**, so we**'re not on speaking terms** at the moment.'

'He was trying to be funny, but he just **made a fool of himself**.'

'I thought he was making a joke, so I laughed – but I'd **got the wrong end of the stick**. It wasn't a joke at all – he was being completely serious.'

Glossary

burst out laughing	suddenly start laughing out loud.
tell sb off (for sth / for doing sth)	INF speak angrily to sb because they have done sth wrong.
pull sb's leg	INF play a joke on sb, often by telling them sth which isn't true.
take sth the wrong way	be upset by a comment which is not intended to be unkind.
make fun of sb	laugh at sb or make others laugh at them, usually in an unkind way. SYN **laugh at sb**.
feel/be sorry for sb	feel sadness and pity for sb.
have the last laugh	be successful or win an argument in the end, when other people thought it was impossible.
go wrong	develop badly and cause problems.
(do sth) for a laugh	(do sth) as a joke.
hit the roof	INF become very angry.
not be on speaking terms	not be prepared to be friendly towards each other, usually because of an argument.
make a fool of yourself	do sth that makes others think you are stupid. (If you **act/play the fool**, you behave in a stupid way in order to make other people laugh.)
get (hold of) the wrong end of the stick	INF understand sth wrongly.

spotlight Expressions with *joke*

If you **make a joke of something**, you laugh at something which is serious or important, and not funny.
If you **can take a joke**, you are able to laugh at a joke about yourself and not get upset.
If you **get a joke**, you understand it. When people tell us a joke we don't understand, we often reply:
Sorry, I don't get it.

1 Match 1–8 with a–h.

1 Don't pull _____	a of him.
2 Don't make fun _____	b of yourself.
3 Don't feel sorry _____	c of it.
4 Don't laugh _____	d his leg.
5 Don't make a fool _____	e him off.
6 Don't make a joke _____	f the wrong way.
7 Don't take it _____	g at him.
8 Don't tell _____	h for him.

2 The same word is missing in each pair of sentences (a and b). Write it in.

1 a It all went _____ .
  b She took it the _____ way.
2 a He _____ a joke about it.
  b He _____ a fool of himself.
3 a I feel sorry _____ her.
  b I did it _____ a laugh.
4 a He can't take a _____ .
  b I didn't get the _____ .
5 a I had the last _____ .
  b They often _____ at him.
6 a He _____ the wrong end of the stick.
  b I don't think she _____ the joke.

3 Circle the correct answer.

1 He made a joke about my driving, but when I passed my test, I had the *final* | *last* laugh.
2 We had an argument and I'm afraid we're not on *speaking* | *talking* terms.
3 I didn't think it was a very funny joke, but everyone else *burst* | *burst out* laughing.
4 She thought I was serious, when, in fact, I was just pulling her *hair* | *leg*.
5 We thought we were doing the right thing, but it all *became* | *went* wrong.
6 I don't know how she misunderstood, but she just got the wrong *part* | *end* of the stick.
7 When my mother saw the mess we'd made she hit the *roof* | *ceiling*.
8 He thinks he's funny, but mostly he's just making *a fool of himself* | *himself a fool*.

4 Complete the sentences on the right, keeping the meaning similar. You will need more than one word.

1 He did it as a joke.	He did it for _____ .
2 She can laugh at herself.	She can take _____ .
3 He was being silly.	He was acting _____ .
4 Why are they laughing at him?	Why are they making _____ ?
5 He misunderstood me.	I'm afraid he got the wrong _____ .
6 Her mother was angry with her.	Her mother told _____ .
7 They suddenly started laughing.	They burst _____ .
8 She got very angry.	She hit _____ .

5 Read each situation, then write a sentence to comment on each one.

▸ It was a joke but she thought I was being serious. *She took it the wrong way.*

1 I told them a funny joke, but they just looked at me. _____

2 He kept running around the room with a saucepan on his head. Nobody else thought it was funny.

_____

3 I said we already had 18 chairs and we needed 24, but he thought I meant we needed 18 plus 24 – in other words, 42. _____

4 We had an argument and she got really angry with me. Now she won't talk to me. _____

5 I was planning to take the train but Bob said there were no trains in the winter. Then I realized he was only joking. _____

6 My aunt had a hard life, and my mother was always very sympathetic towards her.

_____

Review: Communicating with people

Unit 14

1 Match 1–8 with a–h.

1 get hold _____   a in touch
2 drop someone _____   b a ring
3 give someone _____   c touch with someone
4 keep _____   d in the dark
5 keep quiet _____   e of someone
6 keep someone _____   f a word
7 don't breathe _____   g a line
8 lose _____   h about something

Unit 15

1 Complete the text.

There's a man I sometimes meet at the gym who I find really annoying. The thing is, he likes to dominate the conversation, and I find that I can never get a word in (1) _____ . I do my best to get my point of view (2) _____ , but he just ignores everything I say. You always have the feeling that he thinks you're much less knowledgeable or interesting than him, and that he's talking (3) _____ to you. And what's really annoying is that he (4) _____ nonsense most of the time anyway. The other thing about him is that he's very direct, and as a result he can seem rather rude, which sometimes upsets people. In fact, the other day, his girlfriend (5) _____ him _____ for offending someone. But perhaps he just feels it's better to say things to your (6) _____ rather than (7) _____ your back.

Unit 16

1 Complete the crossword. The letters in the grey squares spell out another word. What is it?

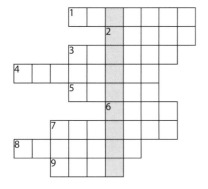

1 I can't give you the answer now, but I'll _____ _____ to you later today with the figures. (3, 4)
2 I spoke to a friend in China for an hour, and the call cost the _____ !
3 Could I speak to Mrs Baker? Yes, _____ _____ , please, and I'll see if she's free. (4, 2)
4 Can I _____ my mobile, please? The battery's flat. (6, 2)
5 I've got to _____ my mobile or I won't be able to make any calls. (3, 2)
6 She was very rude: she _____ up on me in the middle of the call.
7 I tried ringing Danny but I couldn't get _____ : his phone was engaged.
8 The phone company did some work on my landline and it cost a _____ .
9 Hold the _____ please, and I'll try and put you through.
   The word in the grey squares is _____ .

Unit 17

1 Cross out the wrong word; write the correct word at the end.

1 Could you pass me the crisps, please? ~ Sure, here you have. ....
2 I'm not going to class today. ~ Really? Why no? ....
3 Has he brought his dictionary? ~ No, he's forgotten it, as usually. ....
4 You look upset – who's up? ~ Oh, it's my cat; she's very ill. ....
5 Come on, hurry on, we've got to be there by nine o'clock. ....
6 Guess that? The president is coming to visit our school. ....
7 Have some juice. ~ Lovely. ~ Just tell when. ~ That's enough. ....
8 I think it's your turn to drive. ~ Why come? I drove last time. ....
9 OK, class, that's it. Time's over. ~ Oh, no, I haven't finished! ....
10 See you after my holiday. ~ Yeah, all the better. ....
11 Was the restaurant very expensive? ~ Yeah, kind off. ....
12 Shall we go to an Indian restaurant? ~ I don't mind; it's up for you. ....

Unit 18

1 True or false? Write T or F.

1 If you say *To tell you the truth,* you are going to say what you really think. ......
2 If you say *I'd rather not say*, you mean you don't know the answer to something. ......
3 If you say *I'll see what I can do*, you're telling someone that you're going to try and help them. ......
4 If you say *See you around*, you mean that you will see the person later that day. ......
5 If you say *Let's see,* you are giving yourself time to think or remember something. ......
6 If you say, *I told you so,* it means that you had warned someone about something and they didn't pay attention to you. ......
7 If you answer a question with *That would be telling*, it means you are going to give the person the information they want. ......
8 If you say *I couldn't tell you*, you mean you don't know the answer to something. ......

2 Complete the last word of each idiom, and then underline the full idiom in each dialogue.

1 I thought she was awful. ~ You can say that ....
2 Is the pizza restaurant any good? ~ Well, I like it, but go and see for ....
3 Do you think it will work? ~ I'm not sure, but let's see how it ....
4 Was it wet? ~ Yes, and very cold to say the ....
5 Would you like a coffee? ~ Yeah, I wouldn't say ....
6 Can we go in now? ~ Yeah, I don't see why ...., but don't make a noise.
7 Could I come on Thursday? ~ Er, let me .... Yes, that's fine.
8 What are you going to do with the money? ~ Well, to be honest, I'd rather not ....

Unit 19

1 Correct one mistake in each answer. Write the correct idiom at the end.

1 I've had some bad news; I didn't get that flat. ~ Oh, hard lucky. I am sorry. ....
2 Are you selling your flat? ~ I'm not telling you – it's not of your business! ....
3 Manuel's got a new girlfriend. ~ Good heaven! ....
4 Thanks so much for your help. ~ No at all. ....
5 Shall we have pasta or a pizza? ~ It's all the same for me. You decide. ....
6 How long will we have to stay here? ~ Goodness knows it! ....
7 How are you, Manuel? ~ Oh, no bad, thanks. ....
8 I can't come tomorrow. ~ Oh, don't mind. We'll go another day. ....

2 Find answers to the clues by moving horizontally or vertically, backwards or forwards.

YOU'RE	MIND	HEAR	HEAR	GO
JOKING	YOUR	BLESS	YES	AHEAD
BUSINESS	OWN	YOU	AND	NO
I'M	IF	YOU	LIKE	THANK
NOT	I	BEG	NOT	GOODNESS
BOTHERED	PARDON	YOUR	AT	ALL

▶ You say this politely when someone thanks you for something. *Not at all.*
1 You say this when someone sneezes. ....
2 You say this when you give someone permission to do something. ....
3 You say this when you are very relieved about something. ....
4 You say this when you are surprised. ....
5 You say this when you are agreeing with something someone has said. ....
6 You say this when you are saying sorry to someone. ....
7 You say this when you mean 'I don't care'. ....
8 You say this when someone is trying to find out private information that you don't want to give them.
   ....
9 You say this to agree to someone's suggestion. ....
10 You say this when you can't give a very clear answer to certain types of question. ....

Unit 20

1 Tick (✓) the correct column.

	Yes	No
1 *Call by* means 'give someone a ring'.	☐	☐
2 *What have you been up to?* means 'What have you been doing?'.	☐	☐
3 *Crop up* means 'continue'.	☐	☐
4 *Get out of something* means 'do something that you promised to do'.	☐	☐
5 *Wait up for someone* means 'not go to bed until someone else comes home'.	☐	☐
6 *I've got something on tonight* means 'I'm doing something tonight'.	☐	☐
7 *Remember me to your father* means 'Ask your father to remember me'.	☐	☐
8 *Drop someone off* means 'take someone somewhere in your car'.	☐	☐
9 *Six at the latest* means 'no later than six o'clock'.	☐	☐
10 *I'm popping out* means 'I'm staying out'.	☐	☐

2 Complete the sentences using a word from the left and a word from the right.

| wait   after   up   to   about   must   get   my | | to   do   time   together   love   up   dash   all |

1 I'm in a terrible hurry – sorry, I .... See you tomorrow!
2 She was going to be late, so she told her mother not to .... for her.
3 Emily wants to talk to you; I think it's something .... with the wedding.
4 I think it's .... we were leaving. Thanks for a lovely dinner.
5 I've had a tiring day so I don't really feel .... going out tonight.
6 We must try and .... one evening – when are you free?
7 If you see Jamie tonight, will you give him .... ? I really miss him.
8 The film didn't start till 8.00, so we could have got to the cinema on time ....

Unit 21

1 Complete the crossword. The letters in the grey squares spell out an idiom. What is it?

1 As .... as I'm concerned, the risk is too great.
2 What did you .... of his talk? ~ I thought it was brilliant, actually.
3 What you say is true, up to a ....
4 We need more nurses. ~ I couldn't .... more; you're absolutely right.
5 That's true to a certain .... , but don't forget how much it would cost.
6 She says eating meat is wrong, but to be .... , I'd find it hard to give it up.
7 What are the .... and cons of living in a student hostel?
8 He was without .... one of the best leaders our country has ever had.
9 She's been a marvellous employee; her bosses have always thought .... of her.
10 I could never be a pilot; for one .... , I'm terrified of flying.
    The idiom in the grey squares is ....

Unit 22

1 Find answers to the clues by moving horizontally or vertically, backwards or forwards.

TAKE	HIT	MAKE	FUN	OF
A	THE	ROOF	BURST	SOMEONE
JOKE	PULL	SOMEONE'S	OUT	TELL
NOT	TERMS	LEG	LAUGHING	SOMEONE
ON	SPEAKING	FOR	A	OFF
ACT	THE	FOOL	LAUGH	☺

▸ Play a joke on someone by telling them something that isn't true. *pull someone's leg* ....
1 Behave in a silly way to try and make people laugh. ....
2 Criticize someone angrily for doing something wrong. ....
3 Laugh at someone, often in an unkind way. ....
4 An informal way to say 'become very angry'. ....
5 Not prepared to be friendly with each other after an argument. ....
   ....
6 Be able to laugh at a joke about yourself and not get upset. ....
7 Another way of saying 'as a joke'. ....
8 Start laughing suddenly and out loud. ....

23 I can describe actions

1 They're shaking hands.

2 His arms are folded.

3 He's shaking his head (= 'No'). OPP nod your head (= 'Yes').

4 She's standing on tiptoe.

5 She's throwing the carton away.

6 She's got her legs crossed.

7 They're walking hand in hand (also they're holding hands).

8 He's blowing his nose.

9 He's doing his jacket up.

10 He's hanging his jacket up.

11 She's put her jumper on inside out.

12 He's put his jumper on back to front.

13 He's just fallen over.

14 She's tripped him up.

15 The cyclist knocked her over.

16 He's knocked him out.

---

spotlight Phrasal verbs with *knock*

If you **knock sb over/down**, you hit them and make them fall to the ground (see Picture 15).

If you **knock** a building **down**, you destroy it by breaking the walls.

If you **knock sb out**, you make them become unconscious (see Picture 16); or you make them fall asleep, e.g. *The drugs knocked him out.*

1 Match 1–8 with a–h.

1 Don't cross ....
2 He sat with his arms ....
3 Do your ....
4 They've knocked the building ....
5 My top was inside ....
6 I fell ....
7 Blow ....
8 Hang it ....

a over on the grass.
b down.
c folded.
d your nose.
e up behind the door.
f your legs.
g coat up.
h out.

2 Correct the mistake in each sentence.

▶ She sat down and crossed her ~~arms~~. _legs_ ....
1 I think he's nodding his hand. ....
2 He's wearing his T-shirt front to back. ....
3 They're shaking hand. ....
4 The little boy can't do out the buttons on his shirt. ....
5 The drugs completely knocked me over. ....
6 She told the children to fold their hands. ....
7 That stupid boy tripped me down. ....
8 She felt over on the ice. ....

3 Complete the sentences.

1 I didn't fall over – she pushed me and .... me over!
2 He .... me up when I was running for the ball, and I fell on my face.
3 I saw your sister and her boyfriend in the park, and they were walking hand in ....
4 I think you've got your skirt on back to ....
5 Where can I .... up my coat? ~ There's a hook behind that door.
6 You'll be able to see through that window if you stand on ....
7 The children sat on the floor with their legs .... , waiting for the teacher.
8 Please don't throw the newspaper .... ; I haven't read it yet.

4 Use an idiom or phrasal verb to explain what the people are doing, or have done, in these situations.

▶ I think he's saying 'yes'. _He's nodding his head._
1 They're meeting for the first time. ....
2 She doesn't want those old magazines. ....
3 I think he might have a cold. ....
4 The label is showing on his T-shirt. ....
5 I think she's saying 'no'. ....
6 He hit me and I was unconscious for a minute. ....
7 He can only just see over the wall. ....
8 Maybe they're boyfriend and girlfriend. ....

5 ABOUT YOU AND YOUR COUNTRY Write your answers in your notebook, or talk to another student.

1 Do people usually shake hands when they meet?
2 Do people nod their head to mean 'yes'?
3 Is it rude to blow your nose in public?
4 Do young people often hold hands in public places?
5 Do women ever walk hand in hand in your country?
6 Have you ever been knocked out by anyone?
7 Have you ever been knocked over by a bicycle or motorbike?
8 What was the last thing you threw away?

24 I can talk about my family

A Father and son

I **take after** my father. We're both tall – that **runs in the family** – and we both have a passion for the outdoor life. I **was brought up** on a farm and always **looked up to** my father, so it was no surprise when I **followed in** his **footsteps** and joined him on the family farm. Basically farming is **in my blood**, and it's been **our way of life** for five generations. Working with Dad is great. He **knows** the business **inside out**, and enjoys **showing** me **the ropes**. And from his **point of view**, he likes to have someone younger with new ideas – even if they aren't that good!

Glossary

take after sb	look or behave like an older member of your family.
run in the family	be found very often in a family.
bring sb up	care for and teach a child until they are an adult (also **bring sb up to do sth**).
look up to sb	respect and admire sb.
follow in sb's footsteps	do the same job or activity as sb else who did it before you.
in your blood	If sth is **in your blood**, it is a strong part of your character.
a way of life / sb's way of life	the behaviour and customs that are typical of a person or a group.
know sth inside out	have a lot of knowledge of sth (also **know what you are talking about**).
show sb the ropes	INF show sb carefully what to do and how to do it. (👁 See page 144.)
point of view	a way of looking at a situation; an opinion.

1 Complete the sentences with the correct preposition.

1 He hopes to follow .... my footsteps.
2 She has a different point .... view.
3 My sister takes .... my mum.
4 Politics is .... my blood.
5 Baldness seems to run .... my family.
6 It's a different way .... life.

2 Complete the text.

My father was a classical pianist. He knew the works of Mozart inside (1) .... and performed them all over the world. He (2) .... me up to love music as well; it seems to be something that (3) .... in our family. However, I eventually (4) .... in my mother's footsteps and became a doctor, and, by coincidence, it was my uncle (my mother's brother) who showed me the (5) .... when I got my first job in a hospital in London.

3 Complete the questions. (You will answer them in Exercise 4.)

1 Where were you .... up as a child?
2 Who do you most .... after in your family?
3 Would you like to follow in anyone's .... ?
4 Is there anyone you particularly .... up to in your family?
5 Is there a physical characteristic that .... in your family?

4 ABOUT YOU Write your answers to Exercise 3 in your notebook, or talk to another student.

B Sisters

When my mother **gave birth to** twins, I don't suppose she knew what she was **letting herself in for**. Although I'm **nothing like** Elle, we were equally horrible. If she pulled my hair, I **got my own back** by hiding her favourite doll; she always **burst into tears** when I did that. And then we **grew into** even more difficult teenagers. We **stayed out** late, and were always **getting into trouble** at school **for** smoking, wearing make-up, or just being lazy. Our poor mother tried to **turn a blind eye to** some of our behaviour, but it wasn't easy. Then, by some miracle, we **grew up**. We're both quite nice now!

Anna   Elle

Glossary

give birth (to sb)	produce a baby.
let yourself in for sth	INF involve yourself in sth that will probably be unpleasant or difficult.
nothing like sb/sth	completely different from sb/sth (also **not anything like sb/sth**).
get your own back (on sb)	INF do sth unpleasant to sb in return for sth unpleasant they did to you.
burst into tears	suddenly start crying.
grow into sth	gradually develop into a particular kind of person.
get into trouble (for sth)	get into a situation in which you may be punished.
turn a blind eye (to sth)	pretend not to see or notice sth, usually sth bad (in this case, so that she didn't have to do anything about it).
grow up	develop into an adult.

spotlight *stay out/in, stay up*

If you **stay out**, you continue to be away from your home, especially late at night. If you **stay in**, you stay at home and don't go out. And if you **stay up**, you go to bed later than usual.

---

5 Put the words in the correct order and add one missing word.

▶ turned | it | she | eye | to | a   *She turned a **blind** eye to it.*
1 she | why | tears | into | did | ?
2 my | I'll | back | get | her | own
3 birth | she | twins | to | has
4 school | trouble | at | I | got | often
5 watch | he | to | up | a | late | film
6 handsome | he's | man | a | grown | young
7 she | brothers | is | nothing | her
8 yourself | what | in | you | let | have | ?

6 Complete the questions. (You will answer them in Exercise 7.)

1 Where did you grow .... ?
2 Did your parents let you stay .... late to watch TV when you were young?
3 As a teenager, could you stay .... late when you were with friends?
4 Do/Did your parents ever turn a .... eye to things you do/did?
5 Do/Did you ever .... into trouble at school? If so, what for?
6 Do you remember getting your own .... on someone for something horrible they did to you?

7 ABOUT YOU Write your answers to Exercise 6 in your notebook, or talk to another student.

25 I can talk about different generations

A The young about the old

'The older generation are always **going on about** young people. They seem to think we**'re to blame for** everything that goes wrong in the world. Why can't they **leave us alone**?'

'It's true older people **are** a bit **out of touch when it comes to** things like technology, but **on the whole** I think they're probably more open-minded than they used to be.'

'Many older people **are set in their ways**, and that can make them a bit narrow-minded.'

'I sometimes **feel** more **at ease with** older people because they're not trying to impress you. I think maybe it's easier to **be yourself** as you get older.'

Glossary

go on (about sth/sb)	talk about sth/sb for a long time, especially in a boring or complaining way.
be to blame (for sth)	be responsible for sth bad. SYN **be at fault**.
leave sb alone	stop annoying sb.
be out of touch (with sth)	not know or understand what is happening in a particular subject or area.
when it comes to sth / doing sth	= when you are talking about sth / doing sth.
be set in your ways	have attitudes and habits for a long time that you don't want to change.
feel/be at ease (with sb)	feel comfortable and relaxed (with sb).
be yourself	act naturally.

spotlight *on the whole*

There are various idioms we can use to introduce a generalization:

On the whole
In general   } *people become more conservative as they get older.*
By and large

1 Correct the mistake in each sentence. Write the correct idiom at the end.

1 By the whole I enjoyed it. ....
2 Just leave me lone and go away. ....
3 She's largely with fault. ....
4 In generally I don't eat breakfast. ....
5 He's very settled in his ways. ....
6 I feel in ease with them. ....
7 I'm out from touch with computers. ....
8 Who is for blame? ....

2 Rewrite the sentences starting with the words given. The meaning must stay the same.

1 I feel relaxed with Liz and Clive.   I feel at ....
2 Just act naturally.   Just be ....
3 She's to blame.   She's at ....
4 He has very fixed attitudes.   He's very set ....
5 Stop annoying me.   Leave ....
6 I'm not good with numbers.   I'm not good when it ....
7 I don't know much about politics now.   I'm out of ....
8 Don't keep talking about it.   Don't go ....

B The old about the young

'Young people **get up to** all sorts of things nowadays. Parents probably **give in to** them too much, and let them **get away with** things. But in general, they're all right.'

'**More and more** young people still **live off** their parents in their late 20s and early 30s. They should be **standing on their own two feet** at that age.'

'I sometimes find it difficult to **get through to** young people. We seem to **be worlds apart**. Maybe I'm just **behind the times**.'

'I never **take offence** when young people say old people are boring. I felt exactly the same when I was young.'

Glossary

get up to (sth)	INF do sth, especially sth you shouldn't do.
give in (to sb)	stop fighting or arguing with sb and accept you can't win.
get away with sth	not be punished for sth you have done wrong.
more and more	in increasing numbers or at an increasing rate.
live off sb	rely on sb else to provide you with food, money, etc.
stand on your own two feet	not need the help of other people; live or act independently.
get through to sb	make sb understand what you are trying to say.
be worlds apart	be completely different in attitudes, opinions, etc.
behind the times	old-fashioned in your ideas, methods, etc.
take offence (at sth)	feel upset or hurt (by sth).

3 One word is missing. What is it, and where does it go?

▶ The kids always ask for sweets, and in the end I usually ⟨ in. *give*
1 He doesn't understand what I say; I just can't through to him. ....
2 She made a mistake but she was lucky; she got with it. ....
3 The area is becoming more and dangerous. ....
4 What have the children been getting to? ....
5 They're worlds – they have absolutely nothing in common. ....

4 Complete the dialogues. You may need more than one word.

1 I've learnt to be independent. ~ That's right, you can now stand on your ....
2 Does Joe still .... off his parents? ~ Yes, they pay for everything. And he's 40!
3 He's a bit old-fashioned. ~ I agree: he's a bit behind ....
4 The brothers are completely different. ~ Yes, it's strange: they're worlds ....
5 Was she upset at what you said? ~ No, I don't think she took ....
6 There's no point in arguing with him. ~ Yes, it's easier just to ....

5 ABOUT YOU Write your answers in your notebook, or talk to another student.

1 Did your parents give in to you very much when you were younger?
2 Did you get away with things at school when you were younger?
3 Do you ever find it difficult to get through to your parents/children?
4 Do you still live off your parents?
5 Do you think you and your parents are/were worlds apart?

26 I can talk about neighbours

A Getting on with the neighbours

We live **next door to** a young family. When we first **moved in** we invited them for tea to **break the ice**, and, since then, we**'ve got along** well. We **have** a lot **in common**, and they're always willing to **help out**. One day I **got locked out**, and Millie, the wife, **gave** me **a lift** to my husband's office to get a spare key. On the other side there's an old lady living **all by herself** who doesn't **get out and about** much. It's so sad; she needs someone to **keep** her **company**.

Glossary

next door (**to sb/sth**)	in the next house or flat.
move in	start living in a new house or flat. OPP **move out**.
break the ice	say or do sth that makes people feel more relaxed, e.g. at the beginning of a party.
get along	have a friendly relationship (also **get along with sb**). SYN **get on well** (**with sb**).
have sth in common	have similar interests (also **have sth in common with sb**).
help (**sb**) **out**	help sb in a difficult situation. SYN **lend sb a hand**.
lock sb out/in	lock a door so that sb cannot get out or in.
give sb a lift	take sb somewhere in your car.
all by yourself	completely alone ('all' adds emphasis). SYN **on your own**.
get out and about	go to places where you can meet people.
keep sb company	go or be with sb so that they are not alone.

1 Good or bad? Write G or B.

1 We have a lot in common. ....
2 You get along with your neighbour. ....
3 Someone gave you a lift. ....
4 You got locked in. ....
5 Your friend offers to keep you company. ....
6 A noisy neighbour has just moved in. ....
7 You can't get out and about for a month. ....
8 Someone helps you out with your studies. ....

2 Complete the questions. (You will answer them in Exercise 3.)

1 Do you live all .... yourself? If not, who with?
2 What do you have .... common with the people next .... to you?
3 How would you break the .... if you had new neighbours?
4 Do you have any elderly neighbours? Do you ever .... them company?
5 Have any of your neighbours .... you a lift? If so, where to?
6 Have you ever got .... out of your house and asked a neighbour for help?
7 Which of your neighbours do you get .... well with, and why?
8 Do your neighbours ever lend you a .... with things?

3 ABOUT YOU Write your answers to Exercise 2 in your notebook, or talk to another student.

B Throwing a party

Planning to **throw a party**? Here's how to stay **on good terms with** your neighbours!

- Make sure you **let** the neighbours **know** you're having a party, and more or less how long it will **go on**. If you like, **invite** them **round**.

- When it starts to get late, **turn** the music **down** to an acceptable level.

- Keep the windows closed when the party is **in full swing**.

- When the party **is coming to an end**, ask your guests to leave quietly, and not to **stand around** outside chatting. You don't want to **run the risk of** waking your neighbours up.

- If it all goes well, thank the neighbours afterwards for **putting up with** any noise.

Glossary

throw a party	have a party for your friends, family, etc.
on good/bad terms (with sb)	having a good/bad relationship with sb.
let sb know sth	tell sb about sth.
invite sb round	INF ask sb to come to your home.
turn sth down	reduce the volume of sth. OPP **turn sth up**.
in full swing	at the stage when there is the most activity.
come to an end	finish (also **bring sth to an end**).
stand around/about	stand somewhere not doing anything.
run the risk of (doing) sth	do sth that could have a bad result.
put up with sth/sb	accept sth/sb that is unpleasant, without complaining.

spotlight *go on*
(see also page 16)

How long did the party go on? = How long did it last?
What's going on? = What's happening?
Oh, go on – *you can do it!* used to encourage someone to do something.

4 Write sentences using words from each column.

She ✓	me	around outside.
It was	come	on all night.
The guests	invited ✓	of upsetting people.
The party	in full	up with the noise.
Who	stood	the music up?
They couldn't	went	swing by 11.00.
They ran	turned	us around. ✓
When did it	put	know if you can come.
Please let	the risk	to an end?

▶ She invited us around.

1 ....
2 ....
3 ....
4 ....
5 ....
6 ....
7 ....
8 ....

5 Complete the text. Then underline the full idioms and phrasal verbs.

My next-door neighbour decided to (1) .... a party last weekend. Unfortunately, we're on bad (2) .... because the last time he invited some people (3) .... , they all stood (4) .... outside making a lot of noise, and we had to complain. This time, however, he (5) .... us know in advance about the party, and he told us it wouldn't (6) .... on after midnight. I looked out of the window at about 11.30 to see what was going (7) .... , and it was really quiet – he must have turned the music (8) .... , and he actually brought the party to an (9) .... soon afterwards, which was great.

27 I can describe my feelings

A Describing fear

When Bob first suggested we went up in his hot-air balloon, it never **crossed my mind** that I would be nervous. But on the morning of the flight, I was starting to **get butterflies in my stomach**. And by the time we were on **board** and **were about to** take off, I **was shaking like a leaf**. I tried to take **my mind off** it by concentrating on my breathing, but I **was in a terrible state**. And I **jumped out of my skin** when I heard the noise from the gas burner – I just **couldn't help** it. In fact, it was amazing once we were up in the air, and I started to **calm down**. I realized Bob was very experienced and I **was in safe hands**.

Glossary

get/have butterflies in your stomach	feel very nervous before doing sth.
on board	on a ship, plane, hot-air balloon, etc.
be about to do sth	be going to do sth very soon.
shake like a leaf	shake a lot because you are frightened or nervous.
be in a state	INF be very anxious or upset (also **be in a terrible state**).
jump out of your skin	INF make a sudden movement out of fear.
can't help (doing) sth	used to say that sb cannot stop or avoid doing sth.
calm down / calm sb down	become or make sb become more relaxed.
be in safe hands	be with sb who will look after you very well.

spotlight Idioms with *mind*

It never crossed my mind that we would lose. = I never thought that we would lose. (Often used in negatives.)
You've got a lot on your mind. = There are a lot of things that you are thinking and perhaps worrying about.
Going to the gym took my mind off the exams. = made me stop thinking and worrying about them.

---

1 Rewrite the sentences, correcting the mistakes.

1 I've got flies in my stomach. ....
2 She's about for leave. ....
3 He ran out of his skin. ....
4 He's got something at his mind. ....
5 She won't help making mistakes. ....
6 Don't worry, you're on safe hands. ....

2 Complete the text.

I've got a big exam tomorrow and I know I'll be in a terrible (1) .... when I wake up.
I get so nervous – I just (2) .... help it. It has crossed my (3) .... once or
twice that I should really do something about it, and find a way to help myself (4) .... down.
The only thing that seems to (5) .... my mind off it is food, unfortunately! But I know that
tomorrow, I'll be outside the exam room, shaking like a (6) .... , as usual.

3 Complete the questions. (You will answer the questions in Exercise 4.)

1 Have you got a lot .... your mind at the moment?
2 When did you last get butterflies in your .... , and why?
3 Do you feel nervous when you're .... to go on a journey? Why?
4 If someone was .... board a plane and feeling very nervous, what would you suggest to
  .... them down?

4 ABOUT YOU Write your answers to Exercise 3 in your notebook, or talk to another student.

B A range of feelings

If ...	it means
If you're **having the time of your life**, INF	you're enjoying yourself very much.
If you're **thrilled to bits**, INF	you're very happy and excited about sth. SYN **be over the moon** INF (see page 144). **to bits** INF = very much.
If you're **in the mood (for sth)**,	you feel you would like to do sth. e.g. *I'm not in the mood for shopping today.*
If you **go red (in the face)**,	your face becomes red because you are embarrassed.
If you **lose your temper (with sb)**,	you get very angry (with sb). OPP **control your temper**.
If sb's behaviour **makes you sick**, INF	it makes you very angry and upset.
If you're **bored to tears**, INF	you're very bored. SYN **bored stiff** INF.
If you're feeling **on edge**,	you're feeling nervous and unable to relax.
If you **get cold feet** about a decision, INF	you suddenly become nervous about sth you have planned to do.
If you **don't know whether to laugh or cry**,	you feel upset about sth bad that has happened but can also see there is sth funny about it.
If it **breaks your heart** to see or do sth,	you're extremely upset about it. e.g. *It would break my heart to move from this old house.*
If you're feeling **down in the dumps**, INF	you're feeling depressed.

5 Match 1–8 with a–i. Do the sentences express positive or negative feelings? Write P or N at the end.

▶ It broke *f*
1 I wasn't in the ....
2 She saw Louis and just went ....
3 I don't know why she's down ....
4 We were thrilled ....
5 I just felt ....
6 The children had the time ....
7 We were bored ....
8 I completely lost ....

a to tears. ....
b in the dumps at the moment. ....
c of their lives at the adventure playground. ....
d red in the face. ....
e on edge for some reason. ....
f my heart to see my son leave home. N
g mood for going to a party. ....
h my temper with him. ....
i to bits about the wedding. ....

6 Complete the texts. Then underline the full idioms and phrasal verbs.

Poor Jasmine's got her driving test tomorrow and she's terrified. I hope she doesn't get cold (1) .... and not turn up for the exam.

I hate flying, so when I got to the airport I was really on (2) .... And then they announced a four-hour delay on the flight. I didn't know whether to laugh or (3) ....

Gemma was feeling a bit down in the (4) .... and definitely not in the (5) .... for a sad movie, so we went to a jazz café instead. It was fantastic – we had the time of our (6) .... and laughed all the way home.

The man next door is really irritating; he's always leaving his rubbish just outside my front door, and it (7) .... me sick. Whenever I see him I ask him to move it, and then he does; but I find it very hard to (8) .... my temper when I'm talking to him.

A Young love

Ask Claire's advice

SUE: I was very flattered when Chris started **chatting** me **up** at a party because I didn't think I'd **be his type**. But we really **hit it off**, and then started seeing a lot of each other. The thing is, though, his mother **thinks the world of** him and has done everything she can to **come between us** and try to **split us up**. I'd be so upset if we **broke up** because of her – I'm just **crazy about** him.

CLAIRE REPLIES: Start by **putting yourself in** his mother's **shoes**. She can see you've both **fallen in love** and she probably thinks she's losing her son **for good**. Be patient, and try to make friends with her – it's the only solution.

Glossary

chat sb up	INF talk to sb in a friendly way because you are attracted to them.
be your type	INF be someone with the qualities that you find attractive.
hit it off	INF form a good relationship on first meeting (also **hit it off with sb**).
think the world of sb	INF feel great love or affection for sb.
come between people	cause an argument or difficulty between people.
split people up	cause two people to stop having a relationship.
break up	stop having a relationship (also **break up with sb**). SYN **split up** (**with sb**).
crazy about sb	INF very much in love with sb. SYN **mad about sb** INF.
put yourself in sb's shoes	imagine you are in the same situation as sb. SYN **put yourself in sb's place**.
fall in love	start to love each other (also **fall in love with sb**, SYN **fall for sb** INF).
for good	for ever.

1 Tick (✓) the correct phrases. Be careful: one, two, or all three may be correct.

1 I think she's *fallen in love* ☐ *mad about* ☐ *fallen for* ☐ him.
2 I won't let anyone *come between* ☐ *split up* ☐ *break up* ☐ us.
3 Why don't you try and put yourself in his *shoes* ☐ *eyes* ☐ *place* ☐?
4 Do you think Max and Jan will *hit off it* ☐ *hit it off* ☐ *fall for each other* ☐?
5 I'm not sure he will *be Lucy's type* ☐ *chat Lucy up* ☐ *come between Lucy* ☐.
6 She *is crazy about* ☐ *is mad about* ☐ *thinks the world of* ☐ him.

2 Replace the underlined words with a phrasal verb or idiom.

1 He's a terrible liar; I hope she leaves him <u>and never comes back</u>. ....
2 He <u>really loves</u> his little niece. ....
3 She's not <u>the kind of person I find attractive</u>. ....
4 We met at a conference and we really <u>got on very well</u>. ....
5 I wish you would <u>imagine you were in my situation</u>. ....
6 He <u>seemed attracted to me and talked to me</u> in the bar. ....
7 It's sad, but they've decided to <u>separate</u>. ....
8 They're <u>very much in love with</u> each other. ....

B Enduring love

BETTY: Alf **took his time** to **ask** me **out**, but it was **love at first sight** for me, and I **couldn't wait** to get married. It's not all been easy though. You have to **put up with** each other's bad habits; and Alf has a few. But we've **stuck together**, and we're very happy.

ALF: It took me a while to **pluck up the courage to** ask Betty out, but we had lots in common and we **built on** that. Plus we worked hard at our relationship. With some young couples nowadays it seems that if anything **goes wrong**, one of them **walks out**. And lots of couples just seem to **drift apart**.

Glossary

take your time	do sth without hurrying.
ask sb out	invite sb to go somewhere because you want to start a romantic relationship with them.
love at first sight	love or attraction that you feel for sb when you see them for the first time.
can't wait / can hardly wait	If sb **can't** or **can hardly wait** for sth, they are very excited about it.
put up with sth/sb	accept sth/sb that is unpleasant, without complaining.
stick together	INF (of two or more people) stay together and support each other.
pluck up (the) courage (to do sth)	make yourself do sth even though you are afraid to do it.
build on sth	use sth as the basis on which to develop and make progress.
go wrong	develop badly and cause problems.
walk out (on sb)	INF leave sb you are having a relationship with.
drift apart	(of two or more people) slowly become less close or friendly.

3 Write the last word in each sentence.

1 It was great at first, then things started to go ....
2 There's no hurry; take your ....
3 The important thing in our relationship is that we've stuck ....
4 I'm going to ask her out if I can pluck up the ....
5 I saw her at a concert and it was love at first ....
6 We enjoyed the same things, and that gave us something to build ....
7 I'm meeting Gordon after work this evening. I can hardly ....
8 Everyone thought they were in love, then one day, he just walked ....

4 Complete the questions. (You will answer them in Exercise 5.)

1 Do you believe in .... at first sight? Why / why not?
2 Have you ever found it difficult to .... up the courage to ask someone .... ? When, who with, and why?
3 What are the main reasons why relationships .... wrong?
4 Do you know many couples who have .... together for a long time?
5 Which bad habits do you find difficult to .... up with?

5 ABOUT YOU Write your answers to Exercise 4 in your notebook, or talk to another student.

29 I can describe annoying habits

A Brad's annoying habits

Amy:

I love Brad, but some things about him **get on my nerves**!

- He **keeps on** leaving his clothes **all over the place**.
- He doesn't do **his fair share of** the housework.
- He's always **showing off** in front of our friends.
- He spends ages **messing around** on the computer.
- He tells the same jokes **over and over again**.

But I have to **take into account** the fact that he lived **on his own** for years. Being married is completely different – you need a bit of **give and take**.

Glossary

get on sb's nerves	INF annoy sb; make sb angry.
keep (on) doing sth	continue doing sth, often in an annoying way.
all over the place	in a very untidy state.
your fair share of sth	a fair and reasonable amount of sth (often used about work).
show off	try to impress people by showing them how clever you are. (A person who does this is a **show-off**.)
mess around/about	spend time in a relaxed way without a real purpose.
over and over again	many times; repeatedly. SYN **again and again**.
take sth into account	consider sth, especially when you are making a decision.
on your own	alone. SYN **by yourself**.
give and take	INF a situation in which you do things or compromise for other people, and they do things or compromise for you.

1 Circle the correct word.

1 She's messing *along* | *around* upstairs.
2 I said it *out* | *over* and over again.
3 I'll have to *take* | *make* it into account.
4 The papers are all *about* | *over* the place.
5 She's a terrible *show-up* | *show-off*.
6 I keep *on* | *in* forgetting to post it.
7 He tried to do it *by* | *on* his own.
8 He does his *right* | *fair* share of the work.

2 Complete the sentences with a suitable phrasal verb or idiom.

1 He loves being the centre of attention – he's always ....
2 It was terribly untidy; there were books and magazines ....
3 You have to listen to other people's opinions; there has to be some ....
4 Did she get help with that, or did she do it .... ?
5 She's had health problems this year, so when we make a plan we should ....
6 They still don't understand, although I've explained it ....
7 My phone keeps ringing but then there's no one there; it's really ....
8 We spent a relaxing weekend on the boat, just ....

B Amy's annoying habits

> **Brad:**
>
> I love Amy, but these things **drive me round the bend**!
>
> - She's always **putting me down** in front of other people, or making jokes **at my expense**.
> - She's always **tidying** my things **away**, then I can't find them; it **drives** me **up the wall**.
> - When she doesn't want to discuss something important, she just **changes the subject**.
> - She **changes her mind** about what to wear, then **bites** my **head off** if I get impatient.
> - She always **puts off** paying bills till **the last minute**.
>
> But even though we have our **ups and downs**, I love her very much, and it **cheers me up** to see her face every morning.

Glossary

put sb down	INF say things to make a person look stupid or silly.
at sb's expense	against sb, so that they look silly.
tidy sth away	put sth where it is kept in a drawer, cupboard, etc., so that it cannot be seen.
change the subject	start talking about sth different.
change your mind	change your decision or opinion.
bite sb's head off	INF answer sb in a very angry way.
put off doing sth / put sth off	delay doing sth until a later time or date.
the last minute/moment	the latest possible time before sth happens.
ups and downs	a mix of good times and bad times.
cheer sb up	make sb happier (**cheer up!** = be happy).

spotlight Expressing anger

These are two informal ways of saying that something or someone makes you angry, upset, or frustrated:
Her behaviour drives me up the wall.
All this rain drives me round the bend.

3 Is the meaning the same or different? Write S (same) or D (different).

1 She got very angry with me. | She bit my head off. ....
2 He's always putting me down. | He's always trying to make me do something later. ....
3 He sent her a present to cheer her up. | He sent her a present to make her happy. ....
4 Why did you change the subject? | Why did you change your mind? ....
5 It all happened at the last minute. | It all happened at that moment. ....
6 I put my appointment off till Friday. | I changed my appointment to Friday. ....

4 Rewrite the sentences using the word in capitals. The meaning must stay the same.

▸ The noise makes me really upset. WALL *The noise drives me up the wall.*
1 I love putting everything in order. AWAY ....
2 We've had plenty of good times and bad times. UPS ....
3 They all had a good laugh at me. EXPENSE ....
4 Should we delay buying the car? PUT ....
5 Don't get angry with me! BITE ....
6 The kids are driving me up the wall. BEND ....

5 ABOUT YOU Look again at Sections A and B. In your notebook, write six things that other people do which drive you up the wall, or talk to another student.

A Horoscopes

ARIES
21 March – 20 April

Something **is getting in the way of** your happiness. **So far**, you've **kept** your feelings **to yourself**, but **there's no time to lose** – **confide in** that important person in your life. Don't **sit around** doing nothing, **or else** you may regret it.

TAURUS
21 April – 21 May

Today's the day for a big change. You know **your heart isn't in** your work, and it's time to do something else with your life. **If the worst comes to the worst**, you can **count on** your friends to help you **find your feet**.

Glossary

get in the way of sth	prevent or stop sth from happening.
so far	until now.
keep sth to yourself	not tell anyone else about sth.
(there's) no time to lose	used for telling sb to hurry.
confide in sb	tell sb secrets because you feel you can trust them.
sit around	INF spend time doing nothing active or useful. SYN **sit about**.
or else	if not (used to say that there will be a bad result if sth does not happen).
your heart isn't in sth	you are not very interested in or excited about sth you are doing.
if the worst comes to the worst	if the worst possible situation happens.
count on sb/sth	depend on sb/sth; rely on sb/sth.

spotlight Idioms with *feet*

If you **find your feet**, you become confident in a new situation, especially one that is difficult to start with. If you **have** or **keep your feet on the ground**, you have or maintain a sensible, practical attitude to life.

1 Match 1–8 with a–h.

1 There's no time ....
2 If the worst comes ....
3 I don't think we can count ....
4 It's obvious that her heart ....
5 Take the money now, or ....
6 You can't just sit ....
7 Don't let your work get ....
8 I'm sure you'll find ....

a isn't in the job.
b else you might forget about it.
c around all day at home worrying.
d in the way of your happiness.
e to lose.
f your feet very quickly.
g to the worst, I'll leave.
h on Maggie to help us.

2 Rewrite the sentence using the word in capitals. The meaning must remain the same.

▶ Is she reliable? COUNT *Can you count on her?*
1 I can tell Molly any secrets I have. CONFIDE ....
2 Until now, nobody has arrived. FAR ....
3 Keep a sensible attitude to life. GROUND ....
4 If things get really bad, will you help me? WORST ....
5 Don't spend time doing nothing all day! AROUND ....
6 He'll soon become confident in his new job. FEET ....
7 She didn't tell anyone the news. HERSELF ....
8 He's not excited about this project. HEART ....

B Do you believe in horoscopes?

CALGARY
PUBLIC
LIBRARY

Judith Umbach Library
Self Checkout
August,03,2019 13.49

39065141953586   2019-08-24
Perfect phrases for ESL conversation sk
ills : hundreds of ready-to-use phrases
that help you express your thoughts, i
deas, and feelings in English conversat
ions of all types

39065151685771   2019-08-24
Perfecting your English pronunciation :
the most effective way to refine your
accent

39065139070401   2019-08-24
Idioms and phrasal verbs : intermediate

Total   **3 item(s)**

You have 1 item(s) ready for pickup

* <Predictably irrational : the hidden
forces that shape our decisions> ready
for pickup at Judith Umbach Library by
2019-08-13

Register for the Ultimate Summer Challenge
Starts on May 15
http://calgarylibrary.ca/summer

To check your card and renew items
go to www.calgarylibrary.ca
or call 403-262-2928

MOONLOVER Do I believe in ...o – ...rue!

...stn't ...ur

...ng ...ry

AMAL   I dare say there's something in it … **you never know**, do you?

INDY   NO!! **Life's too short** to waste on reading that nonsense.

LEOSCEPTIC   Are they true? It's **anyone's guess.** I just read them **for fun**, and I think most people are too sensible to **base** their lives **on** horoscopes.

...e truth or existence of sth.
...rediction **comes true**, it really happens.

...that was true before is not true now.
...ou do not believe sth that sb has said. (The stress is on the 'on'.)
...aying that sth is possible.
...e are true facts or acceptable ideas in what sb says. OPP **there's**

...you can't be certain of sth.
...ur time doing things or worrying about things that are

...can be certain about.
...ble, and for no other reason.
...s the starting point from which other things can develop.

...**word at the end.**

...e said that is true. ....
...out my life. ....
...ion in the paper? ....
...t was great. ....
...y there no longer. ....
...in! He'll never do that. ....

...**omplete idioms or phrasal verbs.**

...u never .... He might!
...ot. What he told me didn't come ....
...to, but not any ....
...e's .... short to worry about that.
...here's .... in it.
...Who knows! It's anyone's ....

...f so, do you believe in them? Write your answers in

Review: People and relationships

Unit 23

1 Write down five more things that people are doing in the picture; then answer the questions.

▶ *A man is hanging up his jacket.*

1 Has the woman sitting down got her legs crossed?
2 Has she got her arms folded?
3 Has anyone fallen over?
4 Is anyone doing their coat up?
5 Is the boy wearing his cap back to front?
6 Is the man in the white coat shaking his head?

Unit 24

1 Match 1–8 with a–h.

1 show
2 follow
3 get
4 burst
5 turn
6 give
7 run
8 take

a into trouble with the police
b someone the ropes
c a blind eye to something
d in the family
e into tears
f in someone's footsteps
g after someone
h birth

2 Complete the text.

My father (1) _____ up in a small town in Ireland. He was (2) _____ up by his grandparents because his parents both died when he was quite young. My father really (3) _____ up to his grandfather, and always wanted him to feel proud of his grandson. For that reason, perhaps, he never got into serious (4) _____ as a child, and rarely (5) _____ out late in case his grandparents worried about him. I'm afraid I'm (6) _____ like my father in that respect – I never come home before midnight when I go out. But then we live in a city and it's a completely different way of (7) _____ . Also, I know the place inside (8) _____ , so my parents don't worry about me.

Unit 25

1 Complete the sentences using a word from the left and a word from the right in the correct form.

live stand get take give feel	touch ✓ alone in on yourself feet
get be ✓ go leave be	through off offence away ease

▶ If you _are_ out of _touch_ with something, you no longer have recent knowledge or information about it.

1 If you .... someone, it means you depend on someone else for the money or food you need.

2 If you .... to someone, it means you stop arguing with them and accept that you can't win.

3 If someone .... about a subject, it means they talk about it so much that people become bored.

4 If someone asks you to .... them ...., it means they want you to stop annoying them.

5 If you .... at .... with someone, you are comfortable and relaxed when you are with them.

6 If someone .... with a crime, it means they aren't punished for what they have done.

7 If you can .... on your own two ...., it means you are independent and can look after yourself.

8 If you .... at something somebody says, it means you are hurt or upset by it.

9 If you act naturally, it means you can ....

10 If you can't .... to someone, it means you can't make them understand what you want to say.

Unit 26

1 Complete the dialogues.

1 Can you tell me if you decide to have the party? ~ Yes, I'll .... you know immediately.

2 Are you going to help them? ~ Yes, I said I'd .... them a hand.

3 Did you have to walk to the station? ~ No, Edwin gave me a ....

4 Did anyone help you with the cleaning? ~ No! I did it all by .... !

5 The music's a bit loud. ~ Yeah, sorry, I'll .... it down a bit.

6 They share a lot of interests, don't they? ~ Yes, they have a lot in ....

7 Shall we ask her to come for lunch? ~ Yes, I told her we'd .... her round sometime.

8 I've finally found a new flat. ~ Excellent! So when are you .... in?

2 Cross out one wrong word in each sentence. Write the correct word at the end.

1 He's a really annoying neighbour; I don't know how you put out with him. ....

2 You don't want to run the risk in being on bad terms with the people next door. ....

3 Did the meeting come to an end naturally, or did you have to take it to an end? ....

4 Since she's been ill, she's not been able to get round and about much. ....

5 How about the people upstairs – are you getting long with them now? ....

6 She doesn't have many friends so I try to help her off whenever I can. ....

7 He's on his own a lot, so he'd love it if you held him company sometimes. ....

8 We played a game at the beginning to break an ice and it really worked. ....

Unit 27

1 Complete the dialogues.

1 Didn't you realize he would be angry? ~ No, it never _____ my mind.
2 She looked very anxious before the test. ~ Yes, she was in a terrible _____ .
3 Those fireworks gave me a shock. ~ Me too. I nearly jumped out of my _____ .
4 Were you a bit nervous before the interview? ~ Well, I felt a bit on _____ , but not too bad.
5 Was the office party boring? ~ Not at all. We had the time of our _____ .
6 You must have been delighted to win. ~ Yes, I was _____ to bits.
7 Are they going now? ~ Yes, they're _____ to leave.
8 Was the lecture interesting? ~ No, I was bored to _____ .

2 Complete six more idioms by using a word from the left and a picture from the right.

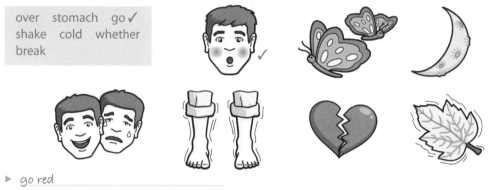

| over   stomach   go ✓ |
| shake   cold   whether |
| break |

▶ go red _____

_____

_____

_____

_____

Unit 28

1 Complete the crossword using the clues. The letters in the grey squares spell out a word. What is it?

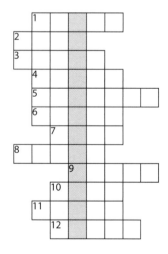

1 It was a case of love at _____ sight.
2 He's very pleasant, but he's not my _____ . I prefer more mature men.
3 He would do anything for his wife; he thinks the _____ of her.
4 Has Jake fallen for Amanda, do you think? ~ Yes, he's _____ about her.
5 I wouldn't like anything to come _____ us.
6 Whatever happens, my parents will always _____ together; they'd never break up.
7 Has he left her for _____ ? ~ Yes, he'll never come back.
8 If anything goes _____ between them, they sit down and talk about the problem.
9 Try putting yourself in your friend's _____ – how do you think she's feeling?
10 He saw me sitting alone and tried to _____ me up – but then my boyfriend turned up!
11 We made a good start in our marriage and managed to _____ on that.
12 It's very sad; I never thought they would _____ up, but they have.

Unit 29

1 Complete the definitions.

1 *drive someone up the wall* = make someone very ....
2 *cheer someone up* = make someone .... than they were.
3 *keep on doing something* = ... doing something.
4 *get on someone's nerves* = make someone ....
5 *bite someone's head off* = answer someone in a very .... way.
6 *change your mind* = change your .... or decision.

2 Complete the sentences using the correct form of the phrasal verbs and idioms in the table. You can move horizontally or vertically, backwards or forwards.

GIVE	OVER	SHOW	BY	PUT
AND	AND	OFF	MYSELF	SOMETHING
TAKE	OVER	AGAIN	THE	OFF
UPS →	AND	MINUTE	LAST	TAKE
ROUND	DOWNS ↓	THE	CHANGE	SOMETHING
THE	BEND	SUBJECT	ACCOUNT	INTO

▶ We've had our *ups and downs* .... , but in general we have a very happy marriage.
1 I didn't want to talk about sport, so I tried to ....
2 He waited until .... before deciding what the team would be.
3 In a relationship you need some .... for it to be successful.
4 Your situation is different from the others, so I'll .... when I make my decision.
5 He leaves all the lights on all the time – it drives me ....
6 The little boy kept saying the same thing ....
7 We can't have the party on Saturday, so we're going to .... until later in the year.
8 He likes to .... on the tennis court, especially when girls are watching.
9 Dad wanted to help me fix the car, but I said I'd prefer to do it ....

Unit 30

1 Complete the phrase that is being defined.

1 If you '........................ in something', you are certain that something exists.
2 'There's no time to .... ' is used to tell somebody to hurry.
3 If something is OK 'so .... ', it is OK until now.
4 If you 'keep your feet on the .... ', you keep a sensible attitude to life.
5 If 'your .... isn't in something', you're not very interested or excited about it.
6 If a wish or hope '........................ true', it really happens.
7 If you do something 'just for .... ', you do it for pleasure, and for no other reason.
8 If you 'find your .... ', you become confident and know what to do in a situation.

2 Complete the horoscope.

GEMINI
22 May – 21 June

Work has taken (1) .... your life in recent months, but it mustn't get in the (2) .... of your personal life over the next two weeks, or (3) .... you could miss a great opportunity. Someone (a member of the opposite sex) has been (4) .... something to themselves for a long time, but not (5) .... longer: and I dare (6) .... you know who I'm talking about! They are going to confide (7) .... you, and – you never (8) .... – it could be the beginning of an important stage in your life. Don't miss it.

31 I can describe the weather

The day will **start off** with a bit of sunshine, but you'll need to **make the most of** it because it'll soon **cloud over**, and by lunchtime **the chances are** we'll all get a shower. The rain may **die out** in the south, where it could even **brighten up** during the afternoon, but further north there will be more showers **here and there**. If you were hoping for better things tomorrow, I'm afraid you're **out of luck**, and Friday could be the third wet day **in a row**. **Looking on the bright side**, though, things may **pick up** by the weekend.

Glossary

make the most of sth	enjoy sth while you have the opportunity.
cloud over	become cloudy.
the chances are (that) …	it is likely/probable (that) …
die out	gradually disappear and stop completely.
brighten up	improve and become brighter (usually with more sunshine).
here and there	in various places.
out of luck	unlucky. OPP **in luck**.
in a row	one after the other.
look on the bright side	be optimistic; think positively.
pick up	improve; get better.

spotlight *start off, start out*

Start off and **start out** both mean 'begin to happen, or begin doing sth', e.g. *We started off/out after breakfast and arrived at lunchtime.*

We often use **start out** to talk about something beginning in one way and developing in another way: *I started out as a vet, then went into business.*

We use **start off** when we talk about something beginning in a particular way: *Let's start off with a review of last week's work.*

1 Choose the correct answer.

1 Even when things are really bad, Harry still looks on the *bright | brighter* side.
2 The centre is quiet now, but the *probabilities | chances* are it'll soon be busy.
3 We were *in luck | out of luck*: we had five cold, wet days in a *line | row*.
4 There's plenty of snow for skiing, so let's make *more | the most* of it.
5 We are expecting a few showers *there and here | here and there* this afternoon.
6 The rain is quite heavy at the moment, but it'll soon *die out | die off*.
7 Business was slow at first, but I'm sure it'll *get up | pick up* soon.
8 Shall we *start off | start out* with soup?

2 Complete the text with suitable words.

We decided to go down to the coast, and were hoping for good weather. We (1) .... off early to avoid the rush hour and also to (2) .... the most of the day. The weather forecast said it had been raining (3) .... and there during the night, but luckily it had (4) .... out by the morning, and it (5) .... up as we got nearer Brighton. It was actually quite sunny when we arrived. Unfortunately it soon (6) .... over again, and by the afternoon it was pouring with rain. Yet again, we were (7) .... of luck.

32 I can talk about sleep

A Morning, Kasha – did you sleep well?

B Yeah, I **had a** really **good night**, thanks – I **fell asleep** immediately. How about you?

A Awful – I **didn't sleep a wink**. Well, that's not entirely true. I eventually managed to **drop off**, but I spent most of the night **tossing and turning**.

B Yeah, I had a similar problem **the night before last**. I was **wide awake** for ages because I was **worried sick about** work.

A Yeah well, never mind. We'll be back home tonight, so we can both **have an early night** and **a lie-in** tomorrow if we want.

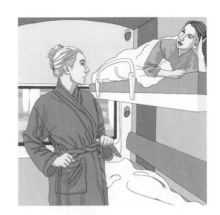

Glossary

have a good/bad night	have a night during which you sleep well/badly.
fall asleep	begin to sleep. SYN **drop off (to sleep)**.
not sleep a wink	INF not sleep at all. OPP **sleep like a log** INF.
toss and turn	be unable to sleep, or sleep badly, changing your position in bed all the time.
the night before last	If today is Saturday, **the night before last** is last Thursday night, i.e. two nights ago.
wide awake	completely awake. OPP **fast asleep** = in a deep sleep.
worried sick (about sth/sb)	INF extremely worried about sth/sb.
have an early / a late night	go to bed earlier/later than usual.
have a lie-in	INF stay in bed later than usual in the morning. **lie in** V.

1 Correct the mistake in each sentence.

▶ I was already ~~wide wake~~ before I had to get up this morning. _wide awake_
1 I sometimes drop out on long train journeys.
2 I didn't wink a sleep last night.
3 I've had several later nights this week.
4 I never fall to sleep watching television.
5 I made a lie-in this morning.
6 If I don't fall asleep quickly, I turn and toss for hours.
7 I had a very good sleep the night before the last.
8 I'm worry sick about my English.

2 Write the opposite using an idiom. More than one answer may be possible.

1 I slept all night.
2 I got up at the usual time.
3 I wasn't worried at all.
4 I didn't move all night.
5 I was fast asleep.
6 I managed to stay awake.
7 I slept badly.
8 I went to bed later than usual.

3 ABOUT YOU Are the sentences in Exercise 1 true for you? If not, change them so that they are true and write them in your notebook, or talk to another student.

▶ I was already wide awake before I had to get up this morning. _No. I was fast asleep._

A Different kinds of spender

← Chloe's very **careful with money**. She's not very **well off**, but she makes sure she's never **in the red**, so if she can't afford something, she just **saves up for** it. She **pays off** her credit card debt immediately, and when times are bad, she just **cuts back on** her spending.

→ The way he behaves, you'd think Luke was **rolling in money**, but he isn't. He finds it hard to **make ends meet**, he**'s** often **in debt**, and he won't admit that he's **hard up**. Some of the time, he **lives off** his parents and I'm sure he never **pays them back**.

Glossary

careful with (your) money	spending money only when it is necessary.
well off	having a lot of money. OPP **badly off**.
in the red	having spent more money than you have in the bank. OPP **in the black**. (👁 See page 144.)
save up (for sth)	keep money so that you can use it later.
cut back on sth	reduce the amount of sth that you spend, use, etc.
rolling in money/it	INF having a lot of money.
make ends meet	manage to buy the things you need with the money you have or earn.
be in debt	owe money to sb.
hard up	INF not having much money.
live off sb	rely on sb else to provide you with food, money, etc.

spotlight Phrasal verbs with *pay*

I paid off my debts. = finished paying the money I owed.
She paid me back. = gave me the money that she had borrowed from me.
I paid in £1000. = put £1000 into my bank account. OPP **take out**.

1 Correct the mistakes with the particles.

1 I'm afraid I'm at the red. ....
2 I cut back in my spending. ....
3 Pay out the money you borrowed. ....
4 He's been on debt for years. ....
5 How will he pay over his debts? ....
6 Go to the bank and pay the cheque on. ....
7 She's absolutely rolling on money. ....
8 You have to save out for it. ....

2 Complete the sentences.

1 I take money .... of my account once a week.
2 I'm not very .... with money; I just spend whatever I have.
3 I find it very difficult to .... back on my spending.
4 Doctors live comfortably and are .... off, but nurses are .... off.
5 Most elderly people are quite .... up.
6 Young people live .... their parents till they are about 18.
7 People who are .... in money have to pay higher taxes.
8 Lawyers find it difficult to make .... meet.

3 ABOUT YOUR COUNTRY Are the sentences in Exercise 2 true about you and your country? Write your answers in your notebook, or talk to another student.

B Money in adverts

Saving for a rainy day?
Look at our new savings account.

✈ **Air travel:**
don't **get ripped off**
– come to
webtravel.co.uk.

Students:
**keep your head
above water**!

Buy
Student Finance Magazine.

Pay for your
electricity online
and we'll **take** 2% **off**.

You've **run up a debt**
and are worried about it?
┌─────────────────┐
│   We can help. │
└─────────────────┘

Don't **run out of**
money abroad:
take

***traveller's
cheques.***

How to **get your money's
worth** when hiring a builder:
read our factsheet and **it
won't cost** you **a penny**.

VISIT
SOUTH AFRICA
on a shoestring!

Our insurance will
COVER THE COST OF
dental work.

Glossary

save for a rainy day	save money for a time when you really need it.
rip sb off	INF cheat sb by charging too much money for sth. **rip-off** N.
keep your head above water	just manage to survive in a difficult situation, especially one in which you don't have enough money.
take sth off sth	make sth cheaper by a certain amount.
run up a debt/bill	If you **run up a debt** or **bill**, you owe sb a lot of money.
run out of sth	use all of sth and have no more left.
get your money's worth	get the full value of the money you have spent.
not a penny	no money at all. (**It didn't/won't cost a penny.**)
on a shoestring	INF using very little money.
cover the cost (of sth)	provide enough money to pay for sth.

---

4 Correct one wrong letter in each sentence. Write the correct word at the end.

▶ If you're lucky, they'll ~~make~~ 10 per cent off your bill. *take*
1 Are you able to cover the post of the transport yourself? ....
2 The concert was disappointing; I didn't feel I'd got my honey's worth. ....
3 Be careful; you don't want to rub up a huge bill for the wedding. ....
4 The taxi driver knew we weren't locals, and we got nipped off. ....
5 It's not always easy to keep your lead above water when you're a student. ....
6 We ran out on money and had to go to the cash machine at the bank. ....
7 Mum said it would be expensive, but it didn't cost a jenny. ....
8 I've always believed you should save for a rainy way. ....

5 Rewrite the sentence using the word in capitals. The meaning must stay the same.

▶ The shopkeeper made it cheaper by €20. OFF *The shopkeeper took €20 off.*
1 He runs the café with little money. SHOESTRING ....
2 I didn't expect him to cheat me like that. RIP ....
3 Keep your money till you really need it. RAINY ....
4 It's hard to survive with the money I've got. WATER ....
5 It was absolutely free. PENNY ....
6 The insurance paid for the hospital. COST ....
7 Did you get good value for money? WORTH ....
8 I haven't got any dollars left. RUN ....

A Going on a diet

NAME Jo Jones
CURRENT WEIGHT 90 kg
TARGET WEIGHT 60 kg

Hi, I'm **going on a diet** – starting tomorrow! I'm worried that if I see a packet of biscuits, I'll just **give in** and eat **one after another**. Please help.

[blond23]   Hi Jo. **If I were you, I'd** just **cut down on** everything sugary. And **whatever you do**, don't **go without** breakfast – it's the most important meal of the day. Remember to do some exercise to **burn up** the calories. Good luck!

[Kima]   Jo, **make sure** you eat <u>lots</u> of fruit, vegetables, and brown rice; **fill yourself up with** them before you eat anything else. The rule is, if you**'re starving**, eat fruit! All the best!

Glossary

go/be on a diet	try to get thinner by eating a limited range of food.
give in (to sth)	If you **give in to sth**, you can't say 'no' to sth you want.
one after another	first one, then the next, etc. SYN **one after the other**.
cut down (on sth)	reduce the amount of sth that you eat, use, etc., or do sth less often.
go without sth	live without sth that you need or would like to have.
burn sth up	use up energy in your body by being physically active.
fill yourself up (with sth)	eat enough food so you no longer feel hungry.
be starving	INF be extremely hungry.

spotlight Giving advice

You can use these phrases when you are giving advice:
If I were you, I'd cut down on bread. = in your situation, I would …
Whatever you do, avoid cheese. used with a warning to sb not to do sth.
Make sure you drink plenty of water. = take the action necessary.

1 Complete the sentences with words from the box. (There are more words than you need.)

in	up	be	another	go	burn	other	cut	go	starving

1 He ate them one after ....
2 Don't give .... to the desire to smoke.
3 What's for dinner? I'm ....
4 You need to .... up the calories.
5 He just fills himself .... with cakes.
6 Try and .... without sugary drinks.
7 Have you .... down on hamburgers?
8 Why don't you .... on a diet?

2 Circle the correct word. (You will complete the sentences in Exercise 3.)

1 If you want to go *in* | *on* a diet, try to eat ....
2 If I *were* | *am* you, I *wouldn't* | *won't* eat ....
3 *Whatever* | *Wherever* you do, don't forget to ....
4 *Make* | *Get* sure you take ....
5 If you're *starving* | *staring*, don't *fill* | *fit* yourself up with ....
6 Try to cut *out* | *down* on drinks like ....

3 ABOUT YOU Complete the sentences in Exercise 2, giving advice to someone who wants to lose weight. If possible, discuss your answers with another student.

B Kitchen tips

All you need to know from kitchenhelp.com

- Freeze an onion before you **chop** it **up**[1]: that way, you won't cry.
- Fish smells can stay on pots and pans used in cooking. If you have a pan that smells, put some tea in it, **turn up** the heat till it boils, then **throw** it **out**. That will **get rid of** the smell.
- Garlic skins **come off** easily if you warm them before peeling. Or put the garlic under a flat knife and hit it with your hand: the skin opens and you can **get** the garlic **out** easily.
- You can **make use of** leftover cold rice by **heating** it **up** in the microwave with a little water. Then add it to a soup: it's a great way to **turn** leftovers **into** something new.

Glossary

chop sth up	cut sth into small pieces.
turn sth up	increase the heat or sound of sth. OPP **turn sth down**.
throw sth out	put sth that you do not want in the dustbin, down the sink, etc.
come off	If sth will **come off**, you can remove it.
get sth out (of sth)	take sth from inside the place where it normally is.
make use of sth	use sth for a particular purpose.
heat sth up	make sth become warm or hot. (**cool down** = become cool, e.g. *Let the vegetables **cool down** before you eat them*.)
turn sth into sth	make sth become sth different.

> **spotlight** *get rid of sth/sb*
>
> If you **get rid of sth/sb**, you take action in order to be free of it/them.
> *Open the door to* get rid of *the smell.* = so that the smell will go away.
> *Let's* get rid of *this stale bread.* = throw it out.
> *I* got rid of *the chef; he was terrible.* = made him leave.

4 Respond to the question in each dialogue using a word from the box in the correct form.

> get ✓   throw   come   heat   rid   turn   use

> ▶ Did you tell that terrible waiter to leave? ~ Yes, I *got rid of him* .
> 1 Was the oven temperature too low? ~ Yes, I had to ....
> 2 The dish wasn't very warm, was it? ~ No, I had to ....
> 3 Can you remove the mark from the saucepan? Yes, it'll .... easily.
> 4 Did you throw that coffee out? ~ Yes, I got ....
> 5 What did you do with all those eggs? ~ I managed to .... ; I made a cake.
> 6 Did you put that awful cake in the bin? ~ Yes, I ....

5 Rewrite the sentences in the correct order, adding one more word.

> ▶ up | I | so | was | the | food | cold | it *The food was cold, so I **heated** it up* .
> 1 pears | throw | don't | those | please ....
> 2 he | chop | needs | the | to | onions ....
> 3 the | out | get | I | olives | jar | couldn't | the ....
> 4 down | please | you | the | oven | could .... ?
> 5 the | turned | I | a | tomatoes | soup ....
> 6 too | let | cool | it's | if | hot | it ....

The Morning News

Thieves get away with antiques valued at €1m

The City Museum was the scene of a major crime last night when thieves **tricked** a security guard **into** believing they were a new team of cleaners …
[read more]

Hold-up at city bank

Two armed men **held up** a city bank yesterday, holding the bank manager prisoner for an hour as they searched for cash. They then **ran off with** €100,000 … [read more]

Break-in at Simpson's Hotel

Police searched **in vain** last night for two men who **broke into** Simpson's Hotel. [read more]

NEWS IN BRIEF

Burglar **caught red-handed**

Police warn residents to **be on the lookout for** thieves

Children 'as young as six' **getting into trouble with** the police

Internet crime **on the rise**

Speeding driver **let off** with warning

Man accused of murder **beaten up** in prison

Drug dealer **behind bars**

Glossary

get away with sth	do sth bad and not be punished for it.
trick sb into sth / doing sth	persuade sb to do sth by making them believe sth which is not true.
hold up sth/sb	rob or try to rob a place or a person by threatening violence. **hold-up** N.
in vain	without success.
break in/into sth	enter a building by force, usually to steal sth. **break-in** N.
catch sb red-handed	catch sb while they are committing a crime. (👁 See page 144.)
be on the lookout for sb/sth	INF pay attention in order to see, find, or avoid sb/sth.
get into trouble (with sb)	get into a situation where you may be punished.
on the rise	increasing. SYN **on the increase**.
let sb off	not punish sb, or punish them less than expected.
beat sb up	attack sb by hitting or kicking them many times.
behind bars	INF in prison.

spotlight Phrasal verbs and idioms with *run*

He ran off with my handbag. = stole it and left quickly.
She ran away from home. = left home secretly to escape from sb or sth.
The prisoner is on the run. = trying to hide or escape from the police.

1 Circle the correct particle.

1 The police searched the area *in | on* vain for the suspects.
2 Two young men are thought to be *at | on* the run after escaping from prison last night.
3 His life started to go wrong after he ran *away | off* from home at the age of 16.
4 The number of burglaries is *in | on* the rise in certain parts of the country.
5 The thief tricked the old couple *into | in* giving him their bank details.
6 I don't think that we will get *away | around* with telling lies for very long.
7 The poor man was beaten *out | up* outside the pub.
8 Police are *in | on* the lookout for two men in their twenties.

2 Write the last word in each sentence.

1 I know the thieves escaped, but are they still on the .... ?
2 If they carry on behaving so anti-socially, they'll soon get into ....
3 Sadly, our efforts to find the person who stole the jewellery were in ....
4 Everyone at the bank was very shocked to hear about last night's break-........................... .
5 What do you think she was running away .... ?
6 The crime figures haven't fallen; on the contrary, they're on the ....
7 It was a silly mistake and the police caught him red-........................... .
8 The boys took his mobile phone, but at least they didn't beat him ....

3 Rewrite the sentence using the word in capitals. The meaning must remain the same.

▶ They threatened violence and stole from the bank. HOLD *They held up the bank.*
1 Dan will be punished for this. TROUBLE ....
2 He committed the crime but wasn't punished. AWAY ....
3 The police are looking for two thieves. LOOKOUT ....
4 The escaped murderer is now back in prison. BARS ....
5 They caught the boy but did not punish him. LET ....
6 She left home to escape from her father. RUN ....
7 The barman was attacked by the gang. BEAT ....
8 We looked for the ring without any success. VAIN ....

4 One word is missing in each line. What is it, and where does it go?

Minor crime is certainly ⟨ the increase in some	*on*
villages; a few teenagers have been into trouble	1 ....
with the police. Residents have been the lookout	2 ....
for any bad behaviour. When one boy into the	3 ....
village shop at night, he was red-handed, but the	4 ....
police just let him with a severe warning. I don't	5 ....
think he should have been able to away with it.	6 ....
But last night two men tricked a resident letting	7 ....
them into his house; they then ran with some	8 ....
very valuable things, and they are still on run.	9 ....
I think that people like that should be bars.	10 ....

A A positive experience

ALAN When you started your apprenticeship, I didn't think you'd **get through** it.

TOM No, neither did I. Working **all hours** for **next to nothing** was hard, and some of the time I wasn't really sure I **was up to** it.

ALAN Yes, I remember old Wilson **giving** you **a hard time** when you **got behind with** work. But you wouldn't have **made it** without him, would you?

TOM No, you're right. He **stood by** me all those years, and I certainly **have** him **to thank for** the fact that I'm now fully qualified.

Glossary	
get through sth	manage to complete a difficult task or deal with a difficult situation.
all hours	If you work **all hours**, you work most of the time or for long periods.
next to nothing	almost nothing (in this case, almost no money).
be up to sth	be skilled or strong enough physically or mentally to do sth.
give sb a hard time	INF make a situation difficult for sb, often by making them work hard or by asking them lots of difficult questions.
get behind (with sth)	not do sth on time, then have more to do later.
stand by sb	support or be loyal to sb, even in a difficult situation.
have sb to thank (for sth)	used when you are saying who is responsible for sth, usually for sth good.

spotlight *make it*

Make it is a common idiom and can be used in different situations:
He'll never make it as a teacher. = be successful in a career (as above).
I can't make it tomorrow. = be present at a particular time or place.

1 Positive or negative? Write P or N.

1 She got through it. ......
2 He made next to nothing. ......
3 I wasn't up to it. ......

4 He got behind. ......
5 They stood by me. ......
6 She made it as a doctor. ......

2 Complete the dialogues.

1 Can you .... it on Wednesday? ~ Yes, I'm free all day.
2 Did you finish the work? ~ Yeah, we eventually .... through it.
3 Is she a difficult boss? ~ Well, she's given me quite a hard ....
4 Did he .... it as an engineer? ~ He did, and he has his uncle to .... for that.
5 Has your boss helped you? ~ Yes, he's always .... by me.
6 Why did Matthew leave? ~ He just wasn't .... to the job, so they dismissed him.

3 One word is missing in each sentence. Where does it go? Write it at the end.

1 The teacher thinks I'm lazy and she's been giving me hard time. ....
2 That poor boy earns next nothing. ....
3 I'm sure she'll make as a nurse; she's very caring. ....
4 She's started to behind with her work, and it's affecting everyone. ....
5 I'm working hours at the moment; I never have a day off. ....
6 The picnic was great, and we have my brother thank for that. ....

B A negative experience

> After university, I **was turned down** by lots of companies before I **was** finally **taken on** by a firm selling farm machinery. I thought it was a **nine-to-five** job but I was wrong. I had to work all hours, and my boss **was** constantly **checking up on** me to make sure I was **hard at it**. **To make matters worse**, we **were dealing with** some difficult farmers. Once I realized that I **wasn't cut out for** the job, I decided to **hand in my notice**. But before I had a chance, they **gave** me **the sack** – they realized I was hopeless!

Glossary

turn sb down	say 'no' to sb when they apply for sth or offer sth.
take sb on	employ sb.
nine-to-five	relating to normal and regular working hours (also as ADV: *work **nine to five***).
check up on sb	watch sb to make sure they are doing their job.
hard at it	INF working hard.
to make matters/things worse	to make a bad situation even worse.
deal with sb/sth	1 do business with sb (as above). 2 take the necessary action to resolve sth, e.g. *I **deal with** customer complaints.*
be cut out for sth / to do sth	INF have the necessary qualities and ability for / to do sth (*He's not **cut out for** teaching / **to be** a teacher*).
hand in your notice	formally tell your employer that you are leaving your job.
give sb the sack	tell an employee that they can no longer work for you because of bad work, their behaviour, etc.

4 Cross out the wrong word. Write the correct word at the end.

1 It's basically a nine-for-five job. ....
2 Why did they give him a sack? ....
3 Is he checking up against you? ....
4 We deal on lots of banks. ....
5 I've been hard with it all day. ....
6 To make matters worst, I failed. ....

5 Agree with the first speaker's comment, but use a different idiom or phrasal verb.

▶ It's regular working hours, isn't it? ~ Yeah, it's a *nine-to-five* .... job.
1 They rejected you! ~ Yes, they ....
2 She's resigned, hasn't she? ~ Yes, she .... yesterday.
3 They've employed more people. ~ Yes, they've .... two drivers.
4 Have they dismissed her? ~ Yes, they .... last week.
5 Has she been watching you at work? ~ Yes, she .... on me all the time.
6 He didn't have the ability for that job. ~ No, he wasn't .... for it.

6 ABOUT YOU Write your answers in your notebook or ask another student.

Have you ever …
… been turned down for anything?
… had a nine-to-five job?
… handed in your notice?
… had someone checking up on you?
… had to do something you weren't cut out for?

37 I can describe a small business

A Taking over a restaurant

Friends thought we **were out of our minds** when we **took over** the restaurant in the High Street. It had been **a going concern** at one time, but **had changed hands** three times in recent years, and on each occasion **had gone out of business**. Someone wanted to **turn** it **into** a baker's, but the deal **fell through** and we **took** it **on**. It needed money spent on it, and we had to **take out** a loan to **bridge the gap**, but we got the business **up and running** very quickly. We **took on** a very good chef, promoted the restaurant widely, and worked day and night to **make a go of** it. We still **have a long way to go**, but we're optimistic.

Glossary

be out of your mind	INF be mad or crazy.
take sth over	get control of sth or responsibility for sth.
a going concern	a business or activity that is making a profit.
change hands	pass from one owner to another.
go out of business	stop operating as a business because there is no more money.
turn sth (from sth) into sth	make sth become sth different.
fall through	fail or not happen.
take out sth	make a financial or legal arrangement with a company, bank, etc. (***take out a loan/insurance***).
bridge the gap	reduce the difference between two things (in this case between the money they have and the money they need).
up and running	(of a business or system) working and being used.
make a go of sth	INF make sth successful.
have a long way to go	need to make more progress before achieving sth.

> **spotlight** *take sth on, take sb on*
>
> If you **take sth on**, you decide to do it or be responsible for it.
> If you **take sb on**, you employ them.

1 Match 1–6 with a–f.

1	bridge	a	insurance
2	take over	b	hands
3	change	c	a new employee
4	take on	d	the gap
5	go out of	e	a company
6	take out	f	business

2 One word is missing in each sentence. Where does it go? Write it at the end.

▶ The company is doing well, so we'll need to take ⟨ more staff. *on* ....

1 We didn't have the money, so we had to take a loan. ....
2 It's not easy to run a café, but they think they can make go of it. ....
3 The shop is making money; they sold it as a concern. ....
4 We're negotiating the deal now, but it could still fall. ....
5 I decided to on the job because I wanted a new challenge. ....
6 You must be out of your to lend money to Karl; he's very unreliable. ....
7 We're doing quite well, but we still have a long to go. ....
8 They soon got the business and running. ....
9 It used to be a shoe shop, but it's been into a chemist's. ....

B Living off the land

Sam Wall had always wanted to **opt out of the rat race**, so when a small farm **came up for sale**, he **handed in his notice** at the bank, and moved his family to the countryside. He thought they could grow their own food and become self-sufficient. Sadly, Sam **was living in a dream world**. He didn't have the skills for farming, and soon found himself **cutting corners** in order to **make ends meet**. It proved to be **a vicious circle** and things gradually **went from bad to worse**. Eventually he was forced to **sell up** and move back to the city.

Glossary

opt out (of sth)	choose not to do sth or take part in sth.
the rat race	a stressful way of life in which people compete for wealth and power.
come up	happen or appear.
for sale	being offered for sb to buy.
hand/give in your notice	formally tell your employer that you are leaving your job.
be (living) in a dream world	have ideas or hopes that are not practical.
cut corners	do sth in the easiest and cheapest way, usually badly.
make ends meet	manage to buy the things you need with the money you have or earn.
a vicious circle	a situation in which one problem causes another problem which then makes the first problem worse.
go from bad to worse	(of a bad situation) get even worse.
sell up	sell your home, business, etc., often when leaving the area.

3 Circle the correct answer(s). Both answers may be correct.

1 They tried to cut *corners* | *edges*.
2 She *gave* | *handed* in her notice.
3 He opted *out of* | *away from* the rat race.
4 It's a *violent* | *vicious* circle.
5 I saw a house *to* | *for* sale.
6 We can make ends *manage* | *meet*.
7 I decided to sell *up* | *off* and move away.
8 It went from bad to *worse* | *worst*.

4 Complete the idioms.

1 hand in your ....
2 a vicious ....
3 make ends ....
4 the rat ....
5 go from bad to ....
6 be living in a dream ....

5 Complete the text.

My father always says I'm living in a (1) .... world if I imagine I can just (2) .... out of the rat (3) .... whenever I want. The truth is, our situations are very different. He has responsibilities, so he can't just hand in his (4) .... and sell (5) .... ; he has to consider the rest of the family. But I don't need a job with lots of money to make (6) .... meet. If something came (7) .... , like the chance to live on a boat for a year, I'd take it.

38 I can talk about shopping

Shopping and you

Have you ever tried to **get** your money **back** on something you bought? ....

Do you like to buy new things as soon as they go **on sale**? ....

Do you ever **send off for** things **rather than** buy them in shops? ....

Do you always **shop around** to get the best price for something? ....

Do you often buy goods which are **on special offer**? ....

When did you last **splash out on** something to wear? What did you buy? ....

When you last bought a present, did the shop **wrap** it **up** nicely for you **for nothing**? ....

Do your local shops often **sell out of** things, e.g. bread? ....

Glossary

get sth back	If you **get your money back**, the money you have paid is returned to you.
on sale	available to be bought, especially in a shop.
send off/away for sth	order sth by post or on the Internet.
rather than	instead of; in place of.
shop around (for sth)	go to several shops before you decide what particular thing to buy.
on (special) offer	on sale at a lower price than normal for a short time.
splash out (on sth)	INF spend a lot of money on sth.
wrap sth up	cover sth, e.g. a present or parcel, completely in paper.
for nothing	for free; without any payment.
sell out (of sth)	If a shop **sells out of sth**, it has no more of that particular thing left to sell.

1 Write sentences using words from each column.

I didn't get	off	back
They've sold	the gift	milk
I sent	on	on a new coat
She splashed	my money	for bargains
The wine is	out of	for a book
He wrapped	out	special offer
I always shop	for	up for me
I got the bike	around	nothing

I ....

They ....

I ....

She ....

The ....

He ....

I ....

I ....

2 Replace the underlined words with another word or phrase with a similar meaning.

1 I don't think I'll be able to get <u>a refund</u> on the holiday. ....
2 We bought the medium size <u>instead of</u> the large one this time. ....
3 When will that computer game be <u>available</u> in the shops? ....
4 He <u>spent a lot of money</u> on presents for his nephews. ....
5 I saw some nice shoes in a catalogue so I <u>ordered them by post</u>. ....
6 Are the CDs <u>cheaper</u> this week? ....
7 Did you <u>go to different shops</u> for the wedding present? ....
8 I was amazed, but she provided the delivery service <u>free</u>. ....

3 ABOUT YOU Write your answers to the questions at the top of the page, or ask another student.

Review: Everyday topics

Unit 31

1 Replace the underlined words and phrases with idioms or phrasal verbs that have the same meaning. Write your answers in the spaces below, using the first words to help you.

It's going to 1) become cloudy, and, according to the weather forecast, 2) it is likely that it will rain before lunchtime. Fortunately, the rain will 3) gradually disappear in the afternoon, and then I think it may 4) become brighter. I'm afraid we may be 5) unlucky at the weekend; they say we're going to have three days 6) running of wet weather, but things will 7) improve by the middle of next week. Let's 8) be optimistic.

1 cloud ....
2 the ....
3 die ....
4 brighten ....

5 out ....
6 in ....
7 pick ....
8 look ....

Unit 32

1 Using all the words, form eight idioms from the word square.

wide	have	like	and	last
not	toss	fall	a wink	a lie-in
sleep	worried	a log	awake	sick
the night	turn	sleep	before	asleep

....

....

Unit 33

1 Complete the dialogues.

1 A Hi, Jen – how's things?
   B Well, OK, but I'm worried about my financial situation. I'm a bit hard (1) .... at the moment and finding it hard to make (2) .... meet.
   A Oh, dear. Look, come and stay with me for a week or two – it won't (3) .... you a penny.
   B That's very kind, but I can't come and (4) .... off you – that's not fair.
   A Well, it's up to you. But I could lend you some money – just (5) .... me back when you're earning more.
   B I appreciate that, and I'll think about it. But in the meantime, I'll just have to (6) .... back on my spending.
2 A Where are you going for your holidays this year?
   B Well, I'm saving (7) .... for a fortnight in the Canary Islands in September. Hey, would you like to come?
   A That would be fantastic, but I really can't afford it at the moment.
   B Well, I tell you what – if you can (8) .... the cost of your travel, I'll pay for the accommodation.
   A Really? Brilliant! I'll be really (9) .... with my money for the next few months.

Unit 34

1 Complete the text.

My favourite meal

Posted by *Mad Matt* on 3 January 2010

One dish I absolutely adore is roast duck, and I make it quite often. First, I (1) _____ up the oven to the maximum temperature, then I put the duck in until the skin starts to go crisp. Meanwhile I (2) _____ up some vegetables such as carrots and potatoes into large chunks. After half an hour, I turn the oven (3) _____ and put the vegetables in as well (but not with the duck, because it is too fatty). I let them both cook for 45 minutes, then take the duck out and let it (4) _____ down slightly (I prefer it warm rather than hot). Then I serve it on top of the vegetables.

When you've eaten the duck, don't get (5) _____ of the bones. You can turn them (6) _____ a delicious soup just by adding vegetables, herbs, water, and seasoning, and cooking it very gently for two hours. You can also (7) _____ good use of the fat from the duck to fry potatoes, so don't throw that (8) _____ either.

One final piece of advice is not to serve roast duck if your dinner guests are (9) _____ a diet or trying to (10) _____ down on fattening food. They won't thank you for it!

Unit 35

1 Write sentences using words from each column.

He won't get	up	with the police.
They broke	away	my wallet.
They beat him	on	a shop.
They caught	for	the run.
They're on the lookout	trouble	with the robbery.
The thief ran off	him	quite badly.
She could get into	into	red-handed.
The prisoner is still	with	the robbers.

2 Complete the second sentence so that it has the same meaning as the first.

▶ The boys escaped without being punished. In other words, they got _away_ _with_ _it_ .

1 They threatened the cashier and demanded money. In other words, it was a _____ .
2 They did it without success. In other words, they did it in _____ .
3 The men will spend ten years in prison. In other words, they will spend ten years behind _____ .
4 They entered the building using force. In other words, there has been a _____ .
5 Crime is increasing. In other words, it's on _____ _____ .
6 She left the house to escape from her parents. In other words, she ran _____ .
7 They didn't punish him for what he did. In other words, they _____ _____ _____ .
8 He could get into a situation where he will be punished. In other words, he could get _____ _____ .

Unit 36

1 Cross out one wrong or unnecessary word in each line of the text.

My workplace difficulties

I haven't been very successful in the workplace. In one job, I worked all ▶ ~~long~~ hours,
and I had a difficult boss who was always checking it up on me; it made work very
hard. She kept on telling me that she didn't think I was up to for the job, and I felt
that she never gave me any support at all. To make the matters worse, my other
colleagues weren't very kind, and they didn't really stand up by me either.
Eventually, I decided that I'd had enough, and I handed them in my notice and
started to look for another job. I was taken down on as a medical secretary, but it
was harder than I'd thought, and I realized that I wasn't really cut off out for it.
And in fact, at the end of the first month, they gave to me the sack.

2 Write the last word in the sentence.

1 I wanted the job, but I didn't have enough experience so they turned me ....
2 I don't really like working nine to ....
3 I looked for another job because my boss was giving me a really hard ....
4 My success is really because of my parents: I have them to ....
5 My sister loves her job, but she earns next to ....
6 There's a meeting tomorrow at 7.30 a.m. Do you think you can make .... ?

Unit 37

1 You own a company. Are the following events good news or bad news? Write G or B.

1 Workers hand in their notice. ......
2 Your company is a going concern. ......
3 A business deal falls through. ......
4 You take people on. ......
5 You start cutting corners. ......
6 You take over another company. ......
7 You make a go of it. ......
8 You are in a vicious circle. ......

2 Complete the sentences with the correct particle.

1 He thinks I must be .... of my mind to work with my uncle.
2 They want to turn the shop .... a café.
3 She has taken .... a lot of responsibility in her new job.
4 The new business will be .... and running soon.
5 I believe the house is .... sale.
6 If an opportunity comes .... , I'm going to take it.

Unit 38

1 Complete the dialogues.

1 Did you have to pay for the repair? ~ No, they did it .... nothing.
2 Did you buy that in a shop? ~ No, I had to .... off for it.
3 Couldn't you get any tickets for the match? ~ No, they'd completely .... out.
4 Did you buy that coat today? ~ Yes, it was on special ....
5 Did you get a present for Magda? ~ Yes, could you .... it up for me?
6 Are you taking that skirt back to the shop? ~ Yes, I want to .... my money back.
7 Why did you get the black necklace .... than the red one? ~ It goes with more things.
8 Do you always shop .... before you buy anything? ~ Yes, I like a bargain.

A A good night out

… and after a hard week, I was hoping for **an early night**, but I **ran into** an old friend who was in town for the weekend, and he was keen for **a night out**. So, we **popped in** for a drink at The Blue Room, then went on to a seafood restaurant **just round the corner**. Seafood's **not my cup of tea** usually, but I quite enjoyed it. I offered to **go halves**, as I always do when I **eat out** with a friend, but Cal insisted on paying as I said I'd **put** him **up** for the night. We **ended up** in a bar until one, so it **turned out to be** quite **a late night** after all …

Glossary

an early night	a night when you go to bed earlier than usual. OPP **a late night**.
run into sb	meet sb you didn't plan to meet. SYN **bump into sb**.
a night out	an evening you spend out of the house enjoying yourself (also **a day out**).
pop in	make a quick visit to see sb or do sth (also **pop over/round**).
(just) round the corner	nearby; not far away. SYN **close by**.
not sb's cup of tea	INF not what sb likes or is interested in.
go halves	(of two people) share the cost of sth.
eat out	eat in a restaurant (**eat in** = eat at home).
put sb up	let sb stay at your home for a short period.
end up (somewhere or doing sth)	find yourself in a place or doing sth, without having planned it.
turn out (to be sth)	happen in a particular way, especially one that you did not expect.

1 Complete the dialogues.

1 Is there a post office close _____ ? ~ Yeah, it's just _____ the corner.
2 Shall we _____ in and see Mandy? ~ Er, I think she might be busy.
3 I _____ into an old school friend yesterday. ~ Really? Who was that?
4 Were you expecting cold weather? ~ Yes, but it _____ out to be very warm.
5 Did you go to the beach? ~ No, we _____ up by the lake instead.
6 Did you have a nice day _____ yesterday? ~ Yes, we went for a walk in the country.
7 Have you been to the Jazz Café? ~ Yes, it's not really my cup of _____ .
8 I've got nowhere to stay tonight. ~ Oh, that's OK, I can _____ you up.

2 Circle the correct answer. (You will answer the questions in Exercise 3.)

1 How often do you have an early *evening* | *night*?
2 How often do you eat *out* | *away*?
3 Do you normally go *half* | *halves* when you go out with a friend?
4 Are there restaurants just round the *bend* | *corner* from your home?
5 How often do you put people *up* | *in* for the night?
6 When was the last time you had a night *out* | *over*?

3 ABOUT YOU Answer the questions in Exercise 2 in your notebook, or talk to another student.

B Not such a good night out

I didn't **feel like** going out, but Malcolm **talked** me **into** it: a club in the square had recently **changed hands** and he thought we should **try** it **out**. It was already busy when we arrived and they were only letting people in **one at a time**, but Malcolm managed to **jump the queue** – something he's very good at. Inside, we were **packed in like sardines**. As usual Malcolm **pushed in** to get a drink, but this time a barman **took exception to** his behaviour. Malcolm started to argue, which **was asking for trouble**, and in the end they **threw** us **out**. In future, I think I'll **keep away from** that place – and from Malcolm!

Glossary

feel like (doing) sth	want (to do) sth.
talk sb into (doing) sth	persuade sb to do sth.
change hands	pass from one owner to another.
try sth/sb out	test sth or sb to see what they are like.
one at a time	separately; individually.
jump the queue	go ahead of other people who have been waiting longer. SYN **push in**.
packed in like sardines	crowded so closely together that there is no space to move.
take exception to sth	be angry about sth and object to it strongly.
be asking for trouble	INF be doing sth that will probably cause problems.
throw sb out	force sb to leave a place. SYN **chuck sb out** INF.
keep away from sb/sth	avoid going near sb/sth.

4 Choose the correct answer(s). Both answers may be correct.

1 They let us in one at a *go | time*.
2 We were making too much noise and they *threw | chucked* us out.
3 She didn't want to go but I talked her *up to it | into it*.
4 The Tube was very busy and we were packed in like *sandwiches | sardines*.
5 Why did she *make | take* exception to your clothes?
6 I was in a hurry, so I tried to *push in | jump the queue*.

5 Complete the sentences.

1 Do you _____ like going out tonight?
2 They _____ us out of the club because we weren't members.
3 Sarah had a terrible time yesterday, so don't mention it; that's _____ for trouble.
4 It makes me very angry when people try to _____ the queue.
5 I would _____ away from that part of town if I were you; it's quite dangerous.
6 Amy's got a new hairdresser; I thought I'd try him _____ to see if he's any good.
7 I didn't want to go, but she talked me _____ it.
8 It used to be an awful place, but it changed _____ last year, and has really improved.

6 ABOUT YOU Write your answers in your notebook, or talk to another student.

1 Do people often talk you into doing things? If so, what kind of thing?
2 Have you ever seen someone being thrown out of a place? If so, where?
3 Has a place near you recently changed hands? If so, what?
4 Do you ever jump the queue? Do you get angry when others push in?
5 Are there any parts of your city that tourists should keep away from?
6 What do you feel like doing this evening?

40 I can describe outdoor activities

A A walk in the country

I can't **keep up with** Josh – I just get **out of breath** – so when he suggested going for a walk, I only agreed to go if we could take my sister Michelle along as well, knowing she would **slow** us **down**. Anyway, we set off, and **sure enough**, after about ten minutes, Michelle started **falling behind**, and Josh was shouting at her, 'Come on! **Get a move on**! You**'re holding** us **up**!' She tried to **run after** us and **catch** us **up**, but eventually she shouted that she**'d had enough of** Josh's military march, and **all of a sudden** she **turned round** and headed home. I was quietly pleased.

Glossary

keep up (with sb)	move at the same speed as sb else.
out of breath	breathing fast and with difficulty.
slow sb down	make sb go/walk more slowly.
sure enough	used to say that sth happened as expected.
fall behind (sb/sth)	move more slowly than other people you are with.
get a move on	INF = hurry up.
hold sb/sth up	cause a delay or make sb/sth late.
run after sb/sth	run to try to catch sb/sth.
catch sb up / catch up with sb	reach sb who is ahead of you by going faster.
have had enough of sth	used when sth is tiring or annoying you, and you want it to stop (*I've had enough of this terrible weather!*).
all of a sudden	quickly and unexpectedly.
turn round/around	change direction and face the other way.

1 Match 1–8 with a–h.

1 This weather's awful. I've had ......
2 We ran to catch ......
3 Sorry I'm late; I was held ......
4 I heard a shout, so I turned ......
5 He got slower and slower and fell ......
6 I was slowed ......
7 He ran ......
8 He shouted at us to get ......

a round and then I saw the man fall.
b a move on.
c enough of it.
d up with the others.
e behind the rest of the runners.
f up in traffic for an hour.
g after the man who had stolen his briefcase.
h down by the strong winds.

2 Complete the dialogues.

1 A Where's Alex?
  B Well, he hurt his ankle and that held us .... for a while. In the end, Leslie and I walked on and Alex started to .... behind. I haven't seen him for two hours.

2 A What happened?
  B Well, I was playing football in the garden with some friends, including my brother, Chris, who's a bit of an idiot, and all of a .... there was a loud crash. I .... around and someone had kicked the ball through the kitchen window. .... enough, it was Chris.

3 A How are your swimming lessons going?
  B Well, I'm getting better, but I'm still out of .... after only 50 metres. My teacher's trying to slow me ...., but I want to .... up with the rest of the class.

B Swimming

I love swimming – your stories

 I **look forward to** the evenings when I can go down to the river and have a swim. It's really helped me **get into shape**.

 Swimming **didn't come easy to** me; I had to **work at** it. But it's just **a question of** practice, and **little by little** I'm getting better, which is great.

 I adore swimming – it just **comes naturally to** me. I **took** it **up** seriously after my accident and it**'s done me** a lot of **good**.

 Last year I decided to **go in for** a two-kilometre charity swim. It was great exercise and it helped to know it **was for a good cause**.

Glossary

look forward to (doing) sth	be thinking with pleasure about sth that is going to happen, or sth that you are going to do.
not come easy/easily (to sb)	be difficult for sb to do.
work at sth	make an effort over a period of time to do sth well.
be a question of (doing) sth	If sth **is a question of** practice, luck, etc., that is all you need for it to happen. SYN **be a matter of (doing) sth**.
little by little	slowly, gradually. SYN **bit by bit**.
come naturally (to sb/sth)	be natural and easy for sb to do.
take sth up	start or learn to do sth, especially for pleasure.
do sb good	have a helpful or useful effect on sb.
go in for sth	take part in a competition or take an exam.
be for/in a good cause	be a good thing to do because it helps others.

spotlight *shape*

If you **get into shape**, you become physically fitter as a result of taking exercise and eating healthy food. If you are **in good shape**, you are physically fit; if you are **out of shape** you are not fit.

3 Circle the correct answer.

1 If you do something in a good cause, it means it will help *you | other people*.
2 If something doesn't come easily, it means *it's hard to learn | you can't find it*.
3 If you plan to get into shape, it means that at the moment you're *in shape | out of shape*.
4 If you do something bit by bit, it means you do it *less and less | little by little*.
5 If you go in for a race, it means you *enter the race | win the race*.
6 If you take up a sport, it means you *enjoy it | start doing it*.

4 Complete the texts.

My sister's an amazing tango dancer. She (1) _____ it up when she was very young, and at first it didn't (2) _____ easy to her. However, bit (3) _____ bit she became more confident, and now she's the local champion. She's going in (4) _____ a national competition next month, and I'm really (5) _____ forward to seeing her perform.

It's strange, but my twin and I are quite different when it comes to sport. Everything (6) _____ naturally to Charlie, and as a result he's in good (7) _____ . But I'm a bit overweight, and for me it's really a (8) _____ of having to work (9) _____ any sport I try. It helps if I feel it's doing me (10) _____ , I suppose, but I'd rather sit and watch him!

5 ABOUT YOU What is your swimming story? Write it in your notebook, using vocabulary from the page. If possible discuss with another student.

41 I can talk about holidays

A A touring holiday

Holidays in Britain

JOE SMITH: We try to **get away** in winter and go somewhere
warm, but this year we decided to stay in England; and it
turned out to be a great success. We didn't plan anything
in advance – we just **set out** in the car, **took our time**,
and **stopped off** whenever we found somewhere nice.
After ten days we'd been **all over the place**. **Getting
around** was so easy with few tourists about, and, it being
out of season, we never had a problem finding a hotel. In
fact, I **got** more **out of** this holiday than one where I just
sit on a beach.

Glossary

turn out (to be)	happen in a particular way that is often unexpected.
in advance (of sth)	before sth happens or is expected.
set out	leave a place and start a journey. SYN **set off**.
take your time	do sth without hurrying.
stop off	make a short visit somewhere during a longer trip.
all over the place	in or through all parts of a place; everywhere.
get around	move from one place to another. SYN **get about**.
out of season	at the time of year when few people go on holiday.
get sth out of sth	get pleasure or benefit from sth. (It can also be used in a negative sense, e.g. *I didn't **get** much **out of** the course.*)

spotlight *get away*

If you plan to **get away**, it
means you are planning to have
a holiday (as above). **Get away
(from a place)** can also mean to
succeed in leaving a place, e.g. *I
won't be able to get away from
work before 6 p.m.* If you **get
away from sb/sth**, you escape
from a person or a place, e.g.
*He got away from the police by
jumping over a wall.*

1 **Circle the correct answer(s). Both answers may be correct.**

   1 We'll stop *of* | *off* for a night on the way.
   2 The hotel turned *up* | *out* to be very nice.
   3 They set *out* | *off* while it was still dark.
   4 It was easy to get *around* | *about*.
   5 He got *away* | *out* from the police.
   6 I can't *leave* | *get away from* work now.

2 **One word is missing in each sentence. Where does it go? Write it at the end.**

   ▶ I like to go to the coast out ⟨ season, when it's quiet. *of* ....
   1 There's no hurry – take time. ....
   2 We set after breakfast so that we would get there in time. ....
   3 I don't have long holidays, but I like to get at least once a year. ....
   4 We expected lots of tourists, but it turned to be very quiet. ....
   5 It was a very educational holiday, and I got a lot of it. ....
   6 During the time I was there, I travelled all the place. ....

3 **Complete the questions. (You will answer them in Exercise 4.)**

   1 Do you usually get .... more than once a year?
   2 Do you often take holidays out of .... when it's quieter?
   3 Do you usually book your holiday .... advance?
   4 When you're on holiday, how do you usually .... around?
   5 Do you often stop .... for a night on your way to a place?

4 **ABOUT YOU Write your answers to the questions in Exercise 3 in your notebook,
   or talk to another student.**

B A riding and camping holiday

Last year I **went away** on my own, so this year I thought it would **make a change** to go with a group. I chose a camping and riding holiday in France with four other people. I'm not very good at **roughing it**, and although I'd ridden **once or twice** before, I'd never spent a week **on horseback**. But I thought, 'Why not?' **As it happened**, the camping was very enjoyable. Everyone **did their bit** with the cooking, and riding's a great way to see the countryside. You get **off the beaten track** so easily, and it's lovely being out **in the open air**. It **did** me **good**, and I'd certainly go again.

Glossary

go away	have a holiday.
make a change	used to say that an activity is enjoyable because it is different from what you usually do.
rough it	INF live with only basic shelter and necessities for a short time.
once or twice	a few times.
on horseback	riding on a horse.
as it happens/happened	used when you comment on sth that is unexpected, or sth connected with what sb else has just said.
do your bit	do an equal amount of a task or job as others.
off the beaten track	far away from buildings and other people.
in the open air	(used in a positive sense) outside; not in a building.
do sb good	have a useful and positive effect on sb.

5 Circle the correct answer.

1 If you **do your bit**, it means you do *an equal amount* | *a bit* of a task that others are doing too.
2 If a place is **off the beaten track**, it is *near* | *not near* where people live.
3 If you **rough it**, you sleep somewhere like *in a tent* | *in an expensive hotel*.
4 If something **makes a change**, it means *you change something* | *it is different from usual*.
5 If something **does you good**, it means *you like it* | *it has a positive effect on you*.
6 If you like being **in the open air**, you are *happy* | *unhappy* to be outside.

6 Complete the text. Then underline the full idioms and phrasal verbs.

I invited my cousin to go on holiday because I thought it would (1) _____ her good to (2) _____ away somewhere nice for a couple of weeks. It would also make a (3) _____ for me to go away with someone else. She was delighted, but she really wanted to go somewhere where we'd be off the beaten (4) _____ , and out in the open (5) _____ most of the time. As it (6) _____ , I was thinking exactly the same thing. I'd been to west Wales (7) _____ or twice before, and I'd already made enquiries about renting a cottage on the coast.

7 Complete the questions. (You will answer them in Exercise 8.)

1 Are you happy to go _____ on holiday on your own?
2 Do you like going off the _____ track when you're on holiday?
3 Do you really enjoy being out in the _____ air?
4 Do you like roughing _____ when you go on holiday?
5 Have you ever spent much time _____ horseback?
6 Do you feel holidays _____ you good, or do you find them tiring?

8 ABOUT YOU Write your answers to the questions in Exercise 7 in your notebook, or talk to another student.

42 I can talk about team sports

A A football match

Brampton were **at full strength** for their last home match, which **kicked off** at the earlier time of 2.30 p.m. Despite **losing the toss** and playing against the wind in the first half, Camborne United **got off to a better start**. They scored after ten minutes and were **on top** for most of the first half. Then, ten minutes into the second half, a United player **was sent off** for a terrible foul on the goalkeeper. Brampton **took advantage of** the extra man and scored an equalizer, and **came close to** adding the winner on several occasions. But despite **being cheered on** by a fanatical home crowd, Brampton had to **settle for** a draw.

'the toss' / 'toss a coin'

Glossary

at full strength	playing with all the best members of your team. OPP **below strength**.
kick off	(of a football or rugby match) start. **kick-off** N.
lose the toss	guess wrongly which side of a coin will face upwards when it lands on the ground (see picture). OPP **win the toss**.
get off to a good/better/bad start	start sth well/better/badly.
on top	in control or leading others (in this case being the stronger team).
send sb off	order a player who has broken a rule to leave the field and not return.
take advantage of sth	make a good use of an opportunity.
come close to sth / to doing sth	almost do sth.
cheer sb on	shout in order to encourage sb in a game, race, etc.
settle for sth	accept sth that is not as good as you wanted.

1 Combine the words and phrases to make six idioms or phrasal verbs.

> kick   win   take   cheer   at full   send   advantage of something
> off   somebody on   somebody off   the toss   strength

....

....

....

2 Complete the dialogues.

1 Do you think we can win? ~ I doubt it. I'd .... for a draw.
2 Are we playing our best team? ~ No, we're not at .... strength.
3 What time does the match .... off? ~ Three o'clock.
4 Did we come .... to scoring? ~ Not really. The other team were .... top.
5 What happened to Kearney? ~ The referee .... him .... for fighting.

3 Complete the text.

I'm not really interested in football, but my boyfriend was playing so I went along to (1) .... him on. The game didn't (2) .... off to a great start for me because it (3) .... off half an hour late, and by then I was freezing. My boyfriend, who was captain, then (4) .... the toss, but that didn't really matter. What did matter was that our goalkeeper was (5) .... off for kicking one of their players, and the other team really took (6) .... of that. In the end, they beat us 5–0. My boyfriend was not happy!

B Sport and language learning

International footballers teach on the field and in the classroom

At a time when many pupils **have had enough of** languages, one class of students is full of enthusiasm. Why? The answer may **be something to do with** their teacher – French International footballer Bacary Sagna. The Arsenal right-back is **taking part in** a project to **liven up** language teaching. **To begin with**, pupils spend 45 minutes with Sagna in the classroom learning French, and **in return** they have 45 minutes trying to **get the better of** him on the football field. And after six weeks, the pupils play on Arsenal's ground in a game refereed in French. The idea **is catching on** fast: 74 schools have now **signed up to** the scheme, and teachers believe it**'s making a** big **difference**.

Glossary

have had enough of sth	used when sth/sb is tiring or annoying you, and you no longer want to do it.
be/have sth to do with sth/sb	be connected with sth/sb.
take part (in sth)	participate; join with other people in an activity. OPP **take no part in sth**.
liven sth up	make sth more interesting and exciting.
to begin with	first; at first. SYN **to start with**.
in return (for sth)	in exchange for sth or as payment for sth.
get the better of sb/sth	defeat or be stronger than sb/sth.
catch on	INF become popular or fashionable.
sign up (for/to/with sth)	agree formally to take part in sth.
make a difference (to sth/sb)	have an effect (on sth/sb). OPP **make no difference / not make any difference**.

4 One word is missing in each sentence. Where does it go? Write it at the end.

▶ Ray Clements is something ⟨ do with the national team. *to*

1 I'm not going to any more lessons: I've had of English. ....

2 We played well, but they the better of us in the end. ....

3 Mariko teaches me Japanese, and in I teach her English. ....

4 They have both signed for the evening course in Italian. ....

5 She was injured so she no part in the race. ....

6 A few new students may help to liven the lessons. ....

7 I can't play today: begin with, I haven't got my boots with me. ....

8 Rock-ball is an interesting new sport, but do you think it will catch? ....

5 Replace the underlined part of each sentence with an idiom or phrasal verb from above.

1 Over 1000 people want to <u>participate</u> in the race. ....

2 They changed the rules to <u>make</u> things <u>more exciting</u>. ....

3 This new sport could <u>become fashionable</u>. ....

4 His job is <u>connected</u> with sports education. ....

5 He changed the team but it didn't <u>have any effect</u>. ....

6 <u>At first</u> we didn't speak very much. ....

43 I can talk about situations on the road

A Driving long distances

When I have to drive long distances, I usually:

- **fill** the car **up** with petrol the day before I travel.
- **load up** the car the night before if necessary.
- **set off** early to avoid rush-hour traffic.
- **stick to** motorways if I can, in order to **get from A to B** as quickly as possible.
- only **break my journey** for 10–15 minutes **at a time**.
- **look out for** any **short cuts** when I'm on minor roads.
- take a map **just in case** I get lost.

Glossary

fill sth up (with sth)	make sth completely full (with sth) (also just **fill up** = fill the car with petrol).
load (sth) up	put a large quantity of things or people onto or into sth.
set off	start a journey (especially a long journey). SYN **set out**.
stick to sth	continue doing or using sth and not change it.
get from A to B	go from one place to another.
break your journey	stop for a short time during a journey.
at a time	on each occasion.
look out for sth/sb	keep a watch for sth/sb.
a short cut	a quicker way to get somewhere (you **take a short cut**).
(just) in case	because of the possibility of sth happening.

1 Make six sentences using words from each column.

We set	up	somewhere to eat
I loaded	to	short cut
I usually stick	a	journey
Let's break	off	the car
We can take	out for	main roads
Please look	the	early

2 Complete the sentences.

1 We'll have to .... the car up with petrol before we get on the motorway.
2 I took some sandwiches just in .... I got hungry.
3 We can go along the main road, or take a short .... through the park.
4 I never drive for more than two hours at a .... before I take a break.
5 My parents .... off after breakfast, so they should be here by lunch.
6 We need to start looking .... for road signs to the town centre.
7 I usually take the motorway: it's the quickest way to get from .... to ....
8 If the weather's really bad, I usually .... to the inside lane of the motorway.

3 ABOUT YOU Read the sentences at the top of the page again. Do you do these things when you drive long distances? Write your answers in your notebook, or talk to another student.

B Problems on the roads

The cars started to **slow down** in front of us, and eventually everything **ground to a halt**.

The police **went after** him because he **jumped the lights**.

We **broke down in the middle of nowhere**, and had to **call out** the emergency services.

The driver **pulled out** without looking, and nearly **knocked** someone **over**.

The car was beginning to **speed up**, so it **didn't stand a chance of** stopping in time.

The taxi started to **pull in**, then suddenly it **drove off** again. I was furious.

Glossary

slow down	go more slowly. OPP **speed up**.
grind to a halt	slowly stop completely. SYN **grind to a standstill**.
break down	(of a car, bus, etc.) stop working.
in the middle of nowhere	a long way from towns or buildings.
call sb out	phone for sb, e.g. a doctor or a plumber, to come and help you.
stand a chance (of sth / of doing sth)	If you **stand a chance of doing sth**, it is possible that you will succeed in doing it (often used in the negative).
go after sb	run after or chase sb in order to catch them.
jump the lights	drive through a red traffic light without stopping.
pull out	(of a car or driver) move away from the side of the road or a queue of cars and into the traffic. OPP **pull in / pull over** move to the side of the road and stop.
knock sb over/down	hit sb and make them fall to the ground.
drive off	(of a car or driver) leave; start moving away.

4 Circle the correct answer(s). Both answers may be correct.

1 It was an emergency so we had to *ask* | *call* out the fire brigade.
2 He was driving so fast, the cyclist didn't *hold* | *stand* a chance.
3 Finally the traffic ground to a *halt* | *standstill*.
4 Why did the police *go* | *get* after him?
5 I broke down in the *centre* | *middle* of nowhere.
6 It's illegal to *jump* | *rush* the lights.

5 Finish each sentence with the correct particle.

1 Why did the car break .... ?
2 He just knocked me ....
3 She got in the car and drove ....
4 The lights were red, so I slowed ....
5 We slowly began to speed ....
6 I saw Paul by the road, so I pulled ....

6 Complete the text.

It all happened very fast. A red car in front of me hit another driver's wing mirror, but drove (1) .... without stopping and (2) .... the lights. Then, in my rear view mirror, I saw a police car (3) .... out from behind me and go (4) .... it. The guy in the red car was driving like a madman. A van coming in the opposite direction tried to pull (5) .... to avoid the red car, but it didn't (6) .... a chance. The red car crashed into the van, then (7) .... over a cyclist waiting at the junction.

7 ABOUT YOU Have you seen or experienced any of the problems on the road at the top of the page? Write your answers in your notebook, or talk to another student.

Review: Out and about

Unit 39

1 One word is missing in each line of dialogue. What is it, and where does it go?

A How was your ⟨ out last Saturday?   ▸ *night*

B Well, I had a cold so I didn't really feel going out,   1 ....

but Connie talked into it, and we went for a meal   2 ....

at the pizza place just the corner from home.   3 ....

B Oh, is it good? I was thinking of it out.   4 ....

A The food was OK, but we were packed like sardines.   5 ....

B Yeah, the thing is, if you eat on a Saturday night,   6 ....

you're asking trouble – it's always busy.   7 ....

A Yeah. Anyway, we bumped Susie when we were   8 ....

leaving and ended back at her flat. I didn't get   9 ....

home till 2.00, so I had a pretty late after all.   10 ....

2 Complete the sentences. The meaning must stay the same as in the sentence on the left.

▸ Is it OK if I stay at your house tonight?   Could you put *me up tonight* ?

1 Shall we go to a restaurant?   Shall we eat .... ?

2 The owner told us to leave immediately.   The owner threw ....

3 He pushed in front of people.   He jumped ....

4 I don't like that sort of music.   That music isn't ....

5 Shall we pay for ourselves?   Shall we go .... ?

6 That shop now has a new owner.   That shop has changed ....

7 He was very angry about Martin's comments.   He took ....

8 I wouldn't go anywhere near her.   I would keep ....

Unit 40

1 Complete the dialogues.

1 Are you going to watch the swimming? ~ Yes, of course. I'm looking .... to it.

2 Do you find ball games difficult? ~ Yes, they don't .... easy to me.

3 Do you enjoy riding? ~ Yes, and I think it's doing me a lot of ....

4 Are the two boys fit? ~ Yes, they're both in good ....

5 Come on. Get a .... on. ~ I'm sorry, I can't go any faster.

6 He ran .... the boys who stole the bag. ~ Really. Did he catch them?

7 When did you start getting .... of breath? ~ It just happened all of a ....

8 Are you going to stop for a rest? ~ Yes, you go on. I'll .... up with you later.

2 One word is missing in each sentence. Where does it go? Write it at the end.

▸ Tell the children to get a move ⟨. We're going to be late! *on*

1 I asked him to slow because I couldn't walk that fast. ....

2 I'm not very fit, so I soon fell the others. ....

3 She was holding everyone so they went on without her. ....

4 He suddenly turned and walked in the opposite direction. ....

5 Golf doesn't come naturally to me; I have to work it. ....

6 I've decided to go in that competition. ....

7 She took swimming to get into shape. ....

8 Louis was going so fast that I couldn't keep with him. ....

Unit 41

1 Complete the texts with words from the box.

away   good   season   happens   get   advance   around   beaten   air   rough

Holidays

Start a conversation

CRAZY CAT Hi, I'm hoping to (1) _____ away for a month travelling in Europe this summer, but I haven't got much to spend. At the same time, I don't want to (2) _____ it too much. Any suggestions?

ERIN Hi, Crazy. First thing is to book your flight a long time in (3) _____ ; that will save you loads of money. And if you can travel out of (4) _____ , do so – it's much cheaper in June than August. As it (5) _____ I'm free in June and hoping to travel in Europe. Would you like a travelling companion? Let me know!

LEROY How about a camping trip? Camp sites these days are really comfortable. That way, the accommodation is cheap, and you'll be in the open (6) _____ , which will do you (7) _____ . If you manage to get off the (8) _____ track, you'll find more bargains in the quiet places – AND you'll get (9) _____ from all those other tourists! Use public transport to get (10) _____ – you know it makes sense. Have a great time.

Unit 42

1 Finish each sentence.

1 At the beginning of a game, you use a coin to find out which team wins the _____ .
2 If a player has to leave the field for breaking a rule, they have been _____ _____ .
3 If you shout to encourage your team, you are _____ them _____ .
4 If you have all your best players playing, you are at full _____ .
5 If you don't join in with something, you take _____ _____ in it.
6 If something catches on, it becomes _____ .

2 Rewrite the sentences starting with the words given. The meaning must stay the same.

1 It has had an effect.   It has made _____ .
2 Anyone can participate.   Anyone can take _____ .
3 His job is connected with sport. His job is something to _____ .
4 We almost won.   We came _____ .
5 I'm tired of training.   I've had _____ .
6 It will make it more interesting. It will liven _____ .
7 I've enrolled for an English course. I've signed _____ .
8 We started very well.   We got _____ .

Unit 43

1 Complete the advice sheet.

Top Tips for New Drivers

- Slow (1) _____ ! Many new drivers go too fast. Remember, if you're driving slowly you (2) _____ a better chance of avoiding an accident if anything unexpected happens.

- Remember to check your seat belt, mirror, etc. before you pull (3) _____ from the side of the road into traffic.

- Don't drive if you're feeling sleepy. If necessary, (4) _____ your journey and have a coffee.

- Be prepared for anything on long journeys if you're alone. Make sure you (5) _____ the car up with petrol, and take a mobile phone with you, just in (6) _____ you break (7) _____ in the middle of (8) _____ .

- Also, on long journeys, check the oil and tyre pressure before you set (9) _____ .

- If your mobile rings, don't answer it. Wait until it is safe to (10) _____ in to the side of the road and then answer the call.

2 Find answers to the clues by moving horizontally or vertically, backwards or forwards.

A	JUMP	THE	SOMETHING→UP	
SHORT	CUT	LIGHTS	LOAD ↑	PULL
SPEED	GRIND	TO	A	OVER
UP	NOWHERE	GO	HALT	OUT
IN	OF	AFTER	CALL	SOMEONE
THE	MIDDLE	SOMEONE	DRIVE	OFF

▶ Put a lot of things or people on to something, in a car, etc. *load something up*
1 start moving away in a car _____
2 drive through a red light without stopping _____
3 a long way from any building or houses _____

4 phone for a plumber, doctor, etc. to come and help you _____
5 go more quickly _____
6 run or chase after something to try to catch them _____
7 slowly stop completely _____
8 move to the side of the road to stop _____
9 a quicker way to get somewhere _____

© Oxford University Press 2010

44 I can say what I want or need

Tell us about you!

I **could do with** some new clothes.

I know I could work harder **if need be**.

I couldn't **do without** my mobile.

I don't usually **feel like** going out in the evenings.

I'**m dying to** get my own flat.

I sometimes **set my heart on** things I know I can't have.

I could **make do with** a smaller car, but I'd rather not.

I **couldn't care less** about money.

I believe you can't always **pick and choose** in life.

Glossary

could do with sth	INF used to say that you need or want to have sth.
if need be	if necessary.
do without sth/sb	manage or survive without sth/sb.
feel like sth / doing sth	want sth or want to do sth (usually used about everyday things, e.g. *I feel like a drink / going out*).
be dying to do sth / for sth	INF want to do sth or want sth very much.
set your heart on sth	want sth very much (usually used about a possession, e.g. a gold ring, or a long-term goal, e.g. becoming a doctor).
make do (with sth)	manage with sth that isn't really good enough.
couldn't care less	INF used to say, often rudely, that you don't think sth/sb is important or worth worrying about. SYN **don't give a damn** INF.
pick and choose	choose only the things you like and want.

1 Correct the mistake in each sentence.

1 I could go and collect them from the station if the need be.
2 Their daughter has put her heart on having her own horse.
3 Do you feel like go out this evening?
4 He'll have to take any job he can get; he can't pick and select.
5 Now they have a baby, they can do with a bigger flat.
6 I'm dying for to have something to eat.

2 Rewrite the sentences using the words in capital letters. The meaning must stay the same.

▶ Football isn't important to me. CARE *I couldn't care less about football.*
1 I want a rest now. FEEL
2 I really need a good dictionary. COULD
3 Can you manage with this small map? MAKE
4 You can't always have what you want. PICK
5 I really want to see his new girlfriend. DYING
6 I must always have my address book with me. DO
7 We can take the car if necessary. NEED
8 She desperately wants a career in music. HEART

3 ABOUT YOU Read the sentences at the top of the page again. Are they true for you? If not, change them so they are true.

▶ I **could do with** some new clothes.   *a new tennis racket*

45 I can discuss plans and arrangements

> Is the wedding **going ahead** as planned?
>> No, they've **put** it **off** until the spring.

> They've **brought** the game **forward** to Saturday.
>> Yes, but they've **put** the kick-off **back** to five o'clock. It**'s** really **messed up** my plans.

> I**'ve got** something **on** this Friday, so I'll have to **call off** our meeting.
>> That's OK – Bob can't **make it** either. Shall we **fix** something **up** for next week?

> You're not **looking ahead to** next year already, are you?
>> Yes. I'm hoping to go to India, if all **goes according to plan**.

Glossary	
go ahead	If sth **goes ahead**, it happens or proceeds (also **go ahead with sth**).
bring sth forward	move sth to an earlier time. OPP **put sth back**.
mess sth up	1 spoil sth or have a bad effect on sth (as above). 2 do sth badly, e.g. *I **messed up** the exam.* SYN **muck sth up** INF (1 and 2).
have (got) sth on	INF have an arrangement to do sth.
call sth off	cancel sth that has been arranged, so it doesn't happen.
make it	manage to do sth or be somewhere.
fix sth up	arrange for sth to happen.
look ahead (to sth)	think about what is going to happen in the future.
go according to plan	happen in the way you intend and expect.

spotlight *put sth off, put sth back*

Both verbs mean to change something to a later time or date: *The meeting was today, but I've put it back / put it off till Friday.*
We also use **put sth off** when we delay something we don't want to do: *I need to go to the dentist, but I keep putting it off.*

---

1 **Circle the correct answer(s). Both answers may be correct.**

1 The exam has been *put back | put off* till Thursday.
2 I'm fairly sure the festival will *go ahead | look ahead* as planned.
3 The game has been *called off | put off* until next Wednesday.
4 Shall we *fix up | mess up* a meeting for Friday week?
5 Mike and Angela have split up, so they've *called off | put back* the wedding.
6 Changing the dates has really *messed up | mucked up* my plans.

2 **Complete the dialogues.**

1 They want to go .... with the meeting. ~ Oh, that'll really muck .... my plans.
2 Where will you be next week? ~ In Peru, if everything goes .... to plan.
3 Six o'clock is a bit early for dinner! ~ Yes, that's why they've .... it back till eight.
4 She thinks about the past too much. ~ Yes, she should be .... ahead to the future.
5 Have you written your essay yet? ~ No, I keep putting it .... ; it's a very hard subject.
6 No one can .... it on Saturday. ~ OK, let's .... the party forward to Friday.
7 Have you rung Gill? ~ Yes, we're going to try and .... something up for the weekend.
8 Have you got anything .... tonight? ~ No, the game's been called ....

46   I can talk about likes and interests

My personal tastes

I used to be **mad about** chips, but I've completely **gone off** them now. ....

I've always **had a sweet tooth**. ....

My dad's **really into** camping, but it's **not my thing**. ....

I **couldn't bear** classical music as a teenager, but it **grows on** you. ....

Most clubs and bars are **too** loud **for my liking**. ....

My life **revolves around** my family. ....

I don't understand people who just **live for** their work. ....

Glossary

mad about sth/sb	INF liking sth/sb very much.
go off sth	INF stop liking sth that you liked in the past.
have a sweet tooth	INF like food that contains a lot of sugar.
be (really) into sth	INF be very interested in sth, especially as a hobby.
not sb's thing	INF not what sb likes or is interested in. SYN **not sb's cup of tea**.
I can't bear (doing) sth	= I hate (doing) sth. SYN **I can't stand (doing) sth**.
grow on sb	If sth or sb **grows on you**, you begin to like it/them more.
too … for my liking	If sth is **too** loud, bright, etc. **for your liking**, you don't like it because it's too loud, bright, etc.
revolve around sb/sth	have sb/sth as the most important part.
live for sth	consider sth to be the most important thing in your life.

1 Complete the sentences. Keep the meaning the same as in the sentences on the left.

▶	I'm not interested in fashion.	Fashion's not _my thing_ .
1	She hates big cities.	She can't ....
2	I don't like football.	Football's not my cup ....
3	He lives for his work.	His life revolves ....
4	I don't like meat any more.	I've gone ....
5	I love anything with sugar in it.	I've got a ....
6	They really like it.	They're mad ....

2 Complete the dialogues with one word.

1 Do you watch war films? ~ No, they're too violent for my ....
2 Do you like Indian food? ~ I used to, but I've .... off it recently.
3 Are you .... rock music? ~ Not at all. I can't .... it.
4 Jazz isn't my .... of tea. ~ No, it's not really my .... either.
5 He likes her a lot, doesn't he? ~ Yes, he's .... about her.
6 I didn't think you liked modern art. ~ I didn't, but it .... on you.
7 All he thinks about is surfing. ~ Yes, his whole life .... around it.
8 She's totally dedicated, isn't she? ~ Yes. She just .... for gymnastics.

3 ABOUT YOU Read the sentences at the top of the page again. Are they true for you? Write your answers in your notebook, or talk to another student.

The bookcase **was falling to pieces** but I managed to **put** it **together** again.

They **knocked** the building **down**[1]; now they're going to **put up** a block of flats **in** its **place**.

My shirt **was torn to bits** in the washing machine. I tried to **sew** it **up**[2], but in the end I had to **throw** it **away**.

Part of the fence **has blown down**[3] in the wind. I hope I can **put** it **up** again.

There was a scene in the film where a car **blew up**[4] and the house next to it **burnt down**.

The car **ran into** a tree. Fortunately no one was hurt, but the car was a **write-off**.

Two young guys stopped outside the bar, **broke** the door **down** and **smashed** the place **up**. It was terrible for the owners, who had just spent a lot of money **smartening** it **up**.

Glossary

put sth together	make or mend sth by joining all the different parts.
put sth up	construct sth such as a building, fence, some shelves, etc.
in sth/sb's place	instead of sth/sb (also **in place of sth/sb**).
throw sth away	get rid of sth that you no longer want. SYN **throw sth out**.
burn down	be destroyed by fire (also **burn sth down**).
run into sth/sb	hit sth/sb with a car, bus, etc. SYN **crash into sth/sb**.
write-off	a car, bus, etc. that has been so badly damaged that it cannot be repaired. **write sth off** v.
break sth down	make sth fall down or open by hitting it hard. SYN **smash sth down**.
smash sth up	destroy sth deliberately (because you want to do it).
smarten sth/sb up	make a place or a person look more attractive.

spotlight *to pieces/bits*

The chair is falling to pieces. = starting to break. SYN **fall to bits / fall apart** (see picture 1).
The chair has fallen to pieces. = it has now broken.
He picked up the paper and tore it to pieces. = destroyed it by tearing it into small pieces. SYN **tear sth to bits**.
Sometimes **to pieces** and **to bits** are used for emphasis and not meant literally (as in the reference to the shirt in picture 3).

1 Match 1–8 with a–h.

1 He ought to smarten ....   a   pieces.
2 The car had to be written ....   b   apart.
3 The wind blew the tree   c   together.
4 You should throw these eggs ....   d   himself up.
5 She tore the letter to ....   e   up.
6 The document was old; it just fell ....   f   down.
7 The chair broke, but I managed to put it ....   g   off.
8 They got into a fight and smashed the room ....   h   away.

2 Complete the dialogues.

1 What happened to the old flats? ~ They .... them down and rebuilt them.
2 Why is she living in a hotel? ~ Oh, her house burnt .... in the forest fires.
3 Where's Mike? ~ He's out in the garden, smashing .... some boxes.
4 I hear his car is a .... ~ Yes, he .... into a wall. Fortunately he wasn't hurt.
5 This table's .... to bits. ~ Never mind, Bob will be able to put it .... again.
6 We need another shelf in the study. ~ Well, I could put one .... if you like.
7 Did the police have to break into the flat? ~ Yes, they had to break the door ....
8 This sheet is torn .... bits. ~ Well, why don't you .... it away?

3 Cross out one word which is not correct.

1 Our neighbour was burnt down his garden shed.
2 I'm going to get a new desk: this one is falling down to pieces.
3 It was very old, so when I picked it up, it just fell to apart in my hands.
4 Suddenly there was a very loud noise and the oil tank blew it up.
5 The dog got hold of my bag and tore it up to pieces.
6 We knocked the garage down and in its place of it we built a small studio.
7 If you don't want those CDs, why don't you just throw them out off?
8 The firemen smashed out the door down so that they could rescue the baby.

4 Rewrite the sentences using the word in capitals. The meaning must stay the same.

▶ I joined all the separate parts of the shelves again. PUT   I put the shelves together again.
1 The building was destroyed by fire. DOWN ....
2 The damage to the car couldn't be repaired. WRITE ....
3 Can't you get rid of those papers? AWAY ....
4 They had to destroy the building. KNOCK ....
5 The book broke into separate parts. BITS ....
6 The motorcyclist hit a brick wall. CRASH ....
7 I repaired the hole in my pocket. SEW ....
8 I sold the chair and put a sofa there instead. ITS ....

5 Complete the text with one word in each gap.

Our house was a terrible mess when we first moved in. In the kitchen, the cupboards were all falling (1) .... and the room was really dirty. The first job was to clean everything up and (2) .... out all the rubbish which the previous owners had left. Then Mark put some new cupboards (3) .... and we were able to unpack our things. In the living room, we had to smarten everything (4) .... : that meant cleaning and redecorating. The curtains were dirty and torn in places, but they were very pretty, so I washed them and spent the afternoon (5) .... them up. There was also an ugly wardrobe in the bedroom which took up a lot of space, so we got rid of it. And in its (6) .... , Mark (7) .... up some shelves and a small cupboard. At last it was starting to feel like home.

I can say how things begin and end

A Different beginnings and endings

I **started off** the race quite well, but I couldn't **keep** it **up** and eventually I **came in fifth**.

She **set out to** write a short story, but **finished up with** a best-selling novel.

The fire **broke out** in the basement.
Have they **put** it **out** yet?

The business **closed down** last month.
They were mad to **set** it **up** anyway.

I recently **took up** golf, but I had to **give** it **up** because of a bad back.

Glossary

start sth off	begin doing sth (also **start off** begin to happen).
keep sth up	continue sth at the same high level.
come in (first, second, etc.)	finish a race in a particular position.
finish (up) with sth	have sth at the end.
break out	(of a fire, a fight, or a war) start.
put sth out	stop sth burning.
close down	(of a business activity) close permanently because it is making no money (also **close sth down**).
take sth up	start or learn to do sth, especially for pleasure.
give sth up / give up doing sth	stop doing sth you have done for a period of time.

spotlight Phrasal verbs with set

If you **set out to do sth**, you begin a job or task to achieve a particular aim (as above).
If you **set sth up**, you start a business, organization, etc. e.g. *I set up the new company two years ago.*

1 Do these sentences describe something that is beginning or ending? Write B or E.

1 Eddie has taken up golf. ....
2 Pedro came in first. ....
3 Lennie set up the café in 2008. ....
4 War has broken out. ....
5 Anna gave up running last year. ....
6 Alec put his cigarette out. ....

2 Write the correct particle.

1 When he first became manager, he set .... to make a lot of changes.
2 Mike set .... the company in 2006, but had to close it .... because of the recession.
3 I took .... tennis because I needed more exercise, but I gave it .... soon afterwards.
4 A fire broke .... in the warehouse, but they managed to put it .... quite quickly.
5 People didn't eat much at the party, so we finished .... with lots of leftover food.
6 It was a good race and Pam started .... quite well. Unfortunately she couldn't quite keep it .... , and in the end I think she came .... third.

B A new beginning

'The 1960s shopping centre was a disaster. It's hard to imagine how it **came about** in the first place, but the council decided to **knock** the whole thing **down** and **start from scratch** with a new development. There were problems **early on**, and it took ages to **get** the project **off the ground**, but the architects finally **came up with** a design that everyone liked. Now, two years later, the centre is really **taking shape**. **Judging by** the look of it, I feel that the designers **started out with** some good ideas, but have **ended up** with something of a compromise. It's quite attractive, but architecturally it doesn't **break** any **new ground**.'

Glossary

come about	happen (often used of sth that is surprising or hard to explain).
knock sth down	destroy a building by breaking the walls.
(start) from scratch	(start) from a new beginning. (See page 144.)
early on	soon after the beginning.
get sth off the ground	If you **get a project off the ground**, you make it start happening successfully. A project can also **get off the ground**.
come up with sth	produce ideas or a solution to sth.
take shape	develop and become more organized and complete.
judging by/from sth	used to say what you think, based on what you have seen, heard, or learnt.
start out with sth	start doing sth with a particular intention.
end up	finish in a situation or place that you didn't expect to be in.
break new ground	do sth that hasn't been done before.

3 Circle the correct answer.

1 Most of the problems happened early *in* | *on*.
2 It took us a couple of years to get the company off the *ground* | *land*.
3 We started *out* | *up* with the aim of creating a youth club.
4 The main part of the sports centre is now taking *form* | *shape*.
5 They're going to knock *down* | *over* all the old houses.
6 I don't know who *went* | *came* up with this idea, but it won't work.
7 Where did you end *up* | *out* last night?
8 He joined the army but I don't know how that came *about* | *off*.

4 Rewrite the sentences using the words in capital letters. Keep the meaning the same.

1 I'm starting my essay from the beginning. SCRATCH ....
2 The problems occurred soon after the beginning. EARLY ....
3 Based on his story, the boys are innocent. JUDGING ....
4 They've done something completely new. BREAK ....
5 The house is developing and looking more finished. SHAPE ....
6 How did these changes happen? COME .... ?
7 They've destroyed the offices. KNOCK ....
8 I'm sure they'll find a solution. COME ....

A Personal time

About me	About you
I often get up **at the crack of dawn**.	
I can get ready to go out **in no time**.	
I go to the doctor **once in a blue moon**.	
I go horse-riding **from time to time**.	
Most of my clothes are a bit **out of date**.	
One day I'm going to travel round the world.	
I'm happy living where I am **for the time being**.	
I do most things **on impulse**.	
I **live from day to day**; I don't think about the future.	

Glossary

at the crack of dawn	INF very early in the morning.
once in a blue moon	INF hardly ever; very rarely. (👁 See page 144.)
out of date	1 old-fashioned (as above). 2 without the most recent information, e.g. *These figures are **out of date***.
one day	at some time in the future.
on impulse	without thinking about sth before you do it. SYN **on the spur of the moment**.
live from day to day	live without thinking about what will happen in the future.

spotlight Idioms with *time*

You will find many idioms with *time* in your dictionary:
in no time very quickly or very soon (also **in next to no time**).
from time to time sometimes, but not regularly or often.
for the time being for now and the immediate future.

---

1 Match the idioms with their opposites.

> at the crack of dawn   in next to no time   for the time being
> out of date   on impulse   once in a blue moon

1 fashionable OPP ....
2 late at night OPP ....
3 planned in advance OPP ....

4 very often OPP ....
5 very slowly OPP ....
6 forever OPP ....

2 Complete the sentences.

1 I buy CDs on the .... of the moment.
2 Hang on, I'll be ready in .... time.
3 This technology is .... of date.
4 I got up at the crack of ....
5 One .... , I'll learn to play the piano
6 She sees him once in a .... moon.
7 I visit them from .... to ....
8 She just lives from .... to ....

3 ABOUT YOU Are the sentences at the top of the page true for you? Write your answers, or talk to another student.

4 ABOUT YOUR DICTIONARY Look up the word *time* in your dictionary and read through the idioms at the end of the entry. Make a note of any new idioms you find interesting, and think how you would translate them into your own language.

B Doing things at the right time

> The other day I **fixed up** a meeting with the staff for 10 o'clock. I was there at ten **on the dot**, and almost everyone else was there **in good time**; everyone, that is, except Kevin. He **kept us waiting** for twenty minutes, then **turned up** with his usual excuse that he**'d been held up** on the train. He does this **over and over again**, and it's the same with his work: he only gets things done **right at the last minute**. I've spoken to him about all this, but I**'m** just **wasting my breath**. It's **only a matter of time** before he has to leave.

Glossary

the other day	recently; a few days ago.
fix sth up	arrange for sth to happen.
on the dot	at exactly the time you mentioned or arranged. (👁 See page 144.)
in good time	before the time you need to be somewhere or do sth.
keep sb waiting	make sb wait for you.
turn up	arrive (often used when sb arrives late or doesn't arrive at all).
hold sb up	(usually passive) cause a delay or make sb late.
over and over again	many times; repeatedly. SYN **time and time again**.
(right) at the last minute	at the latest possible time.
waste your breath	say things that sb doesn't listen to or take notice of.
(only) a matter of time	used to say that sth will definitely happen, but you don't know when.

5 Replace the underlined words and phrases with an idiom or phrasal verb that has a similar meaning.

▶ I'd like to get to the airport <u>before the time we need to be there</u>. *in good* _____ time.

1 She's very punctual – always gets to the office at 9 a.m. <u>exactly</u>. on _____

2 I've told him <u>repeatedly</u>, and it's getting on my nerves. _____ again

3 He <u>made me wait</u>. kept _____

4 Have you <u>arranged</u> your appointment yet? _____ up

5 He cancelled his trip <u>just before it was too late</u>. _____ minute

6 I don't often get <u>delayed</u> on my way to work. _____ up

7 I saw my cousin <u>very recently</u>, just by chance. the _____

8 What time did she <u>arrive</u> last night? _____ up

6 Complete the sentences. (You will answer the questions in Exercise 7.)

1 Do you normally arrive in good _____ for school, college, or work?

2 Do you ever _____ people waiting? If so, when?

3 Do you often _____ up late for social arrangements? If so, when?

4 Do you ever do things at the last _____ ? If so, what?

5 Do you often get held _____ on your way to somewhere? If so, when?

6 Do you ever give people advice, but feel you're wasting your _____ ?

7 ABOUT YOU Write your answers to the questions in Exercise 6 in your notebook, or ask another student.

50 I can talk about numbers

A Quantities, amounts, and times

'If you **count up** all the passwords I have for websites, it's probably about ten **in all**.'

'I **added up** all the hours I had spent at the office and **took away** my lunch breaks: it **came to** an amazing 66 hours a week.'

'I **lost count of** the number of visitors we had, but it must have been **as many as** 50.'

'I would pay €20 for a haircut **at the very most**.'

'We had **dozens of** requests for brochures, and **quite a few** orders as a result.'

'Mila **counted out** €100,000 in €10 notes. **Round about** ten of the notes were badly torn.'

Glossary	
in all	as a total. SYN **in total**.
add sth up	If you **add up** five and four and three, you get twelve.
take sth away	If you **take** four **away** from ten, you get six.
come to sth	add up to a total amount.
as many as	used before a number to show how large and surprising it is.
at the (very) most	not more than, and probably much less than. OPP **at the (very) least**.
dozens of sth	INF a lot of people or things (**a dozen** = twelve).
quite a few / a lot (of sth)	a fairly large amount or number (of sth).
round about	approximately.

spotlight *count*

If you **count sth up**, you count all the people or things in a group. If you **lose count (of sth)**, you forget the number you have counted so far before you have finished counting. If you **count sth out**, you put things down, one by one, as you count them, e.g. when you count money.

1 Find the end of each idiom or phrasal verb.

atthemost|inallattheverleastquiteafewaddupintotallosecountroundabout

2 Put the sentences in order and add one missing word.

▶ sixty | and | were | cups | I | the | out | there   *I counted out the cups, and there were sixty.*
1 the | saw | in | we | dozens | rabbits | fields   ....
2 Dubai | friends | has | few | she | quite | in   ....
3 guests | of | the | lost | we | of | number   ....
4 flight | costs | the | least | at | very | $900   ....
5 €50 | the | that | we | came | surprised | were | bill   ....
6 seven | from | get | you | if | three | away | you | four   ....

3 Complete the dialogues.

1 Eighty people came to the party in .... ~ Really? As .... as that! I'm amazed.
2 Why are you counting .... those beans? ~ Oh, Dad! Now you've made me .... count.
3 I'm planning to invite .... about 20 people. ~ Yes; thirty .... the most.
4 What did it cost, ... total? ~ It .... to £50.80.
5 Did you add all those numbers .... ? ~ Yes, then I .... away 10% and got 60.
6 If you count .... all the residents, there are 600. ~ Really? That's .... a lot.

B Numbers in idioms

	Example	Meaning
1	I had **one or two** ideas about the plans.	**one or two** a few.
1	We went through the points **one by one**.	**one by one** one at a time (i.e. first one, then the next, then the next, etc.)
1st	She **puts** her children **first**.	**put sb/sth first** consider sb/sth to be more important than anyone or anything else.
2	He saw Carrie in a café with Andrew and **put two and two together**.	**put two and two together** guess the truth from what you see or hear.
2nd	I **was having second thoughts** about the flat.	**have second thoughts** change your opinion after thinking about sth again.
3rd	His two previous marriages failed, so he's hoping it will be **third time lucky**.	**third time lucky** used when you have failed to do sth twice and hope it will succeed the third time.
10	**Ten to one** they'll miss the bus again.	**ten to one** very probably.
50	Let's **go fifty-fifty** on dinner at Carlo's.	**go fifty-fifty** share the cost of sth equally.
100	I'm not **a hundred per cent** sure.	**one / a hundred per cent** completely.
100 110	Every player **gave a hundred per cent**. Every player **gave a hundred and ten per cent**.	**give a hundred (and ten) per cent** put as much effort into sth as you can (**and ten** adds emphasis here).
1m	Did you think he would marry her? ~ **Never in a million years!**	**never in a million years** used for emphasizing how impossible it seems that sth could ever happen.

---

spotlight *in his twenties*

He's in his twenties. = between 20 and 29.
She's in her early thirties. = between 31 and 33.

We're in our mid-fifties. = between 54 and 56.
I'm in my late sixties. = between 67 and 69.

---

4 Write in the correct numbers.

1 She's thirty in a year or two, so she's in her late _____ .
2 Did you expect to win the prize? ~ Never in a _____ years; it was a big surprise.
3 I'd failed the first two interviews, so it was a case of _____ time lucky, fortunately.
4 I've met the director on _____ or _____ occasions and he's very friendly.
5 He does his best – he always gives a _____ per cent.
6 I had thought it would be a nice house to live in, but I'm having _____ thoughts.
7 I saw her suitcase and the plane tickets and put _____ and _____ together.
8 Look, the bill's a bit expensive; why don't we go _____ - _____ ?

5 Rewrite the sentences using the word in capitals.

1 I'm not completely certain where he is. A HUNDRED _____
2 He'll very probably be late. TEN _____
3 She changed her mind about the flat. SECOND _____
4 He must be round about forty-five. FORTIES _____
5 They did the first question, then the next, and so on. ONE _____
6 He thinks his work is more important than anything. FIRST _____
7 Shall we share the cost of the petrol? FIFTY _____

A At home

I **haven't a clue** how to work this DVD player.
~ Let's ask Matt. He'll do it **in no time**.

The room's in a mess. There are books and CDs **all over the place**.
~ Don't worry. I'll **sort** them **out**.

I've been doing housework all morning, and **my back's killing me**.
~ You need a nice hot bath. That**'ll do the trick**.

Do you think these trousers **have had it**?
~ Yes, and anyway, they're **a bit on the small side** for you now.

Dan's always **in such a hurry to** finish things.
~ Well, he shouldn't be. He needs to **take his time** and relax.

Glossary

not have a clue	INF used to emphasize that you do not know sth. SYNS **not have the faintest idea** INF, **have no idea** INF.
in no time	so soon or so quickly that it is surprising (also **in next to no time**).
all over the place	in a very untidy state.
sort sth out	arrange sth in a tidy and organized way.
my back/feet etc. **is/are killing me**	INF my back hurts, my feet hurt, etc.
do the trick	INF resolve a problem.
have had it	INF If sth **has had it**, it is in a very bad condition and is no longer useful.
(a bit) on the small/big side	INF slightly too small/big (also **a bit on the heavy/expensive side**, etc.).
in (such) a hurry to do sth	impatient to do sth.
take your time (over sth)	do sth without hurrying.

1 Good news or bad news? Write G or B.

1 The boys sorted everything out. ....
2 Those shoes are on the small side. ....
3 I got there in next to no time. ....
4 My legs are killing me. ....
5 The food was all over the place. ....
6 The thick socks did the trick. ....

2 One word is missing in each sentence. Where does it go? Write it at the end.

1 Were you in hurry to finish? ....
2 The books were over the place. ....
3 He told me to take time. ....
4 The TV has it: it's hopeless. ....
5 We got there no time. ....
6 Who's that ? ~ I haven't clue. ....

3 Replace the underlined words with an idiom that keeps a similar meaning.

1 He is always <u>impatient</u> to get things done. ....
2 I bought a jacket but I think it's <u>slightly too small</u>. ....
3 It's a long walk to my place, but they got here <u>surprisingly quickly</u>. ....
4 After the walk, my feet were <u>really hurting</u>. ....
5 Put some milk on the stain and leave it; that'll <u>solve the problem</u>. ....
6 What time does the train leave? ~ I <u>don't know</u>. ....
7 The children's clothes were <u>in a very untidy state</u>. ....
8 I spent the afternoon <u>organizing and tidying up</u> all the papers. ....

B At work

We**'ll be rushed off our feet** this month.

That's OK. I know a couple of people who can **help** us **out**.

Steve thinks he**'s in with a chance of** getting that job.

Yes, and I**'ve put in a good word for** him – that should help.

Work**'s getting on top of me** at the moment.

That's because you think about it too much. You need to learn to **switch off**.

We can't work any harder – we're already **at full stretch**.

Yes, but we've got more orders **piling up**.

I'm worried I**'ll be out of my depth** in this new job.

Look, just take it **one step at a time** – you'll be fine.

Glossary

be rushed/run off your feet	be extremely busy.
help sb out	help sb, especially in a difficult situation.
get on top of sb	be too much for sb to manage or deal with.
switch off	INF stop thinking about sth.
be out of your depth	be in a situation (often a job) that is too difficult for you to understand or manage.
one step at a time	slowly; gradually.
be in with a chance (of doing sth)	INF have the possibility of succeeding or achieving sth.
put in a (good) word (for sb)	say positive things to another person about sb, to help them get a job, etc.
at full stretch	If sb is working **at full stretch**, they are working as hard as possible.
pile up	become larger in quantity or amount.

4 Match 1–6 with a–f.

1 Work often piles up ......
2 He's been working too hard, and ......
3 It won't be easy to get the job, but ......
4 We're already at full stretch, so ......
5 We'll get there as long as ......
6 The club might accept him as a member if ......

a he's in with a chance.
b we take it one step at a time.
c at this time of the year.
d it's getting on top of him.
e you put in a good word for him.
f we can't provide anything else.

5 Complete the last word in each sentence. Then underline the full idioms and phrasal verbs.

1 It's been terrible today. We've been rushed off our ....
2 Can she win? ~ Yes, I think she's in with a ....
3 Don't hurry. Just take it one step at a ....
4 We can't produce any more; we're already at full ....
5 If things get really difficult, Alex said he would help us ....
6 Is she doing OK? ~ No, to be honest, I think she's out of her ....
7 She worries about things all the time. ~ Yes, her problem is that she can't switch ....
8 Will he get promotion? ~ Yes, I think he will, if I put in a good ....

MARK The university I want to go to has **turned** me **down**: they said I wasn't good enough to study journalism. Now I'm not sure if I want to go to university at all.

TINA **If I were you**, Mark, I'd say to myself: 'OK, **in that case** I'll go to another university and prove I can **make the grade**.'

COLIN Mark, stop **feeling sorry for yourself**; there's more to life than a university degree. **In your shoes**, I'd go out and earn some money.

JED Well, **that's life**, Mark. But if the university thinks you aren't good enough to do journalism, maybe you**'d be better off** applying for something else. **Good luck**.

LISA Mark, you have to **take** a number of things **into account**, but you **could always** do your exams again and apply to the same university next year.

Glossary

turn sb down	say 'no' to sb when they apply for sth or offer sth.
if I were you	used to introduce advice (also **if I were in your place/position/shoes, I'd** …).
in that case	if that is the situation; if that happens or has happened.
make the grade	reach the necessary standard and be successful.
feel sorry for yourself	be unhappy for yourself.
in your shoes	in your situation (followed by *I would / I'd* …).
that's life	used to say that sth is disappointing but you must accept it.
be better off (doing sth)	used to suggest that sb should do sth differently.
good luck	INF used to wish sb success with sth. SYN **(the) best of luck**.
take sth into account	think about sth carefully before making a decision. SYN **take sth into consideration**.
can/could always	used for making a suggestion.

1 Circle the correct answer(s). Both answers may be correct.

1 Don't feel sorry *for | with* yourself.
2 If I were in your *shoes | place*, I'd go.
3 I'm sure you'll make the *mark | grade*.
4 Take it all into *account | consideration*.
5 She'd be better off *to work | working*.
6 You *can | could* always go next year.

2 Complete the dialogues.

1 She doesn't want to sell her car, but she needs the money. ~ Well, that's ....
2 Is it a difficult decision? ~ Yes, there's a lot to take into ....
3 I get my results today. ~ Really? .... of luck.
4 My boss wants to reduce my salary. ~ Well, in that ...., I would leave.
5 I'm in a terrible situation. ~ Oh come on, stop feeling .... for yourself.
6 Did they offer you the job? ~ Yes, but I .... it down.

3 ABOUT YOUR OPINION Read about Penny's situation, then complete the idioms in the first part of each sentence, and finish each one with different advice.

PENNY (secretary) 'I like my job, but the money's not very good. I've been offered a job with more money, but I'm not sure if it will be very interesting. What should I do?'

ABOUT YOU

1 Penny, if I ...., I'd ....
2 Penny, in your ...., I'd ....
3 You .... always ....
4 I think you'd be .... off ....

Review: Concepts

Unit 44

1 Complete the sentences with words from the box. Then write your answers about yourself in the column on the right.

> dying   feel   do   care   need   do   set   could ✓   pick

Write down:

▶ something you _____could_____ do with.

1 one thing you own that you couldn't _____ without.
2 something you couldn't _____ less about.
3 something you've _____ your heart on.
4 something you _____ like doing at the moment.
5 a situation in which you can't _____ and choose.
6 something you're _____ to do soon.
7 something you could sell, if _____ be.
8 something you could make _____ with.

ABOUT YOU

more time to sleep in the morning

Unit 45

1 Complete the crossword. The letters in the grey squares spell out a phrase. What is it?

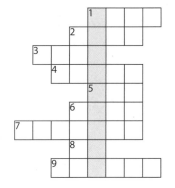

1 If you do a piece of work very badly, you _____ it up.
2 If you cancel something that has been arranged, you _____ it off.
3 If you think about what is going to happen in the future, you _____ ahead.
4 If you make a plan and it goes _____, it means it happens.
5 If you delay something and move it to a later time, you _____ it back.
6 If things happen in the way you expected, they go according to _____.
7 If you move something to an earlier time, you bring it _____.
8 If you've got something _____, it means you have arranged to do something.
9 If something spoils your plans or has a bad effect on them, it _____ them up.

The phrase in the grey squares is _____.

Unit 46

1 Agree with each speaker, using the word in capitals to complete the sentence.

▶ I'm not very keen on aerobics. INTO   ~ No, I'm not really _into it either_ .
1 I don't like this music. MAD   ~ No, I _____ .
2 I don't enjoy going to the gym very much. TEA   ~ No, it's _____ .
3 I learnt to like abstract art after a while. GROWS   ~ Yes, it _____ .
4 I used to love shopping, but not any more. OFF   ~ No, I've _____ .
5 This soup is very spicy. LIKING   ~ Yes, it's _____ .
6 I hate white shoes. BEAR   ~ I agree. I _____ .

Unit 47

1 Put the verbs into the correct column in the table below.

sew sth up   tear sth to pieces   burn sth down   put sth together   smarten sth up   write sth off
fall apart   smash sth up   fall to bits   put sth up   break sth down   crash into sth

DAMAGE or DESTRUCTION		REPAIR or CONSTRUCTION	

2 Complete the sentences using idioms and phrasal verbs from the box in the correct form.

blow up   blow down   throw sth away
tear sth to bits   write sth off   fall to pieces

1   The tree in the back garden .... in the wind.
2   The boy was so angry with his school report that he ....
3   After the accident the insurance company decided to .... the car.
4   There was a bomb in the car. Two people were injured when it ....
5   When she sat on the chair it just .... ; it was quite funny, actually.
6   We don't need these old magazines. Why don't we .... ?

Unit 48

1 The same word is missing in each pair of sentences (a and b). Write it in.

1   a   I think we'll have to start .... scratch.
    b   Judging .... the design, it's going to be a very modern building.
2   a   Who .... up with that brilliant idea?
    b   Who .... in last in the race?
3   a   How did the fire .... out?
    b   The latest dictionary will .... new ground.
4   a   When did your brother .... up the company?
    b   The planners .... out to improve the traffic situation.
5   a   I made good progress at first, but I couldn't keep it ....
    b   We thought about going to a French restaurant, but we ended .... in a pizzeria.
6   a   Did they manage to put .... the fire?
    b   When we started .... , we knew we would need more money.

2 Tick (✓) the answers which are possible. Be careful: one, two, or all three may be possible.

1   Last year they .... a business which has been very successful.
    set out ☐ set up ☐ set off ☐
2   When did the .... break out?
    lesson ☐ fire ☐ war ☐
3   The building project ....
    is taking shape ☐ breaks new ground ☐ is getting off the ground ☐
4   I eventually decided to .... golf.
    take up ☐ give up ☐ start out ☐
5   The shop had to be ....
    put out ☐ knocked down ☐ closed down ☐

Unit 49

1 Find answers to the clues by moving horizontally or vertically, backwards or forwards.

OVER	FOR	ON	THE	SPUR
AND	THE	ON	OUT	OF
OVER	TIME	THE	OF	THE
AGAIN	BEING	DOT	DATE	MOMENT
AT	IN	GOOD	TIME	MINUTE ↑
THE	DAWN	AT →	THE →	LAST ǀ
CRACK	OF	IN	NO	TIME

▸ At the last possible time when something should happen. *At the last minute.*

1 At the exact time which was mentioned or arranged. ....

2 Another way to say 'time and time again'. ....

3 Old-fashioned. ....

4 On impulse; without thinking about something before acting. ....

5 Very early in the morning. ....

6 For now and the immediate future. ....

7 Very quickly or very soon. ....

8 Before the time when you need to be somewhere or do something. ....

2 Complete the sentences using a word from the left and a word from the right in the correct form.

| waste time keep hold |
| once fix turn last |

| up breath moon time |
| minute waiting up up |

1 We waited for hours, and eventually he .... at midnight, without an excuse or apology.

2 I'm sorry I'm so late, but there was a problem on the train and we got .... for an hour.

3 We had an appointment at 4.00, but the manager .... us .... until 4.30.

4 I managed to book my plane ticket at the .... , which was very lucky.

5 We meet up for a meal .... in a blue .... – probably every couple of years.

6 I see Larry from .... to .... – he seems quite well these days.

7 It would be lovely to see you; let's try to .... something .... for the weekend.

8 It's no good telling her not to marry him – you're just .... your ....

Unit 50

1 Use the numbers in the box to help you to complete the sentences. You will need the number and one more word in each sentence.

| 3ʳᵈ   1 ✓   100   2ⁿᵈ   1,000,000   50   dozens   30s |

▸ They let us through *one* .... *by* .... one.

1 He's not the most skilful player, but he always gives a .... cent.

2 You mustn't pay for everything. Let's .... – ....

3 I thought it would be a good idea to get a car, but now I'm having ....

4 There were .... people at the gallery – at least 20 or 30.

5 I've failed my driving test twice, so I'm hoping it will be .... lucky.

6 She had Marcus six years ago when she was 26, so she must be in her ....

7 I never thought in a .... I'd become Managing Director one day.

2 Replace the underlined word(s) with a phrase that has a similar meaning. The first word has been given to help you.

1 There were <u>approximately</u> fifteen.   round ....
2 We had twenty-five students <u>altogether</u>.   in ....
3 If you <u>subtract</u> five, we'll have 21 left.   take ....
4 I don't know exactly how many, but <u>a fairly large number</u>. quite ....
5 If you include Mike and Chloe, <u>the total is</u> 15.   it .... 15.
6 <u>I'm almost sure</u> he'll forget his homework.   ten ....
7 He saw the ring on her finger and <u>guessed the truth</u>. put ....
8 There should be 50 <u>as an absolute maximum</u>.   at ....

Unit 51

1 Complete the crossword. The letters in the grey squares spell out a phrase. What is it?

1 That will solve the problem. = That will do the ....
2 I've been extremely busy. = I've been .... off my feet.
3 You have the possibility of succeeding. = You are in with a
   ....
4 In a very untidy state. = All .... the place.
5 Using everything that is available. = At full ....
6 I haven't a clue. = I haven't the .... idea.
7 The work is too much for me to manage. = The work is getting on
   .... of me.
8 My back hurts. = My back is .... me!
9 I'm in a situation which is too difficult for me to handle. = I'm out of
   my ....
10 I'm taking things slowly. = I'm taking things one .... at a
   time.
11 This washing machine can't be repaired. = This washing machine has
   .... it.
   The phrase in the grey squares is ....

Unit 52

1 Complete Mr Web's letter of advice. Then underline the full idioms and phrasal verbs.

Dear Mr Web,

My neighbours have a ten-year-old son. When he gets home from school, he comes straight to our house. He's a nice boy, but he won't go home and some evenings he even has dinner here. I think his parents both work and don't seem worried about him or want to take responsibility for him. What do you advise me to do? Rhona

Dear Rhona

Poor boy! Well, if I (1) .... you, I would try and think about things from his point of view. Perhaps he's feeling (2) .... for himself, and he probably feels he would be better (3) .... with your family than at home. Think about it: in his (4) ...., would <u>you</u> want to sit around an empty home? He might be afraid, and that would be perfectly natural. You (5) .... always try giving him some little jobs to do, helping you around your home. And you need to take into (6) .... the fact that his parents work, and maybe they don't realize that he is lonely. In that (7) ...., the best thing would be to talk to them gently about it.

The best of (8) .... ,

Mr Web

53 I can use link phrases

'We've lived here **ever since** we got married. It took ages to find the right place, then **at last** we saw this one. We liked it because it's modern, and there's parking for two cars **as well**. Unfortunately, it's near a busy road, but we still bought it **in spite of** that. We had to buy furniture **as soon as** we moved in, and our bed didn't arrive for weeks; **in the meantime**, we slept on the floor! We've been here six years now. **On the one hand** I'd like a bigger house, but **on the other**, we've got great neighbours here, and we can't really afford to move. It looks **as if** we'll stay, but **even if** we sold, we wouldn't move far.'

Glossary

ever since	continuously from the time or event mentioned.
at last	finally, after problems or delays.
in spite of	If you do sth **in spite of** another fact, it is surprising that the other fact didn't stop you doing it. SYN **despite**.
as soon as	at the moment that, or as quickly as possible after. SYN **the minute (that)**.
in the meantime	in the period of time between two times or events.
on the one hand … **on the other (hand)**	used to introduce different points of view, especially when they are opposites.
as if	used for saying how sth or sb appears. SYN **as though**.
even if	used for saying that what follows *if* makes no difference, e.g. ***Even if** we run, we'll be late.*

spotlight *as well, in addition*

We use **as well** and **in addition** when we are adding information. **As well** is more informal than **in addition**. Notice the position of these expressions.
The house is very spacious, and it's close to my parents as well.
The flat is beautifully furnished. In addition, it is in a good location.

1 Circle the correct answer(s). Both answers may be correct.

1 I've worked here *ever since | even if* I left school.
2 Pete's train was an hour late, so *in the meantime | on the one hand* we went for a coffee.
3 It sounds *as if | as though* Patty is enjoying herself in India.
4 I'll let you know *as soon as | the minute* I hear anything.
5 He's already told me that *even if | as if* he's offered the job, he won't accept it.
6 We decided to go on *despite | in spite of* the cost.

2 Complete the sentences with suitable link phrases.

1 I really liked Sophie .... I met her. She was very funny, but we had so much in common ....
2 It took us all day, but .... I found the pair of shoes I wanted.
3 She's been at home .... she had the baby.
4 There are some black clouds coming over, and it looks .... it's going to rain.
5 .... Marie would love to spend more time at home with her family, but .... , I think she would really miss the satisfaction she gets from her job. .... , of course, she may not have enough money to live on.

There are many idiomatic phrases in English where two words are joined by a conjunction, which is usually *and*. The order of the words is almost always fixed (*come and go*, NOT ~~go and come~~), and in many cases the two words are near synonyms or opposites, or words with a repeated sound pattern, e.g. *fast and furious*.

*The pain in my arm **comes and goes**.*

Example	Meaning
Joined by and	
*The pain in my arm **comes and goes**.*	**come and go** be present for a short time, then go away, then return, and so on.
*We can't do anything about it now. We'll just have to **wait and see** what they decide.*	**wait and see** delay action until you know what is going to happen.
*We need to see the **facts and figures** before making a decision.*	**facts and figures** accurate and detailed information.
*The action is really **fast and furious** at the beginning of the film.*	**fast and furious** (of films, games, shows, etc.) full of rapid action and quick changes.
*I've been **up and down** the road, but I can't see them.*	**up and down** the road = along the road in both directions.
*You're up **bright and early** this morning.*	**bright and early** early in the morning.
*I love the **peace and quiet** of the countryside.*	**peace and quiet** calm and silence, especially in contrast to a noisy environment.
***First and foremost** we need to book the hotel.*	**first and foremost** used for emphasizing the main point or the most important reason for sth.
*I've been going **backwards and forwards** all day.*	**backwards and forwards** from one place to another and back again, many times.
Do you see them much? ~ ***On and off**, but not a great deal.*	**on and off** used to say that something happens a few times, then stops for a period, then starts again, and so on. SYNS **off and on**, **now and then**.
*I'm **sick and tired** of all this rain.*	**sick and tired of sth** very unhappy about sth.
Joined by for or or	
*She told me what he said **word for word**.*	**word for word** using exactly the same words.
*We'll get the money **one way or another**.*	**one way or another / the other** INF using one of several possible methods, although you don't know yet which one.
*The books will be here in three weeks, **give or take** a few days.*	**give or take** used to say that the number you have just stated is nearly correct, but not exactly.
*I'll find another job **sooner or later**.*	**sooner or later** at some point in the future.

---

spotlight *lovely and ...*

This informal expression is used when you are emphasizing that something is good because of the quality mentioned:

It's lovely and warm by the fire.   *This water is lovely and cold.*   *It was lovely and quiet without the children.*

1 Complete the phrases.

1 first and ....
2 sick and ....
3 sooner or ....
4 facts and ....
5 one way or ....

6 give or ....
7 on and ....
8 word for ....
9 peace and ....
10 fast and ....

2 Combine the words from the three boxes to make nine idioms. (You can use *and*, *or*, and *for* more than once.)

come one way lovely wait bright word now backwards fast	and or for	see early forwards furious word warm another then go

1 ....
2 ....
3 ....
4 ....
5 ....

6 ....
7 ....
8 ....
9 ....

3 Use one of these words in each sentence below, then complete the phrase.

one way   sick   now   bright   give   backwards   up   wait   peace   word   first ✓

▶ *First* and *foremost* we have to find somewhere to live.
1 She only read it once but she was able to repeat it .... for ....
2 They're not giving out the results yet, so we'll have to .... and ....
3 He had to get up .... and .... to catch the seven o'clock train.
4 I've been helping Sandra, and I've been going .... and .... all day.
5 We still see them .... and .... , but not as much as we used to.
6 People are getting really .... and .... of the terrible pollution from the factory.
7 I'm not sure where the house is, but we'll find it .... or ....
8 We looked .... and .... the road, but there was no one there.
9 You pay £30 for a meal, ... or .... a few pounds.
10 I've got a house in the mountains, and I go there for the .... and ....

4 Rewrite the sentences using a phrase from the opposite page. Keep the meaning the same.

▶ I only see him occasionally.
   I only see him n*ow and then* .
1 We need to see more detailed information.
   We need to see the f........................ .
2 The first half of the game was very quick.
   The first half was f........................ .
3 She repeated his exact message.
   She repeated it w........................ .
4 I'm very unhappy about all this snow.
   I'm s........................ of it.
5 There's no noise in the garden.
   The garden is l........................ .
6 I don't know how, but I'll find them.
   I'll find them o........................ .
7 I get a pain for a bit and then it stops.
   The pain c........................ .
8 I'll paint the room at some point in the future.
   I'll paint the room s........................ .
9 This water's great – it's straight from the fridge.
   This water is l........................ .
10 I meet my old friends now and then.
   I meet my old friends o........................ .

5 ABOUT YOUR LANGUAGE Do you have similar phrases in your language? How would you translate the phrases on the left-hand page? Write your answers in your notebook, or talk to another student who speaks your language.

55 I can use prepositional phrases

A Opposites

Simon said I was **out of tune**, but I think I was the only one singing **in tune**.

In theory the plan sounds great, but I don't think it'll work **in practice**.

The doctor's **off duty** right now, but he'll be back **on duty** at six.

The phones were **in working order** yesterday, but already two are **out of order**.

I don't know if he pushed her **by accident**, or whether he did it **on purpose**.

The crowd was getting **out of control**, but the police now have the situation **under control**.

Glossary

out of tune	singing or playing the wrong musical notes. OPP **in tune**.
off duty	(of nurses, police officers, etc.) not working at a particular time. OPP **on duty**.
by accident	in a way that is not planned or organized. OPP **on purpose**.
in theory	used to say what should happen or be true (often used when it doesn't happen or isn't true).
in practice	used to say what really happens and what is really true.
in working order	(of a machine) functioning properly. OPP **out of order**.
out of control	impossible to manage or control. OPP **under control**.

> **spotlight** *in/out of tune*, etc.
>
> A number of other prepositional phrases form opposites in this way:
> *Tomatoes are in season now.* = growing in large amounts and ready to eat now. OPP out of season.
> *I was in luck – there was one ticket left.* = lucky. OPP out of luck.
> *The lion was just in sight.* = able to be seen. OPP out of sight.

1 Write in the correct preposition(s).

1 The idea sounds good _____ theory.
2 I'm sure she did it _____ accident.
3 Is everything _____ control?
4 He took my pen _____ purpose.
5 I'm afraid the machine's _____ order.
6 She's not at work; she's _____ duty.

2 What are the opposites of these phrases?

1 under control | _____
2 off duty | _____
3 by accident | _____
4 in luck | _____
5 in tune | _____
6 out of order | _____

3 Complete the sentences with the correct word.

1 I don't like eating fruit when it is out of _____ .
2 The group were singing out of _____ ; it sounded horrible.
3 We saw the fox for a minute, then it disappeared out of _____ .
4 They repaired the machines yesterday, so everything should be in working _____ .
5 There was fighting in the street, but the police now have the situation _____ control.
6 It's an interesting proposal in _____ ; but will it work in _____ ?

B A range of prepositional phrases

I spoke to the solicitor **on the phone** this morning. She said they needed confirmation **in writing**, but promised to acknowledge it **by return of post**.

I questioned the two boys **at length. In the end**, I decided that the books had been taken **by mistake**, although the only people who know **for certain** are the two boys themselves.

➡ Remember that you can speak to a counsellor **in confidence**, so if you have anything **on your mind**, come and see us **at once**.

… Yeah, we had the tree cut down. I couldn't get to the shed very easily because the tree was **in the way**, and it looked **out of place** …

Glossary

on the phone	1 by phone (as above). 2 using the phone now.
in writing	in the form of a letter, document, etc.
by return (of post)	in the next available post (usually the next day).
in confidence	If you talk to sb **in confidence**, they agree not to tell anyone else what you have said.
on your mind	If you have sth **on your mind**, you are thinking and perhaps worrying about it.
at once	immediately. SYN **straight away**.
at length	for a long time and in detail.
in the end	finally.
by mistake	If you do sth **by mistake**, you do it accidentally.
for certain	without doubt. SYN **for sure**.
in the/sb's way	stopping sb from moving or doing sth.
out of place	not suitable for the place or situation sth is in.

4 Circle the correct preposition.

1 I can't see the television – you're *in* | *on* the way.
2 We think they're safe, but no one knows *by* | *for* certain.
3 The head teacher spoke to the students *in* | *at* length.
4 You can speak to your doctor *by* | *in* confidence.
5 I can't say *for* | *with* sure, but I think I'll be there around 7.00.
6 They need an answer *by* | *in* writing.
7 I rang the doctor and they said he would come *in* | *at* once.
8 There wasn't anything good on at the cinema, so *at* | *in* the end we stayed at home.

5 Complete the dialogues.

1 Will they send the forms to you? ~ Yes, by return ....
2 Has he got something on his .... ? ~ Yes, I think he's worried about his health.
3 Did he take the coat by .... ? ~ Oh yes, he thought it was his.
4 Is Liselotte free? ~ No, she's on the .... at the moment.
5 Was it a fairly quick conversation? ~ No, I spoke to them at ....
6 Did the ambulance take long? ~ No, it came straight ....
7 Those pictures look out of .... there. ~ I agree. They'd look better on the other wall.
8 Did you move the table? ~ Yes, we had to; it was in the ....

56 I can use phrasal verbs as commands

Certain intransitive phrasal verbs are commonly used as spoken commands in conversation, e.g. *Go away! Get off!* This is also true of some transitive phrasal verbs, e.g. *Put it down! Take it off!* These verbs also have other meanings: see the table below.

Verb	Meaning as a command	Other meanings
Get out!		• (of a piece of information) become known after being secret until recently: *The news **got out**.*
Come on!		• make progress: *Your French is **coming on** very well.* • begin: *I've got a cold **coming on**.*
Go away!		• (of a problem) stop existing; disappear: *The pain has finally **gone away**.* • leave home, especially for a holiday: *I'm **going away** for a few days.*
Get off!		• leave the place where you work at the end of the day: *I **get off** work early on Fridays.* • leave on a journey: *We'd like to **get off** before the traffic gets heavy.*
Get in!		• be accepted to study at a school, university, etc.: *I didn't **get in** to university when I left school, but I went two years later.* • arrive at a place: *The bus won't **get in** till 1.00.*
Sit up (straight)!		• not go to bed until later than usual: *We **sat up** for hours watching TV.*
Pick it up!		• learn sth without making a big effort: *She **picked up** some basic French on holiday.* • go and get sth; collect sth: *Could you **pick** my dry cleaning **up**, please?*
Put it down!		• write sth: *I **put** the appointment **down** in my diary.* • kill an animal because it is old or sick (often passive): *The animal had to be **put down**.*
Hold on (tight)! SYN **Hang on!**		• wait: *Can you **hold on** a minute?* SYN **hang on**. • continue doing sth even though it is very difficult to do so: *They managed to **hold on** till the ambulance arrived.* SYN **hang on**.
Fill it in!		• write the necessary information on a document: *Just **fill in** your name and address.* • use your time doing sth unimportant while waiting for sth: *I'm **filling in** time until 6.00.*

1 Match 1–9 with a–i.

1 The problem won't go ....   a out so quickly?
2 Could you fill this form ....   b up listening to the CD.
3 I put his name ....   c up all night?
4 She picked a few words ....   d down on the list.
5 If you don't go ....   e in and give it back, please?
6 Are you going to sit ....   f away, I'll scream.
7 We had to hold ....   g get in?
8 When does the train ....   h away.
9 How did the information get ....   i on till help arrived.

2 Circle the correct words in the definition.

1 'The cat was put down' means the vet had to *treat the cat | end the cat's life*.
2 'I get off work at 4.00' means I *leave | get to* the office at 4.00.
3 'My headache's gone away' means my headache has *got better | got worse*.
4 'She sat up for hours' means she *went | didn't go* to bed at the usual time.
5 'He had to fill in time' means he had to *write something | wait for something to happen*.
6 'Did you go away last week?' means 'Did you go *out | on holiday* last week?'

3 Use a suitable spoken command to complete the sentences.

▶ I'll give you a lift to school: *get in* ....!
1 Don't leave your coat on the floor: ...., please!
2 We don't want you to come with us, so please ....!
3 You aren't allowed in this room: ....!
4 Don't walk so slowly! ...., hurry up!
5 That vase you're holding is very valuable: please .... immediately!
6 Quick, ...! This is our stop!

4 Complete the dialogues.

1 A Come ....! We'll be late!
   B Just hang .... a minute; I've got to go and get my coat. Anyway, there's no great hurry; Dad's train doesn't get .... till 7.00.
2 A What's wrong?
   B I don't feel too good. I've got a very bad headache coming ....
   A Oh, can I do anything?
   B No, please just go .... and leave me alone.
3 A Is Matthias doing the management course this summer?
   B He's a bit upset, actually; he heard today that he hadn't got ....; the course is full.
4 A How's your Italian coming ....?
   B Oh, not bad. That week I spent in Rome was great; I picked .... a lot of vocabulary.

5 What would you say in these situations? Write your answer using a phrasal verb.

▶ A child is holding a big, angry-looking cat. Put *the cat down* ....!
1 Ask your friend if she's making progress with her English. How ....?
2 Your friend is going near the dry cleaning shop, and you have some trousers that need to be collected. Could ....?
3 Ask your friend if he's having a holiday this summer. Are ....?
4 Ask the ticket inspector the time your train arrives in Paris. When ....?
5 You're on a bus with a child, and the driver is going very fast. What do you say to the child? Hold ....!
6 You want to know what time your friend finishes work. What ....?

Many idioms consist of a verb + (adjective/preposition) + noun.

He's really caught the sun. INF = his face has become red or brown from being in the sun.

She's laying the table. = putting knives, forks, etc. on the table for a meal.

I need to stretch my legs. INF = go for a short walk after sitting for some time.

I tried to catch the waiter's eye. = attract his attention.

Can he tell the time yet? = read the time from a clock.

Come on, let's make a move. INF = begin to leave the place where we are.

Example	Meaning
*You're **missing the point**. I'm not against war; I'm saying <u>this</u> war is wrong.*	**miss the point** not understand the main idea of what sb is saying.
*She'll have to work very hard to **make up for lost time**.*	**make up for lost time** do sth quickly or do more than usual because you couldn't do it before.
*When he started singing, I'm afraid it was hard to **keep a straight face**.*	If you **keep a straight face** you don't laugh or smile even though you find sth funny.
*Could I **pick** your **brain** on a grammar problem?*	**pick sb's brain** (or **brains**) INF ask sb questions because you want to find out more about sth.
*This discussion is hopeless: we're just **going round in circles**.*	**go round in circles** do or discuss sth without making any progress.
*I said I'd **give** him **a hand** when he moved his stuff.*	**give/lend (sb) a hand (with sth)** help sb with sth.
*I'm tired – I**'ve been on the go** all day.*	**be on the go** INF be very active and busy.
*She **has a thing about** fish: she won't eat it unless it has no bones.*	**have a thing about sth/sb** INF have a strong liking for or dislike of sth/sb.
*Why don't you **stay the night** at our flat?*	**stay the night** sleep at sb's house for one night.
*Darren believes in **speaking his mind**, and that can upset people.*	**speak your mind** say exactly what you think in a very direct way.

1 Cross out the mistake in each sentence and correct it.

▶ I'm just going out to stretch my ~~leg~~. _legs_

1 We've had to make up for losing time. _____
2 I've been trying to catch the nurse's eyes for ages. _____
3 Could you lend me an arm with this suitcase? _____
4 I think we're going round in a circle. _____
5 It's late – I'd better do a move. _____
6 We've been on the going since 7 o'clock this morning. _____
7 My brother is sleeping the night at my uncle's house. _____
8 She couldn't keep her face straight. _____
9 When did you learn to say the time? _____
10 I need some ideas. Could I pick your mind for a few minutes? _____

2 Is the speaker pleased, annoyed, or could it be either? Write P, A, or E.

1 We made up for lost time. ___
2 I managed to pick her brains. ___
3 He completely missed the point. ___
4 I think I caught the sun today. ___
5 Nobody has laid the table. ___
6 She gave me a hand with the washing up. ___
7 I've been on the go all day. ___
8 We've been going round in circles all morning. ___

3 Answer the questions.

▶ What do you do if you give someone a hand? _You help them._

1 Why would you pick someone's brains? _____
2 If you have a thing about beards, what do you feel? _____
3 What do you start doing if you can't keep a straight face? _____
4 If someone lays the table, what do they do? _____
5 If you've been on the go, what's been happening? _____
6 What are you doing if you speak your mind? _____
7 What happens if you catch the sun? _____
8 What happens if you miss the point? _____

4 Complete the missing verb in each sentence, in the correct form.

1 Don't worry; if you miss the last train, you can always _____ the night with us.
2 It was so funny, I couldn't _____ a straight face.
3 Do you think you could _____ me a hand with the housework?
4 I was trying to _____ the teacher's eye, but she was very busy.
5 He _____ the table while I was cooking.
6 I did explain it carefully, but I'm afraid he _____ the point.
7 The train leaves in twenty minutes – we ought to _____ a move or we'll miss it.
8 I don't often _____ my mind, but I was just so angry.
9 He went outside to _____ his legs.
10 I think you've _____ the sun on the back of your neck.

5 ABOUT YOU Write your answers in your notebook, or ask another student.

1 Who lays the table in your home, and why?
2 Do you catch the sun easily?
3 Do you have a thing about anything in particular? If so, what?
4 Do you generally speak your mind?
5 When did you last stay the night at a friend's place?
6 Do people ever pick your brains? If so, what about?

A   Positive idioms with *get*

Get through
First Certificate:
five practice tests

A BEGINNER'S GUIDE TO
SKIING

– Don't panic!
You WILL **get**
the hang of it!

How to **get ahead**
in business
IN TEN EASY STEPS

WALKING
in the
BLACK FOREST
– where to **get away from it all**

Get over
a broken marriage
and live again

Get into
ADVERTISING

I0 Ten ways to
get the most out of
your day

Get rid of your bad habits –
and **get on with your life**!

You *and*
your **dog**

– **get the upper**
hand today!

Glossary

get through sth	reach a good enough standard to pass a test.
get away from it all	INF go on holiday to a place where you can relax.
get the hang of sth	INF learn how to do or use sth.
get ahead	be successful and do better than other people in a career.
get over sth	feel normal again after having an unpleasant experience, e.g. an illness or a divorce.
get into sth	start a career in a particular profession.
get the most out of sth	get the maximum benefit or pleasure from sth (also **get sth / a lot out of sth**).
get rid of sth	take action so that you no longer have sth that you do not want.
get on with your life	stop worrying about sth that has happened and start living a normal life again.
get the upper hand	gain an advantage over sb so that you are in control of a situation.

1   One word is missing in each sentence. Where does it go? Write it at the end.

▶   I wasn't expecting to get ⁄ the exam, but I did.   *through*
1   Stop worrying and just get on your life – you're only 21! ....
2   You need to get the hand when your business is under attack. ....
3   I can't get the hang making chips; mine are always too greasy. ....
4   After months of hard work, she just wanted to get away from all. ....
5   My brother showed me how to get the most of my computer. ....
6   What's the best way to get of rats? ....

2   Complete these book titles with a suitable verb from above.

1   Ten things you never learned at college: how to .... in business and beat your rivals

2   101 ways to .... your ex-boyfriend

3   A handbook for junior doctors: how to .... the exams

4   How to .... a career in TV

5   What to do when your enemy gets ....

6   Calling all slimmers! How to .... that fat stomach!

7   Healthy escapes: .... it all by the Red Sea

8   Manage your stress and get .... your life

B Relationships with *get*

What are your cousins like? And do you get on?

I've got a cousin who's **getting on** for forty, but I only **got to know** him quite recently. We **get along** really well, though, and now we **get together** regularly for a chat.

I've got a cousin who **is getting along** really well in his business and earning lots of money, whereas I find it quite hard to **get by** on my salary. He tells me I should **get out of** teaching and work for him.

My cousin's a nightmare. He always **got his own way** as a child, and then later he **got mixed up with** a gang and ended up in prison.

Glossary

be getting on for …	be nearly a particular age, time, or number.
get to know sb	meet sb a number of times and become friends.
get together (with sb)	meet sb socially or in order to discuss sth.
get by	have enough money to buy what you need, but no more.
get out of sth	stop doing sth or being involved in sth.
get your own way	get or do what you want, although other people may want sth different.
get mixed up with sb	INF become involved with sb who is a bad influence on you (also **get mixed up in sth**).

spotlight *get on, get along*

Both **get on** and **get along** can be used with these meanings. **Get on** is more common.
1 *We get on/along well.* = have a friendly relationship. Also **get on/along with sb**, e.g.
  I get on/along with her very well.
2 *He's getting on/along well at school.* = making good progress.

3 Is the meaning the same or different? Write S or D.

1 Did you and Zoe get on? Did you and Zoe get along? ....
2 How did he get mixed up with them? How did he meet them? ....
3 He always gets his own way. He always gets what he wants. ....
4 We often get together in town. We often meet socially in town. ....
5 She gets by on $10 a day. She gets about $10 a day. ....
6 I got to know Sam last year. I became friends with Sam last year. ....
7 My grandmother's getting on for sixty. My grandmother's over sixty. ....
8 How did you get on with her? How did you get to know her? ....

4 Complete the questions. (You will answer them in Exercise 5.)

1 How did you get to .... your best friend?
2 How often do you get .... with all your relatives for a meal?
3 How are you getting .... in your career or with your studies?
4 Do you get your own .... most of the time, or do you give in to others?
5 Who do you get .... with best in your family? Why?
6 Have you ever got mixed .... in something and then regretted it? If so, what?

5 ABOUT YOU Write your answers to the questions in Exercise 4 in your notebook, or talk to another student.

A *Take*

 FORUM Do you hate your boss?

→ I've got a Liverpool accent, and my boss is always **taking** me **off** in front of my colleagues. My dad says, 'Just **take no notice of** him', but it really upsets me.

→ I asked my boss if I could **take** a day **off** to go to a funeral. She just screamed 'NO-O-O!'. I **was** really **taken aback**.

→ Anyone who disagrees with my boss is **taking his life in his hands**. He just goes mad. One day when he was really angry with me, I told him to **take it easy**. What a mistake.

→ When my boss told me he was cutting my salary by 15 per cent, I protested. He just said, '**Take it or leave it**'. I wasn't going to **take** that **lying down**, so I rang my lawyer.

→ He **took against** me the minute we met. But I'm not worried; I can **take care of myself**.

Glossary

take sb off	copy the way sb speaks or behaves, to entertain people.
take (no) notice of sb	pay (no) attention to what sb says.
take (time) off	have a particular amount of time away from work.
be taken aback	be shocked or surprised.
take your life in your hands	put yourself in danger (usually of death; in this example, the speaker is joking).
take it easy	INF used to tell sb not to be angry or worried.
take it or leave it	used to say that you do not care if sb accepts your offer or not.
not take sth lying down	not accept a bad situation without a fight or protest.
take against sb	INF begin to dislike sb, often without a good reason.
take care of yourself	If you can **take care of yourself**, you don't need anybody else to protect you.

1 Cross out one wrong word. Write the correct word at the end.

▶ As usual, she took no notice ~~to~~ what I said. *of* ....

1 It's your decision: you can take it and leave it. ....

2 He's strong; he knows how to take care for himself. ....

3 She was really upset, so I told her to take her easy. ....

4 You need to be careful. You might be taking your live in your hands. ....

5 They said we weren't needed any more. I was really taken back. ....

6 The government decision is wrong, and we won't make it lying down. ....

7 I don't know why he took again her, but she was really upset about it. ....

8 I asked my boss for a few days of because my daughter was ill. ....

2 Rewrite the sentences using the word in capitals. The meaning must stay the same.

1 Just relax and calm down. EASY ....

2 He put himself in a dangerous situation. LIFE ....

3 He copies the way his boss speaks. OFF ....

4 I was really shocked by the job cuts. ABACK ....

5 She's experienced and can protect herself. CARE ....

6 She wasn't at work today because she was ill. OFF ....

B *Look*

What kind of person are you?	About you
Do you **look back on** your childhood as the happiest time of your life?	
Do you **look on the bright side** when you're in a difficult situation?	
Do you **look up to** people who are in positions of power?	
Do you **look out for** other people when they need help?	
Would you **look the other way** if you saw someone stealing from a shop?	
Can you **look** people **in the eye** and tell them the truth all the time?	
Do other people often **look to** you for advice?	
Do you always try to **look your best** when you go out?	
Do you **look young for your age**?	

Glossary

look back on sth	think about sth in your past.
look on the bright side	be cheerful or positive about a bad situation.
look up to sb	respect and admire sb. OPP **look down on sb**.
look out for sb	take care of sb and make sure they are treated well.
look the other way	ignore sth bad that is happening and not try to stop it.
look sb in the eye	look straight at sb, especially to show that you are being honest.
look to sb	hope or expect to get help, advice, etc. from sb.
look your best	look as attractive as possible.
look young for your age	look as though you are younger than you really are.

3 Complete the phrases.

1 look out .... your friend
2 look .... best
3 look young for your ....
4 look up .... someone
5 look on the .... side
6 look someone in the ....
7 look .... on your childhood
8 look .... someone for advice
9 look the other ....
10 look .... on someone you don't respect

4 Complete the dialogues using the phrases from Exercise 3 in the correct form.

1 I don't think he's telling the truth. ~ No, he couldn't look ....
2 Mandy's a very positive person. ~ Yes, she always looks ....
3 I'll get my hair cut before my interview. ~ Good, you need to look ....
4 They don't show Bill any respect. ~ No, they look ....
5 You think a great deal of your mother, don't you? ~ Yes, I really look ....
6 Do you know, that man is nearly 40. ~ I don't believe it! He looks ....
7 People are suffering in the cold. ~ Yes, and the government is just looking ....
8 Does he ask his father if he needs help? ~ Yes, he always looks ....

5 ABOUT YOU Write your answers to the questionnaire, or talk to another student.

A Come

What's all that noise? ~ It's the new neighbours – they've been **coming and going** all day.

Why is she so good at Arabic? ~ I don't know; it just **comes naturally to** her.

How did the accident happen? ~ I don't know. When I **came to**, I was in hospital.

How's your dancing **coming along**? ~ Quite well, actually – I feel I**'ve come a long way**.

Was it a good match? ~ Well, it was a bit dull to start with, but it **came to life** in the second half.

I see they're buying a flat. ~ Yes, they recently **came into** a lot of money.

He had so many plans and ambitions. ~ Yes, how sad that they all **came to nothing**.

How did he die? ~ It's a mystery, but I'm sure the truth will **come out** eventually.

Glossary

come and go	arrive at a place and then leave it, repeatedly.
come naturally to sb	be natural and easy for sb to do.
come to	become conscious again. SYN **come round**. OPP **pass out**.
come along	improve or develop in the way that you want. SYN **come on**.
come a long way	improve a lot or make a lot of progress.
come to life	start to become exciting and lively.
come into sth	If you **come into** money, it becomes yours when sb dies, especially a relative.
come to nothing	be unsuccessful or have no successful result.

> **spotlight** *come out*
>
> **Come out** has several meanings:
> 1 *The true story came out at the trial.* = became known (as above).
> 2 *The book comes out next week.* = becomes available to buy or see (also used of films, CDs, etc.).
> 3 *After the rain, the sun came out.* = appeared.

1 Circle the correct answer.

1 If a CD comes out, it is *unsuccessful* | *available* in the shops.
2 If someone comes to, they become *conscious* | *unconscious*.
3 If skiing comes naturally to you, you *find it easy to do* | *think it is a natural activity*.
4 If you come into money, you *win it* | *receive it from someone who has died*.
5 If a plan comes to nothing, it *costs you nothing* | *doesn't succeed*.
6 If a story comes to life, it *becomes exciting* | *seems realistic*.

2 One word is missing in each sentence. Where does it go? Write it at the end.

1 They're moving house, so they'll be coming and over the next few days. ....
2 She's worked very hard at skating, and she's certainly come a way. ....
3 When the news finally came, nobody could believe it. ....
4 After the operation, it was an hour before he finally came and started talking. ....
5 Imagine it: a warm evening, music, and then the moon came – it was so romantic! ....
6 The pain was terrible – so bad that I out. When I came round, I was on the floor. ....
7 If I ever come any money, I'm going to give it all away. ....
8 Our vegetable garden is coming well, and we'll soon be eating salad and beans. ....

B Go

If everything **goes according to plan**, I'll **go down to** Brighton to stay with friends.

My wife usually decides what we do, and I just **go along with** it.

Dad wants to take us bowling, and **whatever he says goes**.

What are your plans for this weekend?

I've only got £20, and that **won't go far** …

My friend**'s been going through** a bad time, so I**'m going round to** his place to see him.

I think I**'m going down with** flu – I'll probably stay in.

I'm supposed to be **going out with** my boyfriend, but he never rings me. I hope he **hasn't gone off** me.

Glossary

go according to plan	happen in the way that you intend.
go down/up to somewhere	go to a place further south/north from where you are.
go along with sth	agree to do sth that sb else wants to do or wants you to do.
what/whatever sb says goes	used for saying that a particular person has the power to decide what happens in a situation.
not go far	used for saying that you can't buy very much with a particular amount of money.
go through sth	experience sth difficult or unpleasant.
go round (to …)	visit sb or go to a place that is near.
go down with sth	become sick or ill with sth.
go out (with sb)	spend time with sb and have a romantic relationship with them.
go off sb/sth	stop liking sb/sth that you liked in the past.

3 Match 1–8 with a–h.

1 Marcia's started going out ....   a to the coast at the weekend.
2 I used to like pasta, but I've gone ....   b goes.
3 Things didn't go according ....   c down with something.
4 I'm hoping to go down ....   d far these days.
5 I feel awful; I must be going ....   e along with it.
6 She's very dominant; whatever she says ....   f off it recently.
7 The money I earn doesn't go ....   g with my brother.
8 Joe suggested the plan and we just went ....   h to plan.

4 Complete the sentences.

1 Things are better now, but I went .... a bad time last summer.
2 If I'm not busy on Sunday, I might go .... to my friend's for a chat.
3 If everything goes .... to plan, I'll be going abroad this summer.
4 I might go .... to the north coast later this month.
5 How long has Alice been going .... with Gareth?
6 I usually go .... with whatever my friends want to do at the weekends.
7 $20 doesn't go .... if you're going out for the evening where I live.
8 I used to love staying out late, but as I've got older, I've gone .... it.

Unit 53

1 **Are these link words talking about time, making a contrast, or giving extra information? Complete the table.**

> on the other hand   as well   at last   even if   ever since
> in spite of   in addition   as soon as   in the meantime

TIME	CONTRAST	EXTRA INFORMATION

2 **Complete the sentences in a suitable way.**

1 I ordered a sandwich and .... as well.
2 On the one hand, living alone means you can do what you like, but on the other,

  ....
3 They only met in the summer, but they're obviously in love with each other. It looks as if

  .... next year.
4 Even if ...., I still don't think he'll pass his exams.
5 I'll telephone you as soon as I ....
6 She remained quite cheerful in spite of ....
7 We waited and waited, and at last ....
8 He's been very unhappy ever since ....

Unit 54

1 **Complete the sentences below using phrases from the table. You will find them by moving horizontally or vertically, backwards or forwards.**

BRIGHT	AND	AND	THEN	PEACE	AND
GIVE	EARLY	NOW	SICK	WARM	QUIET
OR	UP	AND	AND	AND	LOVELY
TAKE	LATER	DOWN	TIRED	FORWARDS	AND
SOONER	OR	WORD	FOR	WORD	BACKWARDS

▸ I went for a swim and the water was *lovely*   *and*   *warm*   .
1 She's sure to find out the truth of the matter ....
2 My boss complains all the time. I'm .... of listening to him!
3 I looked .... the road, but I couldn't see the car.
4 We spent the morning going .... to the shops.
5 I only meet him ...., usually at his mother's.
6 She repeated what the policeman had told her ....
7 The plane tickets cost about $400, ... a few dollars.
8 We got up .... today, ready for our long journey.
9 My life is so stressful! I just need some ....

Unit 55

1 Write the words below in the correct column.

> theory   mistake   accident   writing   purpose   length   certain
> duty   once   the phone   sure   return of post   season

IN	ON	AT	BY	FOR

2 Replace the underlined words with a prepositional phrase using words from the box.

> duty   length   certain ✓   purpose   end   order   mind   control   tune

▶ We knew <u>without any doubt</u> who was responsible. *for certain*
1 The child was <u>running around wildly</u>.
2 He didn't break the mirror <u>intentionally</u>.
3 She was singing <u>all the wrong notes</u>.
4 That policeman is <u>not working</u> today.
5 The coffee machine's <u>not working</u>.
6 <u>Finally</u>, we got to the theatre.
7 He spoke about the situation <u>for a long time</u>.
8 I've got a lot of things <u>that I'm thinking about</u>.

Unit 56

1 Rewrite the sentences using the word in capitals and making any necessary changes. The meaning must stay the same.

▶ What time do you leave work tonight? OFF *What time do you get off work tonight?*
1 Have you completed the application form? FILL
2 I collected my dry cleaning at 4.00. UP
3 She applied to university but she wasn't successful. IN
4 Hurry up; we're going to be late. COME
5 She is making good progress with her painting. COME
6 Do you know when the train arrives? GET
7 The pain in my leg has disappeared. GO
8 I wrote it in my address book. PUT
9 Could you wait a couple of minutes? ON
10 Don't stand on that chair! OFF

Unit 57

1 Complete the sentences using a word from the left and a word from the right in the correct form.

lay catch speak be give keep make tell	time go move mind face sun hand table

1 The dinner's nearly ready – could you _____ the _____ , please?
2 The little boy was playing his violin so badly; it was hard to _____ a straight _____ .
3 She's been on the beach for hours; she's really _____ the _____ .
4 It's nearly midnight, so I'd better _____ a _____ . I've got a busy day tomorrow.
5 She's really tired. I think she's _____ on the _____ since six this morning.
6 We need to move the bookcase. Could you _____ me a _____ with it?
7 On some websites you are able to _____ your _____ and really say what you think about important issues.
8 I didn't learn to _____ the _____ until I was about seven.

2 Circle the correct word.

1 go round in circles = work hard at something without making *mistakes | progress*.
2 pick sb's brain = ask someone questions because you want to *get to know them | find out information*.
3 make up for lost time = do something *quickly | slowly* because you *couldn't do it before | have plenty of time*.
4 catch sb's eye = *look sb in the eye | make somebody look at you*.
5 miss the point = not *understand | hear* the main part of what someone is saying.
6 stretch your legs = *move your legs | go for a short walk* after sitting for some time.

Unit 58

1 Replace the underlined parts of the sentences using a phrasal verb with *get*, and any other words that are necessary to keep the meaning the same.

▶ I'd like to <u>stop being in</u> the army. *I'd like to get out of the army.*
1 They <u>have a good relationship</u>. _____
2 I'm sure he's good enough to <u>pass</u> the exam. _____
3 It took her some time to <u>recover from</u> the shock. _____
4 I don't know how she <u>started a career in</u> journalism. _____
5 We often <u>meet socially</u> for a coffee in the morning. _____
6 She can't <u>manage financially</u> on £100 a week. _____
7 I think he <u>benefited a lot from</u> the course. _____
8 I think she's <u>making good progress</u>. _____

2 Complete the definitions of these idioms and phrasal verbs, then underline the full idiom or phrasal verb in each sentence.

1 If it is getting on for midnight, it is _____ midnight.
2 If you get the upper hand, you gain an _____ over somebody.
3 If you get ahead in your career, you are _____ .
4 If you get your own way, you do what _____ .
5 If you get the hang of something, you _____ it.
6 If you get mixed up in something, you become involved in something which is _____

Unit 59

1 Are the sentences positive or negative? Write P or N.

1 Mike always looks on the bright side. ....
2 Alain looks down on his neighbours. ....
3 Daisy can't look you in the eye. ....
4 Rebecca looks out for people. ....
5 Rafa takes against people. ....
6 Jorge looks up to his parents. ....
7 Joe won't take things lying down. ....
8 You take your life in your hands when David's driving. ....

2 Replace the underlined parts of the sentence using an idiom or phrasal verb with *take* or *look*.

▶ She <u>pays no attention to</u> anything he says. *takes no notice of* ....

1 I often <u>think about</u> the past. ....
2 Just <u>calm down and relax</u>. ....
3 She <u>appears much younger than she is</u>. ....
4 He has always <u>respected and admired</u> her grandfather. ....
5 I was really <u>shocked and surprised</u> when she said that. ....
6 Whenever there's a problem, he just <u>pretends not to see it</u>. ....

Unit 60

1 Circle the correct answer.

1 I'm happy to *come* | *go* along with whatever my sister decides.
2 Alex lost his job, and then he was ill. He's been *going* | *coming* through a bad time.
3 I used to like Sean, but I've *come* | *gone* off him because he's been horrible to my sister.
4 My brother will make the final decision. Whatever he says, *comes* | *goes*.
5 My cousin Leila is good at all ball games: they just *come* | *go* naturally to her.
6 Margaret Compton's latest book *comes* | *goes* out next month.

2 Complete the crossword. All the answers are idioms or phrasal verbs with *come* or *go*. The letters in the grey squares spell another phrasal verb. What is it?

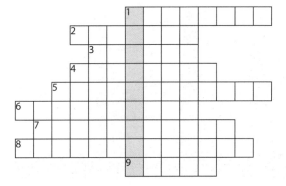

1 When the sun ...., it appears from behind a cloud. (5,3)
2 I'm planning to .... to see my neighbour this evening. (2,5)
3 She fainted, and it was a few minutes before she finally .... (4,2)
4 After his father died, he .... a lot of money. (4,4)
5 You've made so much progress with your English – you've really .... (4,1,4,3)
6 The show was boring at first, but it .... when the dancers came on. (4,2,4)
7 We were hoping to see Rome and Venice, but things didn't .... to plan. (2,9)
8 All his dreams of starting a business sadly .... in the end. (4,2,7)
9 €10 doesn't .... in an expensive city like Paris. (2,3)

Idioms – some interesting histories

How did English idioms come into use? Here we show the meanings behind some idioms, and how some of them developed. 👁 Look at our website www.oup.com/elt/wordskills for more.

a stone's throw (Unit 2)
A stone's throw is the distance that you can throw a stone – in other words, only a short distance from where you are standing.

be over the moon (Unit 27)
In early use, the idiom was to 'jump' over the moon. It spread because of its use in the children's nursery rhyme (= poem):
Hey, diddle, diddle,
The cat and the fiddle,
The cow jumped over the moon.
It means, be extremely happy about something.

brush sth up / brush up on sth (Unit 9)
You could improve the appearance of something like a silk hat or a woollen coat by brushing it. Nowadays, the idiom expresses the idea of improving a skill that you have not used for a long time, e.g. speaking a foreign language.

catch sb red-handed (Unit 35)
If someone was **caught red-handed**, they had blood on their hands after murdering someone or poaching (= killing birds and animals illegally on another person's land). Nowadays if someone is **caught red-handed**, they have been caught while doing something wrong or illegal.

in the red OPP **in the black** (Unit 33)
In bank accounts, if you owed money (i.e. you were in debit), the amount was written in red ink; amounts of money actually in your account were written in black.

on the dot (Unit 49)
On the dot refers to a traditional clock face. The minutes are marked as dots, which the minute hand covers as it moves round the clock.

once in a blue moon (Units 3, 49)
The moon is obviously not blue, and it rarely looks blue; this phrase suggests that if something happens **once in a blue moon**, it rarely or never happens.

show sb the ropes (Unit 24)
In the past, sailing ships had many ropes of different kinds, and sailors had to learn how to handle them. If someone **shows you the ropes**, they teach you a skill or show you how something is done.

start from scratch (Unit 48)
The origin of this phrase is to do with sport. People used to scratch a line on the ground as the starting point of a race, or to show where boxers had to stand at the beginning of a match. It now means to start something again from the beginning, probably because the previous work you did on it was no use.

Answer key

Unit 1

1

1. *Both are correct.*   4 *Both are correct.*
2. on   5 in the distance
3. lose face   6 bell

2

1. He was in a **terrible** state
2. How **on earth** is your sister
3. makes **a lot of** sense
4. every day **without fail**
5. we ran **like mad**
6. situation, but **if all else fails** he can

3

1. steer   4 out of the blue
2. flat out   5 in the distance
3. That   6 lose face

4

1. fail (without fail)
2. bell (rings a bell)
3. sense (makes a lot of sense)
4. eye (turn a blind eye)
5. state (was in a terrible state)
6. come (How come?)

5

1. be unable to decide what you think about sth, or whether to do sth or not
2. after a period of time
3. be lucky that
4. amusing and fun to be with
5. have a lot of money

Unit 2

1

1. never   3 off   5 words
2. bright   4 charge   6 advantage

2

1. through   4 supposed/meant
2. case   5 less
3. throw   6 mind

3

1. getting nowhere   4 thank heavens
2. A piece of cake.   5 get through to
3. Don't ask me. / Search me.   6 stone's throw

4

▶ Type 5 (**trial and error** a way of solving a problem by trying several possibilities and learning from your mistakes; see also Unit 9.)

1. Type 6 (**live on sth** have a particular amount of money to buy the things you need to live.)
2. Type 7 (**Good grief!** used to express surprise, shock, or annoyance; see also Unit 19.)
3. Type 2 (**in the main** mostly; in general.)
4. Type 1 (**find your feet** If you **find your feet**, you become confident in a new situation, especially one that is difficult to start with.)
5. Type 4 (**absence makes the heart grow fonder** used to say that when you are away from someone you love, you love them even more.)
6. Type 3 (**a fact of life** something difficult or unpleasant that cannot be changed and that you have to accept.)

5

making fun of	Get lost
swap places (with)	a pain in the neck
No way!	go away
gets on my nerves	

6

Spoken phrase

No way! = definitely not.

Get lost! a rude way of telling someone to go away.

Verb-based idiom

make fun of sb laugh at sb or make others laugh at them, usually in an unkind way; see also Unit 22.

swap places (with sb) take sb's seat or position so they can take yours; see also Unit 8.

get on sb's nerves annoy sb.

Noun phrase

a pain in the neck INF a person or thing that you find annoying.

Phrasal verb

go away used to tell sb to leave a place or person; see also Unit 56.

Unit 3

1

These answers are based on the Oxford Advanced Learner's Dictionary.

1. moment   4 early   7 thing
2. catch   5 just
3. breath   6 public

2

1 T   2 F   3 T   4 T   5 F   6 F   7 T   8 F
9 T   10 F

3

These answers are based on the Oxford Advanced
Learner's Dictionary.

1 on **our** doorstep
2 at the last **moment**
3 a **bundle** of nerves
4 **give** my love to
5 **stay** out of his way
6 **fresh** blood

4

These answers are based on the Oxford Advanced
Learner's Dictionary.

1 formal
2 old-fashioned, informal
3 informal
4 BrE, informal, humorous
5 old-fashioned, informal
6 BrE, saying
7 informal, especially NAmE
8 formal

Unit 4

1

The correct sentences are: 1, 3, 4, 5, 8.

2

1 the police are looking into **it** at the moment
2 I'm sure he just made **it** up.
3 *Correct.*
4 Who looks after **it** when you go on holiday
5 *Correct.*
6 I came across **it** yesterday on the Internet
7 If you try **it** on and it's too big
8 *Correct.*

3

1 You can check **in** at 5.00.
2 Could you look **up** the number? OR Could you
   look the number **up**?
3 I'm **looking** after my friend's daughter today.
4 He's going out **with** David's sister.
5 CNN stands **for** Cable News Network.
6 Would you like to try this skirt **on**? OR Would
   you like to try **on** this skirt?

4

1 She wasn't happy, but now things are looking
   up.
2 The committee looked into the cause of the
   problem.

3 I didn't know the answer, so I made something
   up.
4 The train's coming in on platform five.
5 We can cut back on the electricity we use.
6 What do the letters FAQ stand for?
7 I had to look up the meaning (in a dictionary).
   OR look the meaning up
8 Our meeting was at 5.00, but Sue never
   showed up.

5

rub sth out (transitive, separable) e.g. *I made a
mistake, so I rubbed it out.*
go in for sth (transitive, inseparable) e.g. *She went
in for the Stage 5 piano exam.*
settle down (intransitive, inseparable) e.g. *They
want to get married and settle down.*
take after sb (transitive, inseparable) e.g. *I take
after my father: we're both very talkative.*
take sth back (transitive, separable) e.g. *The watch
didn't work, so I took it back.*
fall out with sb (transitive, inseparable) e.g. *I fell
out with him because he told me a lie.*

Unit 5

1

1 e   2 f   3 b   4 c   5 h   6 d   7 a   8 g

2

1 keeps on   5 go on
2 go on to   6 went on and on
3 stay on   7 get on with
4 dragged on   8 drove on

3

I saw my dad off at the airport.
We lazed around by the pool.
The town was cut off by the flood water.
We didn't take off until 7.00.
She told me to clear off and leave her alone.
The boys often hang around the street corner.

4

1 hanging   4 lying   7 hang
2 messing   5 went / has gone 8 clear
3 cut   6 see

Unit 6

1

1 b   2 e   3 h   4 c   5 d   6 a   7 f   8 g

2

1 clear ('tidy' is also possible)
2 flicked ('looked' is also possible)

3 used
4 goes
5 tidy ('clear' is also possible)
6 live
7 Drink
8 slept

3
Answers from a Czech person.
1 Yes, we always go through homework in class.
2 I'm afraid I can't remember when I last tidied up my bedroom!
3 Yes, I do often sleep through the alarm clock.
4 Yes, of course I do.
5 No, as I consider it rather impolite.

4

1	took, sent	4	get
2	ring, phone	5	gave, took
3	take, bring, put	6	sent, took

5

1	took	5	brought
2	ring/phone/call	6	got
3	pay	7	get
4	get	8	bring/give

Unit 7

1
1 about five kilos / a lot of weight
2 fire alarm / car alarm
3 *All are possible.*
4 shoes/jacket
5 *All are possible.*

2
1 I see Beverley's ~~got~~ on a few kilos again **put**
2 Could you put the lights ~~down~~ **on**
3 I hope they turn ~~out~~ **up**
4 We've decided to ~~make~~ the living room up **do**
5 She was ~~tidied~~ up this week **tied**
6 I broke ~~away~~ and cried **down**
7 They tied me ~~out~~ **up**
8 I can't do it ~~on~~ **up**

3

1	went	4	broke	7	broke
2	came	5	turn		
3	put	6	tied		

4

1	turn up	4	tied up	7	turned up
2	do up	5	do up	8	broke down
3	going up	6	gone off		

5
1 go 2 put 3 broke 4 do 5 turn 6 going

6
Answers from a New Zealander.
1 We live in a quiet cul-de-sac and never hear car alarms going off.
2 I put on weight during the winter months because it's too cold to go for walks.
3 Once our car broke down at about 10.30 p.m. We rang the AA [Automobile Association] and had to wait half an hour before they came and towed us to the nearest garage.
4 Our home is only 10 years old, but we've started doing it up. So far the ceiling has been painted.
5 If I'm late for class (which is very rare), my students get on with some work or use the time for group discussion.
6 Petrol prices are going up, and that affects the prices of everything else.

Unit 8

1

call it a day	go over something
swap places	hand something out
take it in turns	first of all

2

1	all	4	out
2	give/hand	5	off
3	over/through	6	in

3

1	places	3	turns	5	out
2	away	4	day	6	round

4
1 cross it ~~off~~ **out**
2 ~~top~~ of the iceberg **tip**
3 no use ~~to study~~ grammar **studying**
4 My brother's ~~in~~ home **at**
5 it's ~~not~~ good **no**
6 ~~get~~ back to the beginning **go**

5

1	rough	4	take	7	build
2	iceberg	5	back	8	look
3	crossed	6	good/use		

6
Answers from a British person.
1 When I was studying French I took it very seriously.
2 Yes, it's good to look up words you don't know. But it's also good to see if you can work them out from the context.

3 Now students can prepare their written work on their computers, which is quicker than writing it in rough first.
4 I agree. But it's easy to forget to look back at your notebook.
5 Yes, it's always good to practise speaking with your classmates to build up your confidence.
6 Yes, what you learn in class is only the tip of the iceberg. You go on learning all your life.

Unit 9

1
1 make **myself** understood
2 I'll **get** there eventually
3 got behind **with** his studies
4 make the most **of** it
5 now I have to **catch** up with
6 list of **dos** and don'ts

2

1 make	3 loud	5 get	7 stick
2 heart	4 make	6 error	8 given

3
Answers from a Greek person.
1 I usually make myself understood in English.
2 I've tried to learn phrasal verbs and idioms by heart.
3 I sometimes say words out loud to remember them.
4 I always try to make the most of my time in class.
5 I sometimes get behind with my studies.
6 Trial and error is a good learning method.
7 I generally stick at everything I start.
8 I haven't given up a course.
Best piece of advice: Don't be embarrassed about speaking: the main thing is to make yourself understood.

4
rack your brains
keep your mind on something
go in one ear and out the other
on the tip of my tongue
make sense of something
keep it up

5
1 on, tongue
2 rack
3 keep
4 ear, other
5 pick
6 make
7 in

8 up
9 come

6
Answers from a Brazilian person.
I often find that I have words on the tip of my tongue when I've slept badly and I'm tired.
I'm quite good at languages and I can usually pick things up quite quickly, above all when reading foreign magazines and novels.
I need to brush up on difficult English phrasal verbs; if I don't use them I tend to forget them.

Unit 10

1
1 I must get to the grips with this.
2 You can only do to your best.
3 Keep both your fingers crossed!
4 I did it up to the best of my ability.
5 Best of the luck!
6 He works it out answers to problems.

2

1 get	4 over/through	7 top	
2 ability	5 come	8 world	
3 bogged	6 habit		

3
Answers from a Czech person.
I have to get down to studying in the evening because I'm a distance student, and I'm at work during the day.
I always try to do my best.
Sometimes I do get bogged down in details when I'm learning something new.
I go through my notes shortly before an exam; it isn't as time-consuming as reading a textbook.
It's impossible to guess which topics will come up in an exam; there are usually about a hundred of them for each exam at our university.
If you don't get into the habit of studying regularly, you probably won't be able to pass all the necessary exams before the end of a term.
Feel enthusiasm – I can easily get on top of subjects I like.
I never feel it'll be the end of the world if I fail an exam because I can try each exam three times.

4
1 stayed
2 *Both are correct.*
3 blank
4 eye
5 read
6 stuck, *both are correct.*

5

1 **read** through my notes
2 tried to **breathe** in and out
3 feel my **mind** going blank
4 none of them **made** sense
5 keep my **eye** on the clock
6 I ran **out** of time
7 **miss/leave** out the last question
8 steered **clear** of my friends

6

Answers from a British person.
1 Yes, I always stay up late revising on the night before an exam.
2 I like to be alone and quiet just before an exam, but that's not often possible.
3 I try to keep my eye on the clock, but I find that difficult to do if I'm really concentrating on what I'm writing.
4 Yes, I do try to stick to the question, but I'm not good at doing so.
5 If I get stuck on a question I usually try to write something, even if I know it's not answering the question. I should probably just move on instead.
6 It's a good idea to breathe in and out slowly if your mind goes blank.
7 I never have enough time to read through my answers at the end.

Unit 11

1

1 ~~foot~~   3 ~~worst~~   5 ~~earlier~~
2 ~~compare~~   4 ~~best~~   6 ~~on~~

2

1 She will **go** far in her career.
2 I was **in** my element at university.
3 She came **up** with some good ideas.
4 He sat **back** and did nothing.
5 Why did she drop **out** of college?
6 It went from **bad** to worse.

3

1 comparison (By comparison)
2 early (it's early days)
3 up (it's not up to much)
4 dropped (dropped out)
5 thinking (thinking on his feet)
6 better (be better off)

4

1 start off / get off   5 bring out
2 know   6 think
3 do   7 pull
4 think

5

1 getting   4 pulling   7 foot
2 out   5 stuff   8 do
3 much   6 thanks

Unit 12

1

1 think **straight**   4 think **back**
2 think **ahead**   5 think **twice**
3 think **for** himself   6 think **it** over

2

1 over/through   5 mind
2 back   6 yourself
3 over   7 spur
4 straight   8 twice

3

Answers from a Czech person.
No. I like to think ahead.
It's sometimes good to accept other people's opinions, but I mostly prefer thinking for myself.
I like to solve my problems on my own, but I sometimes consult my close friends.
I try to avoid doing things on the spur of the moment.
That's right. I always tend to start panicking.
Yes, I always think twice before doing anything important.
I hardly ever think back to my time at primary school.

Unit 13

1

1 I'm a bit out of ~~the~~ practice these days.
2 She knows what ~~that~~ she's doing.
3 Would you like to give ~~to~~ it a try?
4 Are you ~~no~~ any good at making things?
5 I'm no ~~much~~ good at maths.
6 I meant to do it but it slipped ~~out~~ my mind.
7 She knew it like the back ~~side~~ of her hand.
8 Are you any good with ~~for~~ electrical things?

2

1 with   4 back   7 hang
2 head   5 good, give   8 out
3 in   6 mind

3

Answers from a New Zealander.
1 I'm good with my hands, especially making and fixing things, e.g. sewing, basic furniture repairs, etc.

2 I've got a good head for figures. Maths was my best subject at high school.
3 I used to be able to take in a lot of factual information but the older I get the less I remember.
4 I know Christchurch like the back of my hand. It's a great place to live and work.
5 I'm pretty good at cooking Kiwi food, but I also love giving Asian food a try.
6 I remember most of my family's birthdays.
7 It must be easier to get the hang of it if they have a good instructor.
8 Yes, I cycle a lot, and so I never get out of practice.

Unit 14

1

1	in	4	from
2	broke	5	*Both are correct.*
3	*Both are correct.*	6	line

2
1 quiet (keep quiet about it)
2 kept (kept him in the dark)
3 touch (got in touch with)
4 broke (broke the news)
5 knowledge (it's common knowledge)
6 hold (get hold of), gave (gave her a ring)

3
Answers from a Norwegian person.
1 I'm a phone person. I use email occasionally, and I only use texting when something is really urgent.
2 I usually give people a ring to thank them. I try to drop them a line as well, because that's what I was taught to do as a child, but I sometimes forget.
3 Quite frequently.
4 Sometimes a lot, sometimes less. I ring friends and family abroad about once a month, but email is a good way to keep in touch with friends abroad.
5 Yes, they do! Mainly because we've moved house a lot. But when I got married, I kept my surname as my middle name, before my husband's surname, as a way for people to be able to find me.

Unit 15

1

1 U 2 H 3 U 4 H 5 U 6 U 7 U 8 U

2

1	speak	4	face, back	7	across
2	talk	5	mind	8	edgeways
3	foot	6	told		

3
Answers from a Syrian person.
1 Yes, I do if the teacher is friendly enough.
2 No, there isn't.
3 No, I haven't as far as I remember.
4 I prefer the former as long as it's objective and not too personal.
5 No, I wouldn't. I tend to be reserved in such situations.
6 No, I haven't.
7 Yes, I sometimes do. It happens when I don't know the exact vocabulary.
8 Yes, it is with some people – those who I consider to be egocentric.

Unit 16

1

1	hung up	4	*Both are correct.*
2	got cut off	5	*Both are correct.*
3	get	6	top

2
1 line (hold the line), through (put you through)
2 charge (charge it up)
3 get (get through to), on (hung up on)
4 hang/hold (hang/hold on), fortune (costing a fortune), up (hung up)
5 off (got cut off)
6 back (get back to)

3
Answers from an Italian person.
1 It happened when I was having an interesting conversation on my mobile and I was a bit annoyed.
2 I have to top up my mobile two or three times a year.
3 Yes, I have. It usually happens when someone phones me to try to advertise their products and sell them to me.
4 No, luckily I don't have that problem.

Unit 17

1

1	up	5	Hurry	9	up
2	come	6	usual/always	10	Guess
3	not	7	of		
4	know	8	when		

2

1 Hurry up!
2 Say when.
3 Time's up.
4 Guess what?
5 What's up?
6 Here goes.
7 All the best.
8 Here you are.

3

1 Kind of.
2 as usual
3 there you are / there you go
4 What's up?
5 It's up to you.
6 all the best

4

1 Time's up.
2 Here goes!
3 Say when.
4 Here's to

Unit 18

1

1 Tell
2 told
3 say
4 say
5 telling
6 say
7 say
8 tell
9 tell
10 say

2

1 say that again
2 whatever you
3 you so
4 say the least
5 Tell, rather not say
6 tell you
7 say no
8 you the truth
9 to say
10 be telling

3

1 I'll see ~~that~~ I can do **I'll see what I can do**
2 ~~seeing~~ you! **see you**
3 let's ~~me~~ see **let's see** OR ~~let's~~ me see **let me see**
4 see yourself **see for yourself**
5 I don't see why ~~no~~ **I don't see why not**.
6 see how ~~a thing goes~~ **see how things go**

4

1 see why not
2 for yourself
3 see you
4 'll see
5 let's see / let me see
6 it goes / things go
7 see what I can do
8 you see

Unit 19

1

1 D 2 S 3 S 4 S 5 D 6 S

2

1 Not bad. / Not too bad.
2 same here
3 if you like
4 Never mind.

5 You're welcome.
6 I'm very / terribly sorry.
7 Yes and no.
8 I'm not bothered.
9 go ahead
10 I beg your pardon?

3

1 none
2 Hear! Hear!
3 *Both are correct.*
4 hard luck!
5 *Both are correct.*
6 For goodness sake!

4

1 bad luck! / hard luck!
2 Mind your own business! / That's none of your business!
3 Good luck! / Best of luck!
4 Well done!
5 Good grief! / Good heavens! / Goodness me!
6 Goodness knows!
7 Bless you!
8 Thank goodness!

Unit 20

1

1 ~~let~~ **get**
2 ~~bash~~ **dash**
3 ~~ill~~ **all**
4 ~~cut~~ **put**
5 ~~bet~~ **get**
6 ~~hot~~ **got**
7 ~~dove~~ **love**
8 ~~day~~ **way**

2

1 cropped
2 on
3 together
4 Remember
5 after
6 by
7 love/regards
8 get
9 something
10 regards/love

3

1 away
2 back
3 earliest
4 pop, about
5 up, wait
6 call/drop

4

1 What's she been up to recently?
2 Meet me at 5.00 at the latest.
3 Could you drop me off at the doctor's?
4 I'll try to get away from work by 7.00.
5 I'm not sure I feel up to it.
6 It's (just) round the corner from where I'm staying.
7 I'm snowed under (with work) at the moment.
8 I'll call by (and see you) on my way home.

Unit 21

1
1 much (don't think much of), be (to be honest)
2 make (make of), concerned (as far as I'm concerned)
3 up (up to a point)
4 point (beside the point)
5 highly / a lot (thinks highly / a lot of), agree (I couldn't agree more)
6 thing (for one thing)

2
1 As far ~~that~~ I'm concerned **as**
2 ~~For~~ be honest **To**
3 I don't think ~~more~~ of **much**
4 think **a** lot of
5 In the ~~large~~ run **long**
6 ~~With~~ a doubt **Without**

3
Answers from a British person.
1 As far as I'm concerned we should learn from the past, in order to avoid the repetition of bad things.
2 It's better if the police don't carry guns, as they can be used in error and can get into the hands of criminals.
3 I agree. We need more efficient trains, and we need more buses in rural areas.
4 I don't agree. People don't seem to think much of him.
5 Yes, in the long run we'll need renewable fuels or energy for cars.
6 We may be dependent on them, but they have advanced our knowledge in a very valuable way.

4
1 D 2 S 3 S 4 D 5 D 6 S

5
1 What are the **pros** and cons
2 Well, **in** some ways
3 I know, but **even** so
4 You've got a **point**
5 And for the **most** part
6 Fair **enough**
7 And the thing **is**
8 To a certain **extent**
9 So, **if** you ask me

Unit 22

1
1 d 2 a 3 h 4 g 5 b 6 c 7 f 8 e

2
1 wrong   3 for   5 laugh
2 made   4 joke   6 got

3
1 last   5 went
2 speaking   6 end
3 burst out   7 roof
4 leg   8 a fool of himself

4
1 laugh   5 end of the stick
2 a joke   6 her off
3 fool   7 out laughing
4 fun of him   8 the roof

5
1 They didn't get it. / No one got the joke.
2 He made a fool of himself. / He was making a fool of himself.
3 He got the wrong end of the stick.
4 We're not on speaking terms.
5 He was pulling my leg.
6 My mother felt sorry for my aunt (because she had a hard life).

Unit 23

1
1 f 2 c 3 g 4 b 5 h 6 a 7 d 8 e

2
1 nodding his ~~hand~~ **head**
2 wearing his T-shirt ~~front to back~~ **back to front**
3 shaking ~~hand~~ **hands**
4 do ~~out~~ the buttons **up**
5 knocked me ~~over~~ **out**
6 fold their ~~hands~~ **arms**
7 tripped me ~~down~~ **up**
8 she ~~felt~~ over **fell**

3
1 knocked   4 front   7 crossed
2 tripped   5 hang   8 away
3 hand   6 tiptoe

4
1 They're shaking hands.
2 She's throwing them away. OR She's throwing away some old magazines.
3 He's blowing his nose.
4 He's wearing his T-shirt inside out. OR He's got his T-shirt on inside out.
5 She's shaking her head.
6 He knocked me out.
7 He's standing on tiptoe.
8 They're holding hands.

5

Answers from an Argentinian person.

1 Yes, but in Argentina, when you meet a friend, you also kiss him or her on both cheeks.
2 Yes, they do.
3 No, it isn't. But, if possible, you don't do it in public.
4 Yes, absolutely.
5 No, women never walk hand in hand in Argentina.
6 No, I haven't.
7 No, I haven't.
8 Some sheets of writing paper.

Unit 24

1

1 in   2 of   3 after   4 in   5 in   6 of

2

1 out   2 brought   3 runs   4 followed   5 ropes

3

1 brought   2 take   3 footsteps   4 look   5 runs

4

Answers from a Czech person.

1 As a child, I was brought up in a small town.
2 I most take after my elder sister.
3 I think I would like to follow in my mother's footsteps.
4 I particularly look up to my husband.
5 I'm not aware of a physical characteristic that runs in our family.

5

1 Why did she **burst** into tears?
2 I'll get my own back **on** her.
3 She has **given** birth to twins.
4 I often got **into** trouble at school.
5 He **stayed** up late to watch a film. or He **stayed** up to watch a late film.
6 He's grown **into** a handsome young man.
7 She is nothing **like** her brothers.
8 What have you let yourself in **for**?

6

1 up   2 up   3 out   4 blind   5 get   6 back

7

Answers from a New Zealander.

1 I grew up in Christchurch, New Zealand. We had a big house with six bedrooms, a huge garden, and a goat.
2 We didn't have TV when I was young, and we were never allowed to stay up late.

3 I was allowed to stay out until 10 p.m., which I thought was far too early.
4 My parents didn't turn a blind eye because they had no idea what we got up to!
5 I was always in trouble at school. I used to break all the rules I could, without it getting back to my parents e.g. not wearing my school hat, riding my bike in the school grounds, etc.
6 I tried to get my own back on one of my sisters and one of my brothers but it didn't seem to bother them at all.

Unit 25

1

1 ~~By~~ the whole **On**
2 Just leave me ~~lone~~ **alone**
3 largely ~~with~~ fault **at**
4 In ~~generally~~ **general**
5 ~~settled~~ in his ways **set**
6 ~~in~~ ease with them **at**
7 out ~~from~~ touch **of**
8 Who is ~~for~~ blame? **to**

2

1 I feel at ease with Liz and Clive.
2 Just be yourself.
3 She's at fault.
4 He's very set in his ways.
5 Leave me alone.
6 I'm not good when it comes to numbers.
7 I'm out of touch with politics now.
8 Don't go on about it.

3

1 can't **get** through to him
2 she got **away** with it
3 becoming more and **more** dangerous
4 been getting **up** to
5 They're worlds **apart**

4

1 own two feet	4	apart
2 live	5	offence
3 the times	6	give in

5

Answers from a British person.

1 No, my parents never gave in to me.
2 No, I was regularly given punishments!
3 I've always been able to get through to both my parents and my children.
4 No. I'm far too old for that!
5 No, we've always understood each other.

Unit 26

1

1 G 2 G 3 G 4 B 5 G 6 B 7 B 8 G

2

1 by	4 keep	7 on/along
2 in, door	5 given	8 hand
3 ice	6 locked	

3

Answers from a Greek person.

1 I live with my husband.
2 We work in the same school.
3 I would make them a cake.
4 No.
5 Yes. To school.
6 No.
7 The neighbours to the right. We have the same interests.
8 Cooking.

4

1 It was in full swing by 11.00.
2 The guests stood around outside.
3 The party went on all night.
4 Who turned the music up?
5 They couldn't put up with the noise.
6 They ran the risk of upsetting people.
7 When did it come to an end?
8 Please let me know if you can come.

5

1 throw/give/have (throw/give/have a party)
2 terms (on bad terms)
3 round (invited some people round)
4 around (stood around)
5 let (let us know)
6 go (go on)
7 on (what was going on)
8 down (turned the music down)
9 end (brought the party to an end)

Unit 27

1

1 I've got ~~flies~~ in my stomach. **butterflies**
2 She's about ~~for~~ leave. **to**
3 He ~~ran~~ out of his skin. **jumped**
4 He's got something ~~at~~ his mind. **on**
5 She ~~won't~~ help making mistakes. **can't**
6 Don't worry, you're ~~on~~ safe hands. **in**

2

| 1 state | 3 mind | 5 take |
| 2 can't | 4 calm | 6 leaf |

3

| 1 on | 3 about |
| 2 stomach | 4 on, calm |

4

Answers from a Brazilian person.

1 Not really. I'm quite relaxed.
2 About five months ago, when I had to do a presentation in front of a big audience.
3 I always feel nervous when I'm about to go on a journey because I'm afraid of flying.
4 I would tell them to watch a movie and do some deep breathing. It always works for me.

5

| 1 g N | 2 d N | 3 b N | 4 i P |
| 5 e N | 6 c P | 7 a N | 8 h N |

6

1 feet (get cold feet)
2 edge (on edge)
3 cry (I didn't know whether to laugh or cry)
4 dumps (down in the dumps)
5 mood (in the mood for)
6 lives (had the time of our lives)
7 makes (makes me sick)
8 control (control my temper)

Unit 28

1

1 mad about / fallen for
2 come between
3 shoes/place
4 hit it off / fall for each other
5 be Lucy's type / chat Lucy up
6 *All are correct.*

2

1 for good
2 thinks the world of
3 my type
4 hit it off
5 put yourself in my shoes/place
6 chatted me up
7 split up / break up
8 mad about / crazy about

3

1 wrong	4 courage	7 wait
2 time	5 sight	8 out
3 together	6 on	

4

| 1 love | 3 go | 5 put |
| 2 pluck, out | 4 stuck | |

5

Answers from a Brazilian person.

1 I don't think so. I believe in attraction at first sight. Love takes time to develop.
2 Yes, I've always found it difficult. And since I have never had good results taking the initiative, I've decided not to do it anymore.
3 That's a tricky one. Maybe because people find they have nothing or little in common, or they lose respect for each other. There are so many possible reasons.
4 No, not many, but I know a few.
5 People smoking near me (I'm allergic), neighbours playing loud music, and people answering mobile phones at the cinema.

Unit 29

1

1 around	4 over	7 on
2 over	5 show-off	8 fair
3 take	6 on	

2

1 showing off
2 all over the place
3 give and take
4 on her own / by herself
5 take that into account
6 over and over again / again and again
7 getting on my nerves
8 messing around/about

3

1 S   2 D   3 S   4 D   5 D   6 S

4

1 I love tidying things/everything away.
2 We've had plenty of ups and downs.
3 They all had a good laugh at my expense.
4 Should we put off buying the car?
5 Don't bite my head off!
6 The kids are driving me round the bend.

5

Answers from a British person.

It drives me mad when my flatmates keep changing channels on the television.
I also get annoyed when they don't do their fair share of the housework.
It especially drives me mad when they leave dirty plates and cups in the sink. Why don't they put them straight in the dishwasher?
I feel upset when my sister's boyfriend puts her down in front of other people.
I hate it when my boss bites my head off before hearing why something has happened.

Unit 30

1

1 e   2 g   3 h   4 a   5 b   6 c   7 d   8 f

2

1 I can confide in Molly.
2 So far, nobody has arrived.
3 Keep your feet on the ground.
4 If the worst comes to the worst, will you help me?
5 Don't sit around all day. / Don't spend time sitting around all day.
6 He'll soon find his feet in his new job.
7 She kept the news to herself.
8 His heart's not in this project. / His heart isn't in this project.

4

1 dare ~~said~~ that is true **say**
2 it's taken ~~out~~ my life **over**
3 based your decision ~~in~~ **on**
4 just for ~~funny~~ **fun**
5 couldn't stay there ~~no~~ longer **any**
6 Come ~~in!~~ **on**

4

1 know (you never know)
2 true (come true)
3 in (believe in), longer (not any longer)
4 too (life's too short)
5 something (there's something in it)
6 guess (anyone's guess)

5

Answer from a South African person.

I read my horoscope when I happen to see it in a magazine. It's good for a bit of fun, but I don't believe in it for a minute.

Unit 31

1

1 bright	5 here and there
2 chances	6 die out
3 out of luck, row	7 pick up
4 the most	8 start off

2

1 started	5 picked/brightened
2 make	6 clouded
3 here	7 out
4 died	

Unit 32

1

1 ~~drop out~~ **drop off**
2 ~~wink a sleep~~ **sleep a wink**
3 ~~later nights~~ **late nights**
4 ~~fall to sleep~~ **fall asleep**
5 ~~made a lie-in~~ **had a lie-in**
6 ~~turn and toss~~ **toss and turn**
7 ~~before the last~~ **before last**
8 ~~worry sick~~ **worried sick**

2

1 I didn't sleep a wink. / I was wide awake all night.
2 I had a lie-in.
3 I was worried sick.
4 I was tossing and turning all night. / I tossed and turned all night.
5 I was wide awake.
6 I managed to drop off (to sleep). / I managed to fall asleep.
7 I slept like a log. / I had a good night.
8 I had an early night.

3

Answers from a Czech person.

1 I always have problems dropping off when travelling by train.
2 No, I had a very good night last night.
3 Yes, I have had three very late nights this week.
4 I hardly ever fall asleep watching television.
5 This morning I had a lie-in. I usually get up late at weekends.
6 Whenever I have problems I toss and turn and cannot fall asleep.
7 If only I could always have such a good sleep as the night before last.
8 I am worried sick, and not only about my English.

Unit 33

1

1 I'm afraid I'm ~~at~~ the red. **in**
2 I cut back ~~in~~ my spending. **on**
3 Pay ~~out~~ the money you borrowed. **back**
4 He's been ~~on~~ debt for years. **in**
5 How will he pay ~~over~~ his debts? **off**
6 Go to the bank and pay the cheque ~~on~~. **in**
7 She's absolutely rolling ~~on~~ money. **in**
8 You have to save ~~out~~ for it. **up**

2

1	out	4	well, badly	7	rolling
2	careful	5	hard	8	ends
3	cut	6	off		

3

Answers from a New Zealander.

1 I don't take money out of my account once a week. I use my credit card as much as possible so I can get air points with Air New Zealand.
2 I'm quite careful with my money. I save as much as possible so I can sometimes afford to do special things.
3 I enjoy the challenge of cutting back on my spending from time to time, e.g. seeing how cheaply I can make a delicious meal instead of eating out or getting takeaways.
4 Senior doctors and specialists are well off. Nurses are underpaid and often try to get a pay rise.
5 Some elderly people are hard up, some are well off, but most would be somewhere in between.
6 A lot of young people live with their parents for longer than 18 years because it's cheaper than renting a flat, and Mum does all the cooking, washing, and cleaning for them.
7 People who are rolling in money have to pay higher taxes, but not enough in comparison with the average person.
8 Lawyers don't usually have any problem making ends meet.

4

1 the ~~post~~ of the transport **cost**
2 my ~~honey's~~ worth **money**
3 to ~~rub~~ up a huge bill **run**
4 we got ~~nipped~~ off **ripped**
5 keep your ~~lead~~ above water **head**
6 ran out ~~on~~ money **of**
7 it didn't cost a ~~jenny~~ **penny**
8 save for a rainy ~~way~~ **day**

5

1 He runs the café on a shoestring.
2 I didn't expect him to rip me off like that.
3 Save (your money) for a rainy day.
4 It's hard to keep my head above water.
5 It didn't cost a penny.
6 The insurance covered the cost of the hospital.
7 Did you get your money's worth?
8 I've run out of dollars.

Unit 34

1

1	another	4	burn	7	cut
2	in	5	up	8	go
3	starving	6	go		

2

1	on	4	Make
2	were, wouldn't	5	starving, fill
3	Whatever	6	down

3

Answers from a British person.

1 If you want to go on a diet, try to eat lots of fresh fruit and vegetables.
2 If I were you, I wouldn't eat so much cheese.
3 Whatever you do, don't forget to drink lots of water.
4 Make sure you take plenty of exercise.
5 If you're starving, don't fill yourself up with biscuits.
6 Try to cut down on drinks like fizzy lemonade.

4

1	turn it up	4	rid of it
2	heat it up	5	make use of them
3	come off	6	threw it out

5

1 Please don't throw **out** those pears. OR … throw those pears **out**.
2 He needs to chop **up** the onions. OR … chop the onions **up**.
3 I couldn't get the olives out **of** the jar.
4 Could you turn the oven **down**, please? OR … turn **down** the oven, please.
5 I turned the tomatoes **into** a soup.
6 If it's too hot, let it cool **down**. OR Let it cool **down** if it's too hot.

Unit 35

1

1	in	4	on	7	up
2	on	5	into	8	on
3	away	6	away		

2

1	run	4	in	7	handed
2	trouble	5	from	8	up
3	vain	6	increase/rise		

3

1 Dan will get into trouble for this.
2 He got away with the crime.
3 The police are on the lookout for two thieves.

4 The escaped murderer is now behind bars.
5 They let the boy off.
6 She ran away from home to escape from her father.
7 The barman was beaten up by the gang. OR The gang beat up the barman.
8 We looked for the ring in vain. OR We looked in vain for the ring.

4

1 been **getting** into trouble
2 been **on** the lookout
3 one boy **broke** into
4 he was **caught** red-handed
5 the police just let him **off**
6 able to **get** away with it
7 tricked a resident **into** letting
8 they then ran **off** with
9 they are still on **the** run
10 should be **behind** bars

Unit 36

1

1 P   2 N   3 N   4 N   5 P   6 P

2

1	make	3	time	5	stood
2	got	4	make, thank	6	up

3

1 giving me **a** hard time
2 next **to** nothing
3 make **it** as a nurse
4 to **get** behind
5 working **all** hours
6 my brother **to** thank for that

4

1 a ~~nine-for-five~~ job **nine-to-five**
2 give him a sack **the**
3 checking up ~~against~~ you **on**
4 deal ~~on~~ lots of banks **with**
5 hard ~~with~~ it all day **at**
6 make matters ~~worst~~ **worse**

5

1 turned me down
2 handed in her notice
3 taken on
4 gave her the sack
5 checks up / has been checking up
6 cut out

6

Answers from a Brazilian person.

Yes, for some job positions.
Not really. I'm a teacher, so my working hours are quite different.
Yes I have – the last time I quit a job.
My boss does that all the time.
No. I've always worked as a teacher, and I'm really cut out for that.

Unit 37

1

1 d   2 e   3 b   4 c   5 f   6 a

2

1 we had to take **out** a loan
2 they think they can make **a** go of it
3 they sold it as a **going** concern
4 it could still fall **through**
5 I decided to **take** on the job
6 must be out of your **mind** to lend money to Karl
7 we still have a long **way** to go
8 got the business **up** and running
9 it's been **turned** into a chemist's

3

1 corners	5	for
2 *Both are correct.*	6	meet
3 out of	7	up
4 vicious	8	worse

4

1 notice	3	meet	5	worse
2 circle	4	race	6	world

5

1 dream	4	notice	7	up
2 opt	5	up		
3 race	6	ends		

Unit 38

1

I didn't get my money back.
They've sold out of milk.
I sent off for a book.
She splashed out on a new coat.
The wine is on special offer.
He wrapped the gift up for me.
I always shop around for bargains.
I got the bike for nothing.

2

1 my money back	5	sent off/away for them
2 rather than	6	on (special) offer
3 on sale	7	shop around
4 splashed out	8	for nothing

3

Answers from a Czech person.
Yes, I have, and I've got it back.
Yes, I do, especially clothes and shoes.
Yes, I do. I prefer to use the Internet to buy electronic gadgets and furniture.
Yes, I browse the Internet first.
No, only when I need them.
It was a year ago. I bought a very nice and very expensive leather jacket.
Yes, it was a huge bunch of flowers in a small shop.
No, never.

Unit 39

1

1 by, round	5	ended
2 pop	6	out
3 ran/bumped	7	tea
4 turned	8	put

2

1 night	3	halves	5	up
2 out	4	corner	6	out

3

Answers from a Norwegian person.
1 I wish I could more often! When my husband is away on business, I take a book to bed for an early night.
2 My husband and I don't eat out often because it's hard to find a babysitter, but we eat out as a family most weekends.
3 Yes, I go halves when I eat out with a friend.
4 Yes, there are several, including a Chinese restaurant.
5 A couple of times a month. We get a lot of family coming to stay with us.
6 When my mum came to stay we went out for a meal; that was about three weeks ago.

4

1 time	4	sardines
2 *Both are correct.*	5	take
3 into it	6	*Both are correct.*

5

1 feel	5	keep
2 threw/chucked	6	out
3 asking	7	into
4 jump	8	hands

6

Answers from an Argentinian person.

1 Sometimes my children ask me little favours, such as driving them to their friends' or buying them a new computer game.
2 No.
3 Yes, a bakery. The first owner retired and sold the shop to a younger couple.
4 No, I am patient and wait for my turn. I get extremely angry when others push in – it's not fair.
5 Yes, some neighbourhoods are more dangerous than others.
6 Nothing much. I plan to relax after a long working day.

Unit 40

1
1 c   2 d   3 f   4 a   5 e   6 h   7 g   8 b

2
1 up, fall   3 breath, down, keep
2 sudden, turned, Sure

3
1 other people   4 little by little
2 it's hard to learn   5 enter the race
3 out of shape   6 start doing it

4
1 took   6 comes
2 come   7 shape
3 by   8 question/matter
4 for   9 at
5 looking   10 good

5

Answers from a Czech person.

Every year I spend my summer holiday at the seaside as I love swimming. I have never had to work at swimming – it just came to me naturally. I am sure swimming must do everybody good. It helps people of any age stay in shape.

Unit 41

1
1 off   4 *Both are correct.*
2 out   5 away
3 *Both are correct.*   6 *Both are correct.*

2
1 take **your** time
2 We set **off/out** after breakfast
3 get **away** at least once a year

4 turned **out** to be
5 got a lot **out** of it
6 all **over** the place

3
1 away   2 season   3 in   4 get   5 off

4

Answers from a New Zealander.

1 We try to get away every long weekend (four to six times a year). Often it's only a short distance, e.g. one or two hours from home. In addition, we usually have two weeks at Christmas to travel round New Zealand.
2 Last year we took a holiday out of season and stayed in motels in camping grounds. We enjoyed it so much; we'll certainly do it again.
3 We book holidays in advance if we're travelling overseas. If we're travelling in New Zealand, we prefer to take a risk and hope we find somewhere nice to stay. So far, so good.
4 We usually get around in our car. We've got a station wagon, so there's plenty of room for luggage for only two people.
5 If we're travelling a long distance we stop off about halfway, but we usually book that accommodation in advance.

5
1 an equal amount
2 not near
3 in a tent
4 it is different from usual
5 it has a positive effect on you
6 happy

6
1 do (do her good)
2 go (go away) ('get' is also possible: get away)
3 change (make a change)
4 track (off the beaten track)
5 air (in the open air)
6 happens/happened (as it happens/happened)
7 once

7
1 away   3 open   5 on
2 beaten   4 it   6 do

8

Answers from a Norwegian person.

1 No, not really. I'd never plan to go away on holiday alone. I've been with friends, though.
2 Yes. We don't like package holidays. We try to find places away from the tourist areas.
3 Yes, very much so. We like to get into the country or go to the seaside.

4 No, I'm not a tent person! I like to go home to a comfortable bed. I used to rough it when I was a student, but those days are gone!

5 No, I haven't.

6 Holidays really do me good.

Unit 42

1

kick off	cheer somebody on
win the toss	at full strength
take advantage of something	send somebody off

2

1 settle   3 kick   5 sent, off
2 full   4 close, on

3

1 cheer   3 kicked   5 sent
2 get   4 lost   6 advantage

4

1 I've had **enough** of English
2 they **got** the better of us
3 in **return** I teach her English
4 signed **up** for the evening course
5 she **took** no part in the race
6 help to liven **up** the lessons
7 **to** begin with
8 do you think it will catch **on**

5

1 take part   4 something to do
2 liven things up   5 make a/any difference
3 catch on   6 To begin with / To start with

Unit 43

1

We set off early.
I loaded up the car.
I usually stick to main roads.
Let's break the journey.
We can take a short cut.
Please look out for somewhere to eat.

2

1 fill   4 time   7 A, B
2 case   5 set   8 stick
3 cut   6 out

3

Answers from a Syrian person.
No, I don't. I fill it up on the way.
Yes, I do. I don't want to rush on the day of travel.
Yes, I try to do that. No one wants to get stuck in traffic or arrive late.

No, I don't.
I do it for five to ten minutes almost every hour.
No, I don't. I focus on driving safely.
Yes, I do – when I have one.

4

1 call   4 go
2 stand   5 middle
3 *Both are correct.*   6 jump

5

1 down   3 off   5 up
2 down/over   4 down   6 in/over

6

1 off   4 after   7 knocked
2 jumped   5 in/over
3 pull   6 stand

7

Answers from a Brazilian person.
I've definitely had some problems on the road. Two months ago I was driving along a road unaware that the speed limit was 100 kph. As I'd left home late, I speeded up so that I would manage to arrive at my appointment on time. A police officer made me pull over and gave me a $100 fine. To make matters worse, my car broke down five miles away from the police station and I had to call out the emergency services and pay another $100. As it's said: it never rains, but it pours!

Unit 44

1

1 if ~~the~~ need be
2 has ~~put~~ her heart **set**
3 feel like ~~go~~ out **going**
4 pick and ~~select~~ **choose**
5 they ~~can~~ do with **could**
6 I'm dying for ~~to have~~ something to eat. OR I'm dying ~~for~~ to have something to eat.

2

1 I feel like a rest now.
2 I could do with a good dictionary.
3 Can you make do with this small map?
4 You can't always pick and choose.
5 I'm dying to see his new girlfriend.
6 I can't do without my address book.
7 We can take the car if need be.
8 She has set her heart on a career in music.

3

Answers from a Brazilian person and a Czech person.
1 I could do with the latest electronic gadgets.

2 I run my own business and so I work unsocial hours six days a week. I know I couldn't work harder. If I did, I'd go crazy.

3 I couldn't do without my laptop and email.

4 I usually feel like going out in the evening, especially if I can sleep late the next day.

5 I'm dying to get my own flat.

6 I don't let myself set my heart on things I know I can't have.

7 I could make do without a car, but I'd rather not.

8 I do care about money. It enables me to do things I enjoy, such as eating out in nice restaurants, getting nice clothes, and travelling.

9 I believe you can't always pick and choose in life.

Unit 45

1
1 *Both are correct.*
2 go ahead
3 put off
4 fix up
5 called off
6 *Both are correct.*

2
1 ahead, up
2 according
3 put
4 looking
5 off
6 make, bring
7 fix
8 on, off

Unit 46

1
1 She can't bear/stand big cities.
2 Football's not my cup of tea.
3 His life revolves around his work.
4 I've gone off meat.
5 I've got a sweet tooth.
6 They're mad about it.

2
1 liking
2 gone
3 into, bear/stand
4 cup, thing
5 mad
6 grows
7 revolves
8 lives

3
Answers from a South African person.
Although I don't like chips as much as I used to, I still enjoy eating them sometimes.
Yes, this is true for me, and my figure has paid the price!
I like camping as long as it is in relative comfort, for instance, at a campsite with hot, running water!
Classical music has grown on me too. I used to think it was quite interesting; now I love it.

Oh, quite so. Some of them make conversation too difficult.
Well, that sounds a little extreme. My family is central, but I try to balance all my interests.
I understand them because my work also sometimes threatens to swallow me up! However, I think they're making a big mistake.

Unit 47

1
1 d 2 g 3 f 4 h 5 a 6 b 7 c 8 e

2
1 knocked
2 down
3 up
4 write-off, ran/crashed
5 fallen/falling, together
6 up
7 down
8 to, throw

3
1 Our neighbour ~~was~~ burnt down
2 this one is falling ~~down~~ to pieces
3 it just fell ~~to~~ apart in my hands.
4 the oil tank blew ~~it~~ up.
5 tore it ~~up~~ to pieces.
6 in ~~its~~ place of it we built a small studio
7 why don't you just throw them out ~~off~~?
8 The firemen smashed ~~out~~ the door down

4
1 The building burnt down.
2 The car was a write-off. OR The car had to be written off.
3 Can't you throw away those papers? OR … throw those papers away?
4 They had to knock down the building. OR … knock the building down.
5 The book fell to bits.
6 The motorcyclist crashed into a brick wall.
7 I sewed up the hole in my pocket.
8 I sold the chair and put a sofa in its place.

5
1 apart
2 throw
3 together/up
4 up
5 sewing
6 place
7 put

Unit 48

1
1 B 2 E 3 B 4 B 5 E 6 E

2
1 out
2 up, down
3 up, up
4 out, out
5 up
6 off, up, in

3

1 on
2 ground
3 out
4 shape
5 down
6 came
7 up
8 about

4

1 I'm starting my essay from scratch.
2 The problems occurred early on.
3 Judging by/from his story, the boys are innocent.
4 They've broken new ground.
5 The house is taking shape.
6 How did these changes come about?
7 They've knocked down the offices. OR They've knocked the offices down.
8 I'm sure they'll come up with a solution.

Unit 49

1

1 out of date
2 at the crack of dawn
3 on impulse
4 once in a blue moon
5 in next to no time
6 for the time being

2

1 spur
2 no / next to no
3 out
4 dawn
5 day
6 blue
7 time, time
8 day, day

3

Answers from a Czech person.

1 No, I never get up at the crack of dawn! I love to have a lie-in.
2 I'm not able to do so as I am a very slow person.
3 No, I always do my best to have a regular check-up.
4 I'm sorry to say that I've never ridden a horse.
5 That's true. I hate fashion and I love shopping in second-hand shops. I definitely prefer feeling comfortable to being dressed up according to the latest fashion.
6 Yes, I hope so.
7 That's right. Nevertheless I can imagine myself living in another country without any problems.
8 No, I'm not that type of person.
9 I always think about the future. I could never live from day to day.

5

1 on the dot
2 over and over again / time and time again
3 kept me waiting
4 fixed up
5 at the last minute
6 held up
7 the other day
8 turn up

6

1 time
2 keep
3 turn
4 minute
5 up
6 breath

7

Answers from a New Zealander.

1 I do more than arrive in good time! I prefer to get to work nice and early so my day can start in a relaxed way.
2 I never keep people waiting unless something totally out of the ordinary stops me arriving early.
3 I don't turn up late for social arrangements because it's considered impolite.
4 I seldom do things at the last minute. I normally do things well ahead of time.
5 I sometimes get held up if the Director of Studies wants to discuss something with me, but my class is able to continue without me for a few minutes.
6 I don't feel as if I'm wasting my breath when I give advice, because my students are very keen to learn.

Unit 50

1

in all | at the very least | quite a few | add up | in total | lose count | round about

2

1 We saw dozens **of** rabbits in the fields.
2 She has quite **a** few friends in Dubai.
3 We lost **count** of the number of guests.
4 The flight costs $900 at **the** very least.
5 We were surprised that the bill came **to** €50.
6 If you **take** three away (OR **take** away three) from seven, you get four. OR If you **take** four away from seven you get three.

3

1 all/total, many
2 out, lose
3 round, at
4 in, came
5 up, took
6 up, quite

4

1 twenties
2 million
3 third
4 one, two
5 a hundred / a hundred and ten
6 second
7 two, two
8 fifty-fifty

5

1 I'm not a hundred per cent certain where he is.
2 Ten to one he'll be late.
3 She had second thoughts about the flat.
4 He must be in his mid-forties.
5 They did the questions one by one.

6 He puts his work first.
7 Shall we go fifty-fifty on the petrol?

Unit 51

1
1 G 2 B 3 G 4 B 5 B 6 G

2
1 in **a** hurry
2 were **all** over the place
3 take **my** time
4 has **had** it
5 **in** no time
6 I haven't **a** clue

3
1 in (such) a hurry
2 (a bit) on the small side
3 in (next to) no time
4 killing me
5 do the trick
6 haven't (got) a clue / haven't (got) the faintest idea / 've no idea
7 all over the place
8 sorting out

4
1 c 2 d 3 a 4 f 5 b 6 e

5
1 feet (rushed off our feet)
2 chance (is in with a chance)
3 time (one step at a time)
4 stretch (at full stretch)
5 out (help us out)
6 depth (out of her depth)
7 off (switch off)
8 word (put in a good word)

Unit 52

1
1 for
2 *Both are correct.*
3 grade
4 *Both are correct.*
5 working
6 *Both are correct.*

2
1 life
2 account/consideration
3 Best
4 case
5 sorry
6 turned

3
1 were you
2 shoes/place/position
3 can/could
4 better

Answers from a British person.
1 Penny, if I were you, I'd try to find out more about the new job.
2 Penny, in your shoes, I'd take the job with more money. It could lead to other things.
3 You could always ask your present boss for a pay rise.
4 I think you'd be better off doing an interesting job, even if the money's not very good.

Unit 53

1
1 ever since
2 in the meantime
3 *Both are correct.*
4 *Both are correct.*
5 even if
6 *Both are correct.*

2
1 as soon as / the minute (that), as well
2 at last
3 ever since
4 as if / as though
5 On the one hand, on the other (hand), In addition

Unit 54

1
1 foremost
2 tired
3 later
4 figures
5 another / the other
6 take
7 off
8 word
9 quiet
10 furious

2
come and go
one way or another
lovely and warm
wait and see
bright and early
word for word
now and then
backwards and forwards
fast and furious

3
1 word for word
2 wait and see
3 bright and early
4 backwards and forwards
5 now and then
6 sick and tired
7 one way or another
8 up and down
9 give or take
10 peace and quiet

4
1 facts and figures
2 fast and furious
3 word for word
4 sick and tired
5 lovely and quiet
6 one way or another / the other

7 comes and goes
8 sooner or later
9 lovely and cold
10 on and off / off and on

Unit 55

1
1 in
2 by
3 under
4 on
5 out of
6 off

2
1 out of control
2 on duty
3 on purpose
4 out of luck
5 out of tune
6 in working order

3
1 season
2 tune
3 sight
4 order
5 under
6 theory, practice

4
1 in
2 for
3 at
4 in
5 for
6 in
7 at
8 in

5
1 of post
2 mind
3 mistake
4 phone
5 length
6 away
7 place
8 way

Unit 56

1
1 h 2 e 3 d 4 b 5 f 6 c 7 i 8 g 9 a

2
1 end the cat's life
2 leave
3 got better
4 didn't go
5 wait for something to happen
6 on holiday

3
1 pick it up
2 go away
3 get out
4 come on
5 put it down
6 get off

4
1 on, on, in
2 on, away
3 in
4 on, up

5
1 How is your English coming on?
2 Could you pick my trousers up (for me)? OR pick up my trousers (for me)
3 Are you going away this summer?
4 When does the train get in to Paris?
5 Hold on (tight)!
6 What time do you get off work?

Unit 57

1
1 make up for ~~losing~~ time **lost**
2 catch the nurse's ~~eyes~~ **eye**
3 lend me ~~an arm~~ **a hand**
4 going round ~~in a circle~~ **in circles**
5 I'd better ~~do~~ a move **make**
6 been on the ~~going~~ since 7 o'clock **go**
7 ~~sleeping~~ the night **staying**
8 keep ~~her face straight~~ **a straight face**
9 learn to ~~say~~ the time **tell**
10 Could I pick your ~~mind~~ **brain/brains**

2
1 P 2 P 3 A 4 E 5 A 6 P 7 E 8 A

3
1 To get some ideas or information.
2 You either like them very much, or you dislike them.
3 You start laughing.
4 They put the plates, knives, forks, etc. on the table ready for a meal.
5 You've been very busy.
6 You're giving your opinion in a very direct way.
7 Your skin becomes red or tanned.
8 You don't understand the main point of what someone has been saying.

4
1 stay
2 keep
3 give/lend
4 catch
5 laid
6 missed
7 make
8 speak
9 stretch
10 caught

5
Answers from an Italian person.
1 I usually do it because I'm the first back home after work.
2 Yes, but I use a lot of suncream to avoid sunburn.
3 I can't stand eating lamb because my mum made me eat it very often when I was a child.
4 Well, I try not to do that unless I am with my husband or my dearest friends; anyway, I always try to be tactful, and not too direct.
5 When I was a university student. It was fun.
6 I would like my students to do that but it rarely happens.

Unit 58

1
1 get on **with** your life
2 get the **upper** hand
3 get the hang **of** making chips

4 get away from **it** all.
5 get the most **out** of my computer.
6 get **rid** of rats

2

1 get ahead	5 the upper hand
2 get over	6 get rid of
3 get through	7 get away from
4 get into	8 on with

3

1 S 2 D 3 S 4 S 5 D 6 S 7 D 8 D

4

1 know	4 way
2 together	5 on/along
3 on/along	6 up

5

Answers from a Brazilian person.
1 We met in college and immediately hit it off.
2 Hardly ever. Only on special occasions, such as weddings and Christmas.
3 I'm doing well, I believe. I'm always trying to improve my skills, though.
4 Not as often as I'd like. I give in to others more frequently than I should.
5 No one in particular. I don't have much in common with anyone in my family.
6 Not that I can recall.

Unit 59

1

1 you can take it ~~and~~ leave it **or**
2 he knows how to take care ~~for~~ himself **of**
3 I told her to take ~~her~~ easy **it**
4 taking your ~~live~~ in your hands **life**
5 I was really taken ~~back~~ **aback**
6 we won't ~~make~~ it lying down **take**
7 I don't know why he took ~~again~~ her **against**
8 I asked my boss for a few days ~~of~~ **off**

2

1 Just (relax and) take it easy.
2 He took his life in his hands.
3 He takes off his boss. OR He takes his boss off.
4 I was really taken aback by the job cuts.
5 She's experienced and can take care of herself.
6 She took a day off (work) today because she was ill.

3

1 for	5 bright	9 way
2 your	6 eye	10 down
3 age	7 back	
4 to	8 to	

4

1 me/you in the eye	5 up to her
2 on the bright side	6 young for his age
3 your best	7 the other way
4 down on him	8 to him for help/advice

5

Answers from a British person.
1 I was a happy child, but I've been happiest as an adult with my own children.
2 Yes, I'm an optimistic person, and I'm usually able to look on the bright side.
3 I used to look up to people in positions of power, but I don't any more. They often don't impress me at all.
4 I know I should look out for other people who need help, but I sometimes fail to do so.
5 If the person seemed to be hungry or in need, I might look the other way.
6 I really believe in telling the truth and I can usually look people in the eye when I do.
7 People occasionally look to me for advice – usually this would be my daughters, but sometimes my colleagues.
8 Yes, I do try to look my best when I go out.
9 Unfortunately I don't look young for my age!

Unit 60

1

1 available
2 conscious
3 find it easy to do
4 receive it from someone who has died
5 doesn't succeed
6 becomes exciting

2

1 coming and **going** over the next few days
2 come a **long** way.
3 finally came **out**, nobody could believe it
4 he finally came **to/round** and started talking
5 the moon came **out** – it was so romantic
6 so bad that I **passed** out
7 come **into** any money
8 coming **along/on** well

3

1 g 2 f 3 h 4 a 5 c 6 b 7 d 8 e

4

1 through	5 out
2 round	6 along
3 according	7 far
4 up	8 off

Answer key to review units

Introduction to idioms and phrasal verbs

Unit 1

1

1 suddenly
2 very fast
3 always
4 stupid/silly
5 anxious/upset
6 see/notice

2

1 How **come**, **make** sense
2 steer **clear** of him, rings a **bell**
3 in **the** distance, running flat **out**
4 How **on** earth, running **like** mad

Unit 2

1

1 don't ask me
2 more or less
3 better late than never
4 a stone's throw
5 thank heavens
6 a piece of cake
7 famous last words
8 change your mind
9 get nowhere

2

1 main (in the main)
2 fonder (absence makes the heart grow fonder)
3 grief (Good grief!)
4 nerves (gets on your nerves)
5 error (trial and error)
6 life (a fact of life)

Unit 3

1

1 once in a blue moon
2 pulling my leg
3 on my doorstep
4 fresh blood
5 go public
6 with reference to

2

1 the back ~~part~~ of a lorry
2 it's still ~~too~~ early days
3 caught ~~up~~ my eye
4 on ~~her~~ purpose
5 and by ~~in~~ the way
6 it's a long ~~time~~ story

Unit 4

1

1 drink less coffee
2 taking care of them
3 put on a piece of clothing
4 behaves like him
5 they've had a row
6 represent

2

1 rub it out
2 came across
3 look up ('pick up' would also be possible)
4 show up ('turn up' would also be possible)
5 check in
6 made it up
7 going out with
8 look it up

Unit 5

1

1 She went on and **on** about her illness.
2 Brenda was messing **about/around** in the garden.
3 The village was cut **off** by deep snow.
4 The children carried **on** working until lunchtime.
5 The boys were hanging **around/about** outside the club.
6 There was a lot of money lying **around/about**.

2

1 lazed around / lazed about / messed around / messed about
2 get on
3 see my brother off
4 going on
5 lying around / lying about
6 keeps on
7 dragged on
8 stayed on

Unit 6

1

1 bring
2 up
3 *Both are correct.*
4 get
5 go
6 *Both are correct.*

2

1 Please tidy up the office / tidy the office up.
2 I'll have to take these trousers back (to the shop) / take back these trousers.
3 When do you think he'll get back from lunch?
4 I flicked through the magazine.

5 Maggie rang – she wants you to phone/ring/call her back.
6 Did you go through / look through the figures?

Unit 7

1

1	goes	5	doing	9	breaks
2	turns	6	breaks	10	go
3	put	7	goes	11	goes
4	tied	8	do	12	turns

2

1	go off	4	switch on	7	broke down
2	go down	5	come up	8	done up
3	do up	6	put on	9	go off

Thinking, learning, and knowledge

Unit 8

1

1 b   2 a   3 b   4 a   5 b   6 b

2

1 It's just the tip of the iceberg.
2 Make sure you go over your work carefully.
3 OK, let's call it a day.
4 Mark, swap places with Eve.
5 It's no good if you don't listen.
6 He's taking the course seriously.
7 First of all, turn to page 45.
8 You can leave out Exercise 3. OR You can leave Exercise 3 out.

Unit 9

1

1	understand	4	know, remember
2	concentrate/focus	5	learn, effort
3	difficult/hard	6	forget

2

1	getting	6	error
2	catch	7	get
3	keep	8	heart
4	up	9	racking
5	in	10	come

Unit 10

1

1	grips	5	through
2	work	6	steer

3	crossed	7	run
4	world	8	breathe

2

1 My mind just **went** blank in the exam.
2 I decided to miss **out** the first question.
3 I read the letter but it didn't **make** sense.
4 She did it to the **best** of her ability.
5 I must **get** down to some work now.
6 I **get** bogged down in too much detail. OR I **get** much too bogged down in detail.

Unit 11

1

1 f   2 c   3 g   4 h   5 a   6 e   7 d   8 b

2

1 it's **early** days
2 got **off** on the wrong foot
3 pulling **his** weight
4 appears to **sit** back
5 Her tutor **thinks**
6 she's in **her** element
7 does her **best**
8 she'll **go** far
9 to bring **out** the best
10 gets **on** better

Unit 12

1

1	making	4	for himself
2	twice	5	over
3	it over	6	straight

Unit 13

1

1 knows it like the **back** of her hand
2 no **good** at it
3 **slipped** my mind
4 **take** it in
5 good with my **hands**
6 out of **practice**
7 knows what he's **doing**

Communicating with people

Unit 14

1

1 e   2 g   3 b   4 a   5 h   6 d   7 f   8 c

Unit 15

1
1 edgeways
2 across
3 down
4 talks
5 told him off
6 face
7 behind

Unit 16

1
1 get back
2 earth
3 hold on
4 charge up
5 top up
6 hung
7 through
8 fortune
9 line
The word in the grey squares is 'telephone'.

Unit 17

1
1 here you ~~have~~ **are/go**.
2 Why ~~no?~~ **not**
3 as ~~usually~~ **usual/always**
4 ~~who's~~ up? **what's**
5 hurry ~~on~~ **up**
6 Guess ~~that?~~ **what**
7 Just ~~tell~~ when **say**
8 ~~Why~~ come? **How**
9 Time's ~~over~~ **up**
10 all the ~~better~~ **best**
11 kind ~~off~~ **of**
12 it's up ~~for~~ you **to**

Unit 18

1
1 T 2 F 3 T 4 F 5 T 6 T 7 F 8 T

2
1 again (You can say that again)
2 yourself (see for yourself)
3 goes (see how it goes)
4 least (to say the least)
5 no (I wouldn't say no)
6 not (I don't see why not)
7 see (let me see)
8 say (I'd rather not say)

Unit 19

1
1 hard ~~lucky~~ **luck**
2 It's ~~not~~ of your business **none**
3 Good ~~heaven!~~ **heavens**
4 ~~No~~ at all **Not**
5 It's all the same ~~for~~ me **to**
6 Goodness knows ~~it~~
7 ~~no~~ bad **not**
8 ~~don't~~ mind **never**

2
1 Bless you.
2 Go ahead.
3 Thank goodness.
4 You're joking.
5 Hear! Hear!
6 I beg your pardon.
7 I'm not bothered.
8 Mind your own business.
9 If you like.
10 Yes and no.

Unit 20

1
1 No
2 Yes
3 No
4 No
5 Yes
6 Yes
7 No
8 Yes
9 Yes
10 No

2
1 must dash
2 wait up
3 to do
4 about time
5 up to
6 get together
7 my love
8 after all

Unit 21

1
1 far
2 make
3 point
4 agree
5 extent
6 honest
7 pros
8 doubt
9 highly
10 thing
The idiom in the grey squares is 'fair enough'.

Unit 22

1
1 act the fool
2 tell someone off
3 make fun of someone
4 hit the roof
5 not on speaking terms
6 take a joke
7 for a laugh
8 burst out laughing

People and relationships

Unit 23

1

A man is hanging up his jacket / hanging his jacket up, a boy is standing on tiptoe, a doctor is shaking hands with someone, a couple are holding hands, the receptionist is throwing something away, a man is blowing his nose, a woman is sitting with her legs crossed and her arms folded.

1 yes   2 yes   3 no   4 no   5 yes   6 no

Unit 24

1

1 b   2 f   3 a   4 e   5 c   6 h   7 d   8 g

2

1 grew	4 trouble	7 life
2 brought	5 stayed	8 out
3 looked	6 nothing	

Unit 25

1

1 live off
2 give in
3 goes on
4 leave (them) alone
5 feel (at) ease
6 gets away
7 stand (on your own two) feet
8 take offence
9 be yourself
10 get through

Unit 26

1

1 let	4 myself	7 invite
2 lend	5 turn	8 moving
3 lift	6 common	

2

1 put ~~out~~ with him **up**
2 run the risk ~~in~~ **of**
3 ~~take~~ it to an end **bring**
4 ~~round~~ and about **out**
5 getting ~~long~~ with them **along**
6 help her ~~off~~ **out**
7 ~~held~~ him company **kept**
8 break ~~an~~ ice **the**

Unit 27

1

1 crossed	4 edge	7 about
2 state	5 lives	8 tears
3 skin	6 thrilled	

2

have/get butterflies in your stomach
over the moon
I didn't know whether to laugh or cry
get cold feet about sth
it breaks your heart (to see or do sth)
shake like a leaf

Unit 28

1

1 first	5 between	9 shoes
2 type	6 stick	10 chat
3 world	7 good	11 build
4 crazy	8 wrong	12 split

The word in the grey squares is 'relationship'.

Unit 29

1

1 angry/frustrated/upset
2 happier
3 continue
4 angry/annoyed
5 angry
6 opinion

2

1 change the subject
2 the last minute
3 give and take
4 take it into account
5 round the bend
6 over and over again
7 put it off
8 show off
9 by myself

Unit 30

1

1 believe	4 ground	7 fun
2 lose	5 heart	8 feet
3 far	6 comes	

2

1	over	4	keeping	7	in
2	way	5	any	8	know
3	else	6	say		

Everyday topics

Unit 31

1

1	over	5	of luck
2	chances are	6	a row
3	out	7	up
4	up	8	on the bright side

Unit 32

1

wide awake, have a lie-in, sleep like a log, toss and turn, the night before last, not sleep a wink, worried sick, fall asleep

Unit 33

1

1	up	4	live	7	up
2	ends	5	pay	8	cover
3	cost	6	cut	9	careful

Unit 34

1

1	turn/heat	5	rid	9	on
2	chop	6	into	10	cut
3	down	7	make		
4	cool	8	out		

Unit 35

1

He won't get away with the robbery.
They broke into a shop.
They beat him up quite badly.
They caught him red-handed.
They're on the lookout for the robbers.
The thief ran off with my wallet.
She could get into trouble with the police.
The prisoner is still on the run.

2

1	hold-up	5	the rise / the increase
2	vain	6	away from home
3	bars	7	let him off
4	break-in	8	into trouble

Unit 36

1

checking ~~it~~ up on me
I was up to ~~for~~ the job
To make ~~the~~ matters worse
stand ~~up~~ by me either
I handed ~~them~~ in my notice
I was taken ~~down~~ on as a medical secretary
I wasn't really cut ~~off~~ out for it
they gave ~~to~~ me the sack

2

1	down	3	time	5	nothing
2	five	4	thank	6	it

Unit 37

1

1 B   2 G   3 B   4 G   5 B   6 G   7 G   8 B

2

1	out	3	on	5	for
2	into	4	up	6	up

Unit 38

1

1	for	4	offer	7	rather
2	send	5	wrap	8	around
3	sold	6	get		

Out and about

Unit 39

1

1 feel **like** going out
2 talked **me** into it
3 just **round** the corner
4 thinking of **trying** it out
5 packed **in** like sardines
6 eat **out** on a Saturday night
7 you're asking **for** trouble
8 we bumped **into** Susie
9 ended **up** back at her flat
10 a pretty late **night** after all

2

1 Shall we eat out?
2 The owner threw us out.
3 He jumped the queue.
4 That music isn't my cup of tea.
5 Shall we go halves?
6 That shop has changed hands.
7 He took exception to Martin's comments.
8 I would keep away from her.

Unit 40

1

1	forward	4	shape	7	out, sudden
2	come	5	move	8	catch
3	good	6	after		

2

1 to slow **down**
2 fell **behind** the others
3 holding everyone **up** so they went on
4 turned **round/around** and walked
5 I have to work **at** it
6 to go in **for** that competition
7 She took **up** swimming
8 keep **up** with him

Unit 41

1

1	get	5	happens	9	away
2	rough	6	air	10	around
3	advance	7	good		
4	season	8	beaten		

Unit 42

1

1	toss	4	strength
2	sent off	5	no part
3	cheering them on	6	popular/fashionable

2

1 a difference
2 part
3 do with sport
4 close to winning
5 enough of training
6 it up
7 up for an English course
8 off to a good start

Unit 43

1

1	down	5	fill	9	off/out
2	stand	6	case	10	pull
3	out	7	down		
4	break	8	nowhere		

2

1 drive off
2 jump the lights
3 in the middle of nowhere
4 call someone out
5 speed up
6 go after someone
7 grind to a halt
8 pull over
9 a short cut

Concepts

Unit 44

1

1	do	4	feel	7	need
2	care	5	pick	8	do
3	set	6	dying		

Answers from a British person.
1 I couldn't do without a car.
2 I couldn't care less about looking younger than I am.
3 I've set my heart on a holiday walking with friends.
4 At the moment I feel like reading my book – it's very gripping!
5 You can't pick and choose how wealthy you become.
6 I'm dying to go to the coast soon, to walk along a wild and windswept beach.
7 If need be I could sell the jewellery my mother-in-law left to me – but I'd much rather not.
8 I could make do with a smaller car.

Unit 45

1

1 mess ('muck' is also possible)
2 call
3 look
4 ahead
5 put
6 plan
7 forward
8 on
9 messes
The phrase in the grey squares is 'make plans'.

Unit 46

1

1 No, I'm not mad about it either.
2 No, it's not my cup of tea either.
3 Yes, it grows on you.
4 No, I've gone off it too / as well.
5 Yes, it's too spicy for my liking too / as well.
6 I agree. I can't bear them either.

Unit 47

1

DAMAGE or DESTRUCTION
tear sth to pieces
burn sth down
write sth off
fall apart
smash sth up
fall to bits
break sth down
crash into sth
REPAIR or CONSTRUCTION
sew sth up
put sth together
smarten sth up
put sth up

2

1 blew down   4 blew up
2 tore it to bits   5 fell to pieces
3 write off   6 throw them away

Unit 48

1

1 from   3 break   5 up
2 came   4 set   6 out

2

1 set up
2 fire / war
3 *All are possible.*
4 take up / give up
5 knocked down / closed down

Unit 49

1

1 on the dot
2 over and over again
3 out of date
4 on the spur of the moment
5 at the crack of dawn
6 for the time being

7 in no time
8 in good time

2

1 turned up   5 once in a blue moon
2 held up   6 time to time
3 kept us waiting   7 fix something up
4 last minute   8 wasting your breath

Unit 50

1

1 hundred per   5 third time
2 go fifty-fifty   6 early thirties
3 second thoughts   7 million years
4 dozens of

2

1 round about
2 in all/total
3 take away
4 quite a few/lot
5 comes to
6 Ten to one
7 put two and two together
8 at the (very) most

Unit 51

1

1 trick   5 stretch   9 depth
2 rushed   6 faintest   10 step
3 chance   7 top   11 had
4 over   8 killing
The phrase in the grey squares is 'I have no idea'.

Unit 52

1

1 were (if I were you)
2 sorry ('s feeling sorry for himself)
3 off (would be better off)
4 shoes/place/position (in his shoes/place/
   position)
5 could/can (could always)
6 account/consideration (take into account/
   consideration)
7 case (In that case)
8 luck (The best of luck)

Language

Unit 53

1

TIME
at last
ever since
as soon as
in the meantime
CONTRAST
on the other hand
even if
in spite of
EXTRA INFORMATION
as well
in addition

2

Possible answers.
1 a cup of coffee / a bowl of soup
2 it can be lonely / you have to pay all the bills
3 they'll get married
4 he works really hard
5 get home / get the information / know the answer
6 all her problems / her poor health
7 he turned up / the train arrived
8 his wife left him / he lost his job

Unit 54

1
1 sooner or later
2 sick and tired
3 up and down
4 backwards and forwards
5 now and then
6 word for word
7 give or take
8 bright and early
9 peace and quiet

Unit 55

1

IN
theory   writing   season
ON
purpose   duty   the phone
AT
length   once
BY
mistake   accident   return of post

FOR
certain   sure

2
1 out of control   5 out of order
2 on purpose   6 In the end
3 out of tune   7 at length
4 off duty   8 on my mind

Unit 56

1
1 Have you filled in the application form? OR Have you filled the application form in?
2 I picked up my dry cleaning at 4.00. OR I picked my dry cleaning up at 4.00.
3 She didn't get in to university. OR She applied to university but she didn't get in.
4 Come on, we're going to be late.
5 Her painting is coming on well.
6 Do you know when the train gets in?
7 The pain in my leg has gone away.
8 I put it down in my address book.
9 Could you hold/hang on for a couple of minutes?
10 Get off that chair!

Unit 57

1
1 lay, table   5 been, go
2 keep, face   6 give, hand
3 caught, sun   7 speak, mind
4 make, move   8 tell, time

2
1 progress
2 find out information
3 quickly, couldn't do it before
4 make somebody look at you
5 understand
6 go for a short walk

Unit 58

1
1 They **get on well / get along well**.
2 I'm sure he's good enough to **get through** the exam.
3 It took her some time to **get over** the shock.
4 I don't know how she **got into** journalism.
5 We often **get together** for a coffee in the morning.
6 She can't **get by** on £100 a week.

7 I think he **got a lot out of** the course. OR I think he **got the most out of** the course.
8 I think she's **getting on/along well**.

2
1 nearly/almost (is getting on for)
2 advantage (get the upper hand)
3 successful / doing well (get ahead)
4 you want (get your own way)
5 learn how to do it (get the hang of something)
4 bad or wrong (get mixed up in something)

Unit 59

1
1 P 2 N 3 N 4 P 5 N 6 P 7 P 8 N

2
1 look back on
2 take it easy
3 looks young for her age
4 looked up to
5 taken aback
6 looks the other way

Unit 60

1
1 go   3 gone   5 come
2 going   4 goes   6 comes

2
1 comes out   6 came to life
2 go round   7 go according
3 came to   8 came to nothing
4 came into   9 go far
5 come a long way
The phrasal verb in the grey squares is 'come along'.

List of spotlight boxes

Unit	Title of spotlight box	Page
4	Intransitive and transitive verbs	15
4	Phrasal verbs in dictionaries	15
5A	*go on*	16
6B	*get back*	19
8A	*hand sth in/out/round*	26
9B	Remembering and forgetting	29
10A	Idioms with *best*	30
11B	*think the world of sb/sth, not think much of sb/sth*, etc.	33
13	Idioms with *good*	35
14	*in touch*	39
16	*hang on, hang up, hang up on sb*	41
17	*be up to sb*	42
18B	Greetings	45
19A	*I beg your pardon*	46
19B	More idioms with *goodness*	47
20A	Sending greetings to other people	48
21A	*point*	50
22	Expressions with *joke*	52
23	Phrasal verbs with *knock*	58
24B	*stay out/in, stay up*	61
25A	*on the whole*	62
26B	*go on*	65
27A	Idioms with *mind*	66
29B	Expressing anger	71
30A	Idioms with *feet*	72
31	*start off, start out*	78
33A	Phrasal verbs with *pay*	80
34A	Giving advice	82
34B	*get rid of sth/sb*	83
35	Phrasal verbs and idioms with *run*	84
36A	*make it*	86
37A	*take sth on, take sb on*	88
40B	*shape*	97
41A	*get away*	98
45	*put sth off, put sth back*	108
47	*to pieces/bits*	110
48A	Phrasal verbs with *set*	112
49A	Idioms with *time*	114
50A	*count*	116
50B	*in his twenties*	117
53	*as well, in addition*	125
54	*lovely and …*	126
55A	*in/out of tune*, etc.	128
58B	*get on, get along*	135
60A	*come out*	138

Word list / Index

Here is an index of all the idioms and phrasal verbs, in alphabetical order according to the first word. The numbers are unit numbers. (If you cannot remember the first word, see the list of key words on page 187.)

(a bit) on the big/small side 51
a (good) laugh 1
a bag/bundle of nerves 3
a fact of life 2
a going concern 37
a laugh 1
a matter of time 49
a night/day out 39
a pain in the neck 2
a piece of cake 2
a short cut 43
a stone's throw 2
a vicious circle 37
a way of life / sb's way of life 24
a/one hundred per cent 50
absence makes the heart grow fonder 2
act/play the fool 22
add sth up 50
after all 20
again and again 29
all by yourself 26
all hours 36
all of a sudden 40
all over the place (= everywhere) 41
all over the place (= in an untidy state) 29, 51
all the best 17
an early / a late night 39
answer (sb) back 15
any moment 3
anyone's guess 30
as always 17
as far as I'm concerned 21
as if 53
as it happens/happened 41
as many as 50
as regards 3
as soon as 53
as though 53
as usual 17
as well 53
ask sb out 28
at a time 43
(at) any moment 3
at full stretch 51
at home 8
at last 53
at length 55
at once 55
at sb's expense 29

at the (very) least 50
at the (very) most 50
at the crack of dawn 49
at the earliest 20
at the last minute/moment 3
at the latest 20
at the least 50
at the most 50

back to front 23
backwards and forwards 54
bad luck! 19
badly off 33
base sth on sth 30
be (living) in a dream world 37
be (really) into sth 46
be a good thing (that) 1, 3
be a matter of (doing) sth 40
be a question of (doing) sth 40
be about to do sth 27
be asking for trouble 39
be at fault 25
be better off (doing sth) 11, 52
be bored to tears 27
be common knowledge 14
be cut out for sth / to do sth 36
be dying to do sth / for sth 44
be for/in a good cause 40
be fresh out of sth 3
be getting on for … 58
be in debt 33
be in the mood (for sth) 27
be in touch (with sb) 14
be in two minds about sth 1
be in with a chance (of doing sth) 51
be in / get into a state 1, 27
be meant to do sth 2
be on the go 57
be on the lookout for sth/sb 35
be out of touch (with sth) 11, 25
be out of your depth 51
be out of your mind 37
be over the moon 27
be rolling in money 1
be rushed/run off your feet 51
be set in your ways 25
be snowed under 20
be starving 34
be supposed to do sth 2

be taken aback 59
be thrilled to bits 27
be tied up 7
be to blame (for sth) 25
be up to sth 36
be up to you/him/her, etc. 17
be worlds apart 25
be your type 28
be yourself 25
be/go on a diet 34
be/have sth to do with sth/sb 20, 42
be/keep sb in the dark 14
beat sb up 35
behind bars 35
behind sb's back 15
behind the times 25
believe in sth 30
beside the point 21
best of luck 10, 19, 52
better late then never 2
bit by bit 40
bite sb's head off 29
bless you! 19
blow (sth) up 47
blow down 47
blow your nose 23
bored stiff 27
break down (= start crying) 7
break down (of a vehicle = stop working) 7, 43
break in/into sth 35
break new ground 48
break out (of a fire, fight, etc. = start) 48
break sth down 47
break the ice 26
break the news 14
break up (with sb) 28
break your heart 27
break your journey 43
break-in 35
breathe in/out 10
bridge the gap 37
bright and early 2, 54
brighten up 31
bring out the best/worst in sb 11
bring sb up (to do sth) 24
bring sth back 6
bring sth forward 45
bring sth to an end 26
brush sth up / brush up on sth 9
build on sth 28
build sth up 8
bump into sb 39
burn (sth) down 47
burn sth up 34

burst into tears 24
burst out laughing 22
by accident 55
by and large 21, 25
by comparison 11
by mistake 55
by yourself 29
by return (of post) 55
by the way 20
call by 20
call in 20
call it a day 8
call sb out 43
call sth off 45
calm down / calm sb down 27
can always 52
can't bear (doing) sth 46
can't help (doing) sth 27
can't stand (doing) sth 2, 46
can't wait / can hardly wait 28
careful with money 33
carry on (doing sth) 5
catch on 42
catch sb red-handed 35
catch sb up / catch up with sb 40
catch sb's eye 3, 57
catch the sun 57
catch your death of cold 3
change hands 37, 39
change the subject 29
change your mind 2, 29
charge sth up 16
chat sb up 28
check in 4
check up on sb 36
cheer sb on 42
cheer sb up 29
cheer up! 29
chop sth up 34
chuck sb out 39
clear off 5
clear sth up 6
close by 39
close down 48
cloud over 31
come a long way 60
come about 48
come across sth/sb 4
come along 60
come and go (= be present then go away) 54
come and go (= arrive then leave) 60
come back to sb 9
come between sb (and sb) 28
come close to sth / to doing sth 42

come in (= arrive) 4
come in (first, second, etc.) 48
come into sth 60
come naturally (to sb/sth) 40, 60
come off 34
come on! (= hurry up!) 56
come on (= improve / make progress) 56, 60
come on (of an illness = begin) 56
come on! (= showing disbelief) 30
come out (= appear, e.g. the sun) 60
come out (= become available to buy or see) 60
come out (= become known) 60
come round 60
come to 60
come to an end 26
come to life 60
come to nothing 60
come to sth 50
come true 30
come up (= happen or appear) 10, 37
come up with sth 11, 48
confide in sb 30
cool down 34
cost a fortune 16
cost the earth 16
could always 52
could do with sth 44
couldn't care less 44
count on sb/sth 30
count sth out 50
count sth up 50
cover the cost (of sth) 33
crash into sth/sb 47
crazy about sth 28
crop up 20
cross sth out 8
cross your legs 23
cross your mind 27
cut back on sth 4, 33
cut corners 37
cut down (on sth) 34
cut sb off 16
cut sth off (sth) 5

deal with sth/sb 36
die out 31
do sb good 40, 41
(do sth) for a laugh 22
do sth to the best of your ability 10
do sth up (= fasten) 7, 23
do sth up (= renovate) 7
do the trick 51
do without sth/sb 44
do your best 10, 11
do your bit 41

don't ask me 2
don't give a damn 44
dos and don'ts 9
down in the dumps 27
dozens of sth 50
drag on 5
drift apart 28
drink sth up 6
drive off 43
drive on 5
drive sb round the bend 29
drive sb up the wall 29
drop by 20
drop off (to sleep) 32
drop out (of sth) 11
drop sb a line 14
drop sb/sth off 20

early on 48
eat in 39
eat out 39
eat sth up 6
end up (somewhere / doing sth) 39, 48
even if 53
even so 21
ever since 53

facts and figures 54
fair enough 21
fair share 29
fall apart 47
fall asleep 32
fall behind (sb/sth) 40
fall for sb 28
fall in love with sb 28
fall out with sb 4
fall over 23
fall through 37
fall to bits 47
fall to pieces 47
fall/come off the back of a lorry 3
famous last words 2
fast and furious 54
fast asleep 32
feel like sth / doing sth 39, 44
feel sorry for yourself 52
feel up to (doing) sth 20
feel/be at ease (with sb) 25
feel/be sorry for sb 22
fingers crossed 10
fill in time 56
fill sth in (= fill sth completely) 56
fill sth in (= write on a form) 56
fill sth up (with sth) 43
fill yourself up (with sth) 34
find your feet 2, 30

finish (up) with sth 48
finish sth off 8
first and foremost 54
first of all 8
fix sth up 45, 49
flat out 1
flick through sth 6
fold your arms 23
follow in sb's footsteps 24
for a laugh 22
for certain 55
for fun 30
for good 28
for goodness sake! 19
for nothing 38
for one thing 21
for sale 37
for sure 55
for the most part 21
for the time being 49
from scratch 48
from time to time 49
get (hold of) the wrong end of the stick 22
get a joke 22
get a move on 40
get about 41
get ahead 58
get along (= make progress) 58
get along (with sb) (= have a friendly
    relationship) 26, 58
get around 41
get away (from sb/sth) (= succeed in leaving sb or a
    place) 20, 41
get away (= go on holiday) 41
get away from it all 58
get away with sth 24, 35
get back 6
get back to sb 16
get back to sth 6
get behind (with sth) 9, 36
get bogged down (in sth) 10
get by 58
get cold feet 27
get down to sth 10
get from A to B 43
get hold of sb 14
get in (= be accepted to study at a school, etc.) 56
get in (= arrive) 56
get in (= enter a vehicle) 56
get in the way of sth 30
get in touch (with sb) 14
get into shape 40
get into sth 58
get into the habit of doing sth 10

get into trouble (for sth) 24
get lost! 2
get mixed up in sth 58
get mixed up with sb 58
get nowhere 2
get off (= leave a bus, train, etc.) 56
get off (= leave on a journey) 56
get off (= leave work with permission) 56
get off to a good/better/bad start 42
get on (= make progress) 11, 58
get on (with sb) (= have a friendly relationship) 26, 58
get on for 58
get on sb's nerves 2, 29
get on top of sb 51
get on top of sth 10
get on with sth 5
get on with your life 58
get out (= leave a place) 56
get out (of information = become known) 56
get out and about 26
get out of sth (= stop doing sth) 58
get out of sth (= avoid a responsibility) 20
get over sth 58
get rid of sth 34, 58
get sth across (to sb) 15
get sth back 6, 38
get sth off the ground 48
get sth out (of sth) (= remove sth) 34
get sth out of sth (= benefit from sth) 41, 58
get stuck (on sth) 10
get the better of sb/sth 42
get the hang of sth 13, 58
get the most out of sth 58
get the upper hand 58
get there 9
get through (to sb) (= make contact by phone) 2, 16
get through to sb (= make sb understand) 25
get through sth (= complete a task) 36
get through sth (= pass a test) 58
get to grips with sth 10
get to know sb 58
get together (with sb) 20, 58
get up to (sth) 25
get your money's worth 33
get your own back (on sb) 24
get your own way 58
get/have butterflies in your stomach 27
get/start off on the wrong foot 11
give a hundred (and ten) per cent 50
give and take 29
give birth (to sb) 24
give in (to sb) 25
give in (to sth) 34
give my love to sb 20

give my regards to sb 20
give or take 54
give sb a hard time 36
give sb a lift 26
give sb a ring/call 14
give sb my love 20
give sb the sack 36
give sth a try 13
give sth back 6
give sth out 8
give sth up / give up doing sth 48
give up (= stop trying to do sth) 9
go according to plan 45, 60
go after sb 43
go ahead 19
go ahead (with sth) 45
go along with sth 60
go away (= leave home for a holiday) 41, 56
go away! (used to tell sb/sth to leave) 56
go away (of a problem = stop existing) 56
go back (to …) 8
go blank 10
go down (= become lower) 7
go down (of the sun = disappear) 7
go down to … 60
go down with sth 60
go far 11
go fifty-fifty 50
go from bad to worse 11, 37
go halves 39
go in for sth 4, 40
go in one ear and out the other 9
go off (= explode) 7
go off (= ring) 7
go off (= leave) 5
go off (of lights, etc. = stop working) 7
go off sb/sth 46, 60
go on (= continue without changing) 5
go on (= last) 26
go on (= happen) 26
go on (about sth/sb) 5, 25
go on to sth 5
go on! (used for encouragement) 26
go out of business 37
go out with sb 4, 60
go over sth 8, 10
go public 3
go red (in the face) 27
go round (to…) 60
go round in circles 57
go through sth (= check sth carefully) 6, 8, 10
go through sth (= experience sth difficult) 60
go without sth 34
go wrong 22, 28

good at sth 13
good grief! 2, 19
good heavens! 19
good luck 52, 19
good with sb 13
good with your hands 13
goodness knows! 19
goodness me! 19
grind to a halt/standstill 43
grow into sth 24
grow on sb 46
grow up 24
guess what? 17
hand in your notice 36, 37
hand in hand 23
hand sth in 8
hand sth out 8
hand sth round 8
hang around/about 5
hang on (= continue doing sth difficult) 56
hang on (= wait) 16, 56
hang on (= keep holding sth) 56
hang sth up 23
hang up 16
hang up on sb 16
hard at it 36
hard luck! 19
hard up 33
have (got) sth on 20, 45
have a (good) head for sth 13
have a good/bad night 32
have a lie-in 32
have a long way to go 37
have a sweet tooth 46
have a thing about sth/sb 57
have an early / a late night 32
have had enough of sth/sb 40, 42
have had it 51
have no idea 51
have sb to thank (for sth) 36
have second thoughts 50
have sth in common 3, 26
have the last laugh 22
have the time of your life 27
have/keep your feet on the ground 30
hear from sb 14
hear! hear! 2, 19
heat sth up 34
help sb out 26, 51
here and there 31
here goes 17
here to stay 21
here you are 17
here's to sb/sth 17

hit it off (with sb) 28
hit the roof 22
hold hands 23
hold on (= wait) 16, 56
hold on (tight) (= keep holding sth) 56
hold on (= continue doing sth difficult) 56
hold sb up 49, 40
hold the line 16
hold up sth (= rob) 35
hold-up 35
how come? 1, 17
hurry up 17

I beg your pardon 19
I couldn't agree more 21
I couldn't tell you 18
I dare say 30
I don't see why not 18
I have to / must say (that) 18
I know 17
(I) must dash 20
I told you (so) 18
I wouldn't say no 18
I'd rather not say 18
I'll say 3
I'll see what I can do 18
I'm not bothered 19
(I'm) sorry? 19
I'm very/terribly sorry 19
if I were in your place/position/shoes 52
if I were you 34, 52
if need be 44
if the worst comes to the worst 30
if all else fails 1
if you ask me 3, 21
if you like 19
in (next to) no time 49, 51
in (such) a hurry to do sth 51
in a row 31
in addition 53
in advance (of sth) 41
in all 50
in case 43
in charge (of sb/sth) 2
in confidence 55
in full swing 26
in general 25
in good time 49
in luck 31, 55
in his twenties, etc. 50
in no time 49, 51
in place of sth/sb 47
in practice 55
in return (for sth) 42
in rough 8

in safe hands 27
in season 55
in shape 40
in sight 55
in some ways 21
in spite of 53
in sth/sb's place 47
in that case 2, 52
in the black 33
in the distance 1
in the end 1, 55
in the long run 21
in the long term 21
in the main 2
in the meantime 53
in the open air 41
in the red 33
in the/sb's way 55
in theory 55
in total 50
in tune 55
in vain 3, 35
in working order 55
in writing 55
in your blood 24
in your element 11
in your shoes 52
inside out 23
invite sb round 26
it/that depends 3
it's a long story 3
it's about time 20
it's all the same to me 19
it's early days 3, 11
it's no good (doing sth) 8
it's no use (doing sth) 8
it's none of your business! 19
it's not the end of the world 10

judging by/from sth 48
jump out of your skin 27
jump the lights 43
jump the queue 39
(just) for fun 30
(just) in case 43
(just) round the corner 20, 39

keep a straight face 57
keep away from sb/sth 39
keep in touch (with sb) 14
keep it up 9
keep on doing sth 5, 29
keep quiet (about sth) 14
keep sb company 26
keep sb waiting 49
keep sth to yourself 30

keep sth up 48
keep to sth 10
keep up (with sb) 9, 40
keep/have one eye on sth 10
(keep your) fingers crossed 10
keep your head above water 33
keep your mind on sth 9
keep/control your temper 27
keep/stay out of sb's way 3
kick off v 42
kick-off n 42
kind of 17
knock sb out 23
knock sb over/down 23, 43
knock sth down 23, 47, 48
know sth inside out 24
know sth like the back of your hand 13
know what you are doing 13
know what you are talking about 24
know your stuff 11

laugh at sb 22
laugh sth off 2
lay the table 57
laze around/about 5
learn sth (off) by heart 9
leave sb alone 25
leave sb out 8
leave sth out 8, 10
lend/give (sb) a hand (with sth) 26, 57
let sb know 26
let sb off 35
let sb/yourself in for sth 24
let's see / let me see 18
lie around/about 5
lie in 32
life's too short 30
like mad 1
little by little 40
live for sth 46
live from day to day 49
live off sb/sth 25, 33
live on sth 2
live through sth 6
liven sth up 42
load (sth) up 43
lock sb in/out 26
look after sb/sth 4
look ahead (to sth) 45
look back on sth 59
look down on sb 59
look forward to (doing) sth 40
look into sth 4
look on the bright side 31, 59
look out for sb (= take care of sb) 59

look out for sth/sb (= keep trying to find sb/sth) 43
look sb in the eye 59
look sth up 4, 8
look the other way 59
look through sth 6
look to sb 59
look up 4
look up to sb 24, 59
look young for your age 59
look your best 59
lose count (of sth) 50
lose face 1
lose touch (with sb) 14
lose your temper (with sb) 27
lose/win the toss 42
lots of love 3
love at first sight 28
lovely and warm/quiet/cold 54

mad about sb (= in love with sb) 28
mad about sth/sb (= liking sb/sth very much) 46
make a change 41
make a fool of yourself 22
make a go of sth 37
make a joke of sth 22
make a move 57
make a/some/any/no difference 42
make do (with sth) 44
make ends meet 33, 37
make fun of sb 2, 22
make it (= be present) 36, 45
make it (= be successful) 36
make it (= survive) 36
make of sb/sth 21
make sense (= be practical) 1
make sense (= have a clear meaning) 10
make sense of sth (= manage to understand sth) 9
make sth up 4
make sure 34
make the grade 52
make the most of sth 9, 31
make up for lost time 57
make up your mind 12
make use of sth 34
make you sick 27
make yourself understood 9
mess around/about (with sth) 5
mess around/about 29
mess sth up 45
mind out! 19
mind your own business! 19
miss sth out 10
miss the point 57
more and more 25
(more than) your fair share of sth 29

more or less 2
move in 26
move on to sth 5
move out 26
muck sth up 45
must dash 20
my back/feet etc. is/are killing me 51

never in a million years 50
never mind 19
new/fresh blood 3
next door (to sb/sth) 26
next to nothing 36
nine to five 36
no chance 3
(no) good at sth 13
no time to lose 30
no way! 2
nod your head 23
not (too) bad 19
not a penny 33
not any longer / no longer 30
not at all 19
not bad 19
not be on speaking terms 22
not be up to much 11
not breathe/say a word (about/of sth) 14
not come easy (to sb) 40
not exactly 19
not get a word in edgeways 15
not go far 60
not have a clue 51
not have the faintest idea 51
not just yet 3
not know whether to laugh or cry 27
not my thing 46
not sb's cup of tea 46
not sleep a wink 32
not take sth lying down 59
not think much of sb/sth 11, 21
(not) think straight 12
not your cup of tea 39
nothing like sb/sth 24
now and then 54

off duty 55
off the beaten track 41
on (special) offer 38
on a shoestring 33
on and off / off and on 54
on board 27
on duty 55
on edge 27
on good/bad terms with sb 26
on horseback 41
on impulse 49

on offer 38
on purpose 3, 55
on sale 38
on the big/small side 51
on the dot 49
on the increase 35
on the one hand … on the other (hand) 53
on the phone (= by phone) 55
on the phone (= using the phone) 55
on the rise 35
on the run 35
on the spur of the moment 12, 49
on the tip of your tongue 9
on the whole 21, 25
on the/your doorstep 3
on tiptoe 23
on top 42
on your mind 27, 55
on your own 26, 29
once in a blue moon 3, 49
once or twice 41
one after another / the other 34
one at a time 39
one by one 50
one day 49
one or two 50
one step at a time 51
one way or another 54
(only) a matter of time 49
opt out (of sth) 37
or else 30
out loud 9
out of breath 3, 40
out of control 55
out of date 49
out of luck 31, 55
out of order 55
out of place 55
out of practice 13
out of season (= when few people go on holiday) 41
out of season (= not growing or ready to eat) 55
out of shape 40
out of sight 55
out of the blue 1
out of tune 55
over and over again 29, 49

packed in like sardines 39
pass out 60
pay sb back 6, 33
pay sth in 33
pay sth off 33
peace and quiet 54
phone sb back 6
pick and choose 44

pick sb's brain 57
pick sth up (= collect sth) 56
pick sth up (= learn sth without effort) 9, 56
pick sth up (= take sth from a lower level) 56
pick up (= improve) 31
pile up 51
pluck up (the) courage (to do sth) 28
point of view 24
pop in/over/round 39
pop out 20
pros and cons 21
pull in 43, 45
pull out 43
pull over 43
pull sb's leg 3, 22
pull your weight 11
push in 39
put in a (good) word (for sb) 51
put off doing sth 29
put sb down 29
put sb through 16
put sb up 39
put sb/sth first 50
put sth away 8
put sth back (= postpone sth) 45
put sth back (= return sth to its place) 6
put sth off 29, 45
put sth on (= become fatter) 7
put sth on (= dress yourself) 7
put sth on (= make sth start working) 7
put sth out (= leave sth outside) 20
put sth out (= stop sth burning) 48
put sth together 47
put sth up 47
put two and two together 50
put up with sb/sth 26, 28
put your foot in it 15
put yourself in sb's shoes/place 28

quite a few / a lot (of sth) 50

rack your brain(s) 9
rather than 38
read sth through 10
remember me to sb 20
revolve around sb/sth 46
(right) at the last minute 49
ring a bell 1
ring sb back 6, 20
rip sb off 33
rip-off 33
rolling in money/it 33
rough it 41
round about 50
round the corner 20, 39
rub sth out 4, 8

run after sb/sth 40
run away (from somewhere) 35
run in the family 24
run into sb (= meet sb by chance) 39
run into sth/sb (= hit sb in a car, bus, etc.) 47
run off with sth 35
run out of sth 10, 33
run sth up 33
run the risk of doing sth 26

same here 19
save for a rainy day 33
save up (for sth) 33
say when 17
see for yourself 18
see how it goes 18
see how things go 18
see sb off 5
see you (later/around/soon) 18
sell out (of sth) 38
sell up 37
send off/away for sth 38
send sb off 42
send sth back 6
send/give my love to sb 3
set off 41, 43
set out 41, 43
set out to do sth 48
set sth up 48
set your heart on sth 44
settle down 4
settle for sth 42
sew sth up 47
shake hands 23
shake like a leaf 27
shake your head 23
shop around (for sth) 38
show off 29
show sb the ropes 24
show up 4
show-off 29
sick and tired 54
sign up (for/to/with sth) 42
sink in 9
sit about/around 30
sit back 11
sit up (= not go to bed) 56
sit up (= sit in an upright position) 56
sleep like a log 32
sleep through sth 6
slip your mind/memory 13
slow down 43
slow sb down 40
smarten sth/sb up 47
smash sth down 47

smash sth up 47
so far 30
something to do with 20
sooner or later 54
sorry? 19
sort of 17
sort sth out 51
speak up 15
speak your mind 15, 57
speed up 43
splash out (on sth) 38
split sb up 28
split up (with sb) 28
stand a chance (of sth / of doing sth) 43
stand around/about 26
stand by sb 36
stand for sth 4
stand on your own two feet 25
(start) from scratch 48
start off (= begin in a particular way) 48
start off/out (= begin doing sth) 31
start out (= begin with an intention) 48
stay in 24
stay on 5
stay out 24
stay the night 57
stay up 10, 24
stay/steer clear of sb/sth 1, 10
stick at sth 9
stick to sth (= write/talk about one thing) 10
stick to sth (= continue doing sth and not
    change it) 43
stick together 28
stop off 41
straight away 55
stretch your legs 57
sure enough 40
swap places with sb 2, 8
switch off 51
switch sth on 7
take (no) notice of sb 59
take (time) off 59
take a joke 22
take advantage of sth 2, 42
take after sb 4, 24
take against sb 59
take care 17
take care of yourself 59
take exception to sth/sb 39
take it easy 59
take it/sth in 13
take it in turns 8
take it or leave it 59
take money off 33

take no part (in sth) 42
take off 5
take offence (at sth) 25
take out (a loan/insurance) 37
take over sth 30
take part (in sth) 42
take sb off 59
take sb on 36, 37
take shape 48
take sth away 50
take sth back 4, 6
take sth in 13
take sth into account 29, 52
take sth into consideration 52
take sth off 7
take sth on 37
take sth out (of a bank account) 33
take sth over 37
take sth seriously 8
take sth the wrong way 22
take sth up 40, 48
take the lead 42
take your life in your hands 59
take your mind off sth 27
take your time 28, 41, 51
talk down to sb 15
talk it/sth over 12
talk nonsense 15
talk sb into (doing) sth 39
talk sense 15
talk sth over 12
tear sth to bits/pieces 47
tell me, … 18
tell sb off (for sth / for doing sth) 15, 22
tell the time 57
ten to one 50
thank goodness! 19
thank heavens 2
thanks to sb/sth 11
that would be telling 18
that/it depends 1
that's life 52
(the) best of luck 10, 19, 52
the chances are (that) 31
the last minute 29
the last moment 29
the middle of nowhere 43
the minute (that) 53
the night before last 32
the other day 49
the rat race 37
the thing is 21
the tip of the iceberg 8
there is nothing in it 30

(there's) no time to lose 30
there is something in sth 30
there you are/go 17
think a lot of sb/sth 11
think ahead (to sth) 12
think back (to sth) 12
think for yourself 12
think highly / a lot of sb/sth 21
think on your feet 11
think it/sth over/through 12
think straight 12
think the world of sb 11, 28
think twice 12
third time lucky 50
throw a party 26
throw sb out 39
throw sth away 23, 47
throw sth out 34, 47
tidy sth away 29
tidy sth up 6
tie sb/sth up 7
time and time again 49
time's up 17
to a certain extent 21
to be honest 21
to begin/start with 42
to bits 27
to make matters/things worse 36
to say the least 18
to sb's face 15
to some extent 21
to tell you the truth 18
too … for my liking 46
top up (your mobile) 16
toss and turn 32
touch wood 3
trial and error 2, 9
trick sb into sth / doing sth 35
trip sb up 23
try sth on 4
try sth/sb out 39
try your best 10
turn a blind eye (to sth) 1, 24
turn around/round 40
turn out (to be) 41, 39
turn sb down 36, 52
turn sth down 26, 34
turn sth (from sth) into sth 34, 37
turn sth on 7
turn sth up 26, 34
turn up (= arrive) 7, 49
turn up (= be found) 7

under control 55
up and down 54

up and running 37
up to a point 21
ups and downs 29
use sth up 6

wait and see 54
wait up (for sb) 20
(walk) hand in hand 23
walk out (on sb) 28
waste your breath 49
watch out! 19
well done! 19
well off 33
what do you make of sb/sth? 21
what have you been up to? 20
what/whatever sb says goes 60
what's up? 17
whatever you do 34
whatever you say 18
when it comes to sth / doing sth 25
why not? 17
why (how, where, who, etc.) on earth 1
wide awake 32
with reference to sth 3
without (a) doubt 21
without fail 1
word for word 54
work at sth 40
work sth out 10
worried sick (about sth/sb) 32
wrap sth up 38
write sth down 4
write sth off 47
write-off 47

yes and no 19
you can say that again 18
you never know 30
you see 18
you/they, etc. can/could always … 52
you'll see 18
you're joking! 19
you're kidding! 19
you're welcome 19
you've got a point 21
your fair share of sth 29
your heart isn't it sth 30

Key words

If you cannot remember the first word of an idiom, look here for other key words that are used in the idiom. The numbers are unit numbers.

A 43
aback 59
ability 10
about 26, 27, 50
absence 2
accident 55
account 29, 52
addition 53
advance 41
advantage 2, 42
after 20
again 18, 29, 49
age 59
agree 21
air 41
all 8, 19, 50
alone 25
always 17, 52
another 34
apart 47
arms 23
ask 2, 3, 21, 39
asleep 32
awake 32
away 39, 55, 58
B 43
back 3, 13, 15, 23
backwards 54
bad 11, 19, 37
badly 33
bars 35
bear 46
beaten 41
before 32
beg 19
begin 42
behind 15, 25, 35
bell 1
bend 29
beside 21
best 10, 11, 17, 19, 52, 59
better 2, 11, 52, 00
between 28
birth 24
bit 40, 41
bite 29
bits 27, 47
black 33
blame 25

blank 10
bless 19
blind 1, 24
blood 3, 24
blow 23
blue 1, 3, 49
board 27
bog 10
bored 27
bothered 19
brain(s) 5, 9
break 48, 26, 14, 27, 43
breath 3, 40, 49
breathe 14
bridge 37
bright 2, 31, 54, 59
burst 24, 22
business 19
butterflies 27
cake 2
call N 14
call V 8
care N 17, 59
care V 44
case 2, 43, 52
catch 35, 3, 57,
cause 40
certain 55
chance N 3, 43, 51
chances N 31
change 41
change V 2, 29, 37, 39
charge 2
choose 44
circle N 37
circles N 57
clear 1, 10
close 39, 42
clue 51
cold ADJ 27
cold N 3
common 3, 14, 26
company 26
comparison 11
concern 37
concerned 21
confidence 55
cons 21
consideration 52

control 55
corner 20, 39
corners 37
cost N 33
cost V 16
count 50
courage 28
cover 33
crack 49
crazy 28
cross 10, 23, 27
cry 27
cup 39, 46
cut N 43
cut V 37
cut out 36

damn 44
dare 30
dark 14
dash 20
date 49
dawn 49
day 8, 33, 39, 49
days 3, 11
death 3
debt 33
depend 1, 3
depth 51
die 44
diet 34
difference 42
distance 1
don't 2, 44
don'ts 9
done 19
door 26
doorstep 3
dos 9
dot 49
doubt 21
down ADV 27, 54
downs N 29
dozens 50
dream 37
drive 29
drop 14
dumps 27
duty 55

ear 9
earliest 20
early 2, 3, 11, 32, 48, 54
earth 1, 16
ease 25
easy 40, 59

edge 27
edgeways 15
element 11
else 30
end N 1, 10, 22, 26, 55
ends N 33, 37
enough 21, 40, 42
error 2, 9
even 21, 53
ever 53
exactly 19
exception 39
expense 29
extent 21
eye 1, 3, 10, 24, 57, 59

face 1, 15, 27, 57
fact 2
facts 54
fail 1
faintest 51
fair 21, 29
fall 3, 28, 32, 47
family 24
famous 2
far 11, 21, 30, 60
fast 54, 32
fault 25
feel 39, 44, 52, 20, 25, 22
feet 2, 11, 25, 27, 30, 51
few 50
fifty-fifty 50
figures 54
fill 56
find 2, 30
fingers 10
first 8, 28, 50, 54
five 36, 50
flat 1
fold 23
follow 24
fonder 2
fool 22
foot 11, 15
footsteps 24
foremost 54
fortune 16
forwards 54
fresh 3
front 23
fun 2, 22, 30
furious 54

gap 37
general 25
give 29, 54

go 37, 57
going 37
good 2, 8, 13, 19, 28, 40, 41, 49, 51, 52
grade 52
grief 2, 19
grind 43
grips 10
ground 30, 48
guess N 30
guess V 17

habit 10
half 39
halt 43
halves 39
hand N 13, 23, 26, 53, 57, 58
hand V 36, 37
hands 13, 23, 27, 37, 39, 59
hang 13, 58
happen 41
hard 36, 19, 33
have (in *had it*) 51
head 13, 23, 29, 33
hear 2, 19
heart 2, 9, 27, 44
heavens 2, 19
help 27
here 17, 19, 31
highly 21
hold N 14
hold V 23, 16
hold-up 35
home 8
honest 21
horseback 41
hours 36
how 1, 17
hundred 50
hurry 51

ice 26
iceberg 8
idea 51
impulse 49
in 30
increase 35
inside 23, 24
into 46
it 30, 33

joke N 22
joke V 19
journey 43
judge 48
jump 27, 39, 43
just 3

kick-off 42
kid 19
kill 51
kind 17
know 17, 26, 27, 30, 58
knowledge 14

large 21, 25
last 2, 3, 22, 29, 32, 49, 53
late 2, 32
later 54
latest 20
laugh N 1, 22
laugh V 22, 27
lay 57
lead 42
leaf 27
least 18, 50
leave 59
leg N 3, 22
legs N 23, 57
lend 26, 57
length 55
less 2
let 26
lie 59
lie-in 32
life 2, 24, 27, 30, 52, 58, 59, 60
lift 26
lights 43
like 19
liking 46
line 14, 16
little 40
log 32
long 3, 21, 37, 60
longer 30
look 31, 59
lookout 35
lorry 3
lose 1, 14, 27, 30, 50, 00
lost 2, 57
lot 11, 21, 50
loud 9
love 3, 20, 28
lovely 54
luck 10, 19, 31, 55, 52
lucky 50

mad 1, 28, 46
main 2
many 50
matter N 40, 49
matters N 36
meant 2
meantime 53

memory 13
middle 43
million 50
mind N 1, 2, 9, 12, 13, 15, 27, 29, 37, 55, 57
mind V 19
minute 3, 29, 49, 53
miss 57
mistake 55
mixed 58
moment 3, 12, 29, 49
money 1, 33
mood 27
moon 3, 27, 49
more 25, 29, 2
most 9, 31, 50, 58
move 40, 57
much 11, 21
myself 29

naturally 40, 60
neck 2
need 44
nerves 2, 3, 29
never 2, 19, 30
news 14
next 26
night 32, 39, 57
nine 36, 50
no 18, 19
nod 23
nonsense 15
nose 23
nothing 24, 30, 36, 38, 60
notice 36, 37, 59
now 54
nowhere 2, 43

off 28, 33, 54, 59
offence 25
offer 38
on 20, 45, 54
once 3, 41, 49, 55
one 21, 50
open 41
order 55
other 34, 49
out 26
over 29, 49
own 24, 26, 29

pack 39
pain 2
pardon 19
part 21, 42
party 26
peace 54

penny 33
per cent 50
phone 55
pick 44, 57
piece N 2
pieces N 47
place N 28, 29, 41, 47, 51, 52, 55
places N 2, 8
plan 45, 60
pluck 28
point 21, 24, 57
position 52
post 55
practice 13, 55
pros 21
public 3
pull 3, 22, 11
purpose 3, 55

question 40
queue 39
quiet 14, 54
quite 50

race 37
rack 9
rainy 33
rat 37
rather 38
red 27, 33
red-handed 35
reference 3
regards 3, 20
return 42, 55
rid 34, 58
ring N 14
ring V 1
rip-off 33
rise 35
risk 26
roll 1, 33
roof 22
ropes 24
rough N 8
rough V 41
round 5
row 31
run V 24, 26, 51
run N 21, 35
running 37
rush 51

sack 36
safe 27
sale 37, 38
same 19

sardines 39
save 33
say 3, 14, 17, 18, 30
scratch 48
season 41, 55
second 50
see 18, 54
send 3
sense 1, 9, 10, 15
seriously 8
set 25
shake 23, 27
shape 40, 48
share 29
shoes 28, 52
shoestring 33
short 30, 43
show 24
show-off 29
sick 27, 32, 54
side 31, 51, 59
sight 28, 55
since 53
skin 27
sleep 32
slip 13
snow 20
something 20, 30, 50
soon 53
sooner 554
sorry 19, 22, 52
sort 17
speak 15, 22, 57
spite 53
spur 12, 49
stand 2, 25, 43, 46
standstill 43
start N 42
start V 11, 48
starve 34
state 1, 27
stay 1, 3, 10, 21, 57
steer 1, 10
step 51
stick 22
stiff 27
stomach 27
stone 2
story 3
straight 12, 55, 57
stretch N 51
stretch V 57
stuck 10
stuff 11

subject 29
sudden 40
sun 57
supposed 2
sure 34, 40, 55
swap 2, 8
sweet 46
swing 26
table 57
take 29, 54
talk 15, 24
tea 39, 46
tear V 47
tears N 24, 27
tell 18, 57
telling 18
temper 27
ten 50
term N 21
terms N 22, 26
thank V 2, 19, 36
thanks N 11
then 54
theory 55
there 9, 17, 31
thing 1, 3, 21, 46, 57
things 18, 36
think 11, 12, 21, 28
third 50
though 53
thoughts 50
thrilled 27
throw 2, 26
tie 7
time N 17, 20, 27, 28, 30, 36, 39, 41, 43, 49, 50, 51, 57, 59
times N 25
tip 8, 9
tiptoe 23
tired 54
tongue 9
too 46
tooth 46
top 10, 42, 51
toss N 42
toss V 32
total 50
touch N 11, 14, 25
touch V 3
track 41
trial 2, 9
trick 51
trouble 24, 39
true 30

truth 18
try N 13
try V 10
tune 55
turn V 32
turns N 8
twenties 50
twice 12, 41
two 50
type 28

under 55
understood 9
up ADV 11, 17, 20, 21, 37, 54
up to sb 17
up to sth 36
upper 58
ups N 29
use 8, 34
usual 17

vain 3, 35
vicious 37
view 24

wait 28, 49, 54
wall 29
waste 49
water 33
way 2, 3, 20, 22, 24, 30, 37, 54, 55, 59, 60
ways 21, 25
weight 11
well 19, 33, 53
what 17
whatever 34, 60, 18
when 17
whole 21, 25
why 17
wide 32
wink 32
without 44
wood 3
word N 14, 15, 51, 54
words N 2
working 55
world 10, 11, 28, 37
worlds 25
worried 32
worse 11, 36, 37
worst 11, 30
worth 33
write-off 47
writing 55
wrong 11, 22, 28

years 50
yes 19
yet 3
young 59
yourself 12, 18, 25, 26, 30